Lord's Justice

Lord's Justice

SHELDON ENGELMAYER
AND ROBERT WAGMAN

Anchor Press/Doubleday
Garden City, New York
1985

Library of Congress Cataloging in Publication Data

Engelmayer, Sheldon D.
Lord's justice.

1. Grudem, Diane—Trials, litigation, etc.
2. A.H. Robins Company—Trials, litigation, etc.
3. Trials (Products liability)—Minnesota—
Minneapolis. 4. Lord, Miles. 5. Judicial power—
Minnesota—Minneapolis. 6. Judicial error—Minnesota—
Minneapolis. 7. Intrauterine contraceptives—
United States. I. Wagman, Robert J. II. Title.
KF228.G78E54 1985 346.7303'82'0269
ISBN 0-385-23051-6 347.3063820269

Library of Congress Catalog Card Number 85-6114

PRINTED IN THE UNITED STATES OF AMERICA
FIRST EDITION

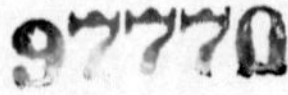

AUTHORS' NOTE

The story we tell in *Lord's Justice* involves the marketing by a major U.S. company of a birth-control device that led to the injury of thousands of women and children, and even a number of deaths; the company's response to the complaints it received about the device; the legal effort on the part of many of the injured women to obtain "justice" through lawsuits filed against the company; and one judge's efforts to resolve the dispute.

The story in its entirety is by no means a simple one. Nearly eleven thousand lawsuits have been filed against the company in question in practically every state in the Union, tens of thousands of pages of documents have been introduced into evidence, and millions of words of testimony have been given. A portion of these lawsuits have been filed in state courts; another portion went to the federal court system. Many judges have sat on the cases over the twelve-year history of these suits and scores of attorneys have served as counsel for either side. Thus, the cast of characters in this real-life drama is huge.

To tell the whole story in detail would confound the reader as much as the writers. However, the story is too important to be buried under its own heavy weight. So we have chosen to tell it as a sort of "docudrama," the story unfolding mainly through the eyes, words, and deeds of a limited number of people in the narrow setting of a "single" case. Nevertheless, the crucial elements of the larger story are all here.

The words spoken by the "actors" in this drama are taken from actual certified court transcripts or from documents written by those actors, or are based on their recollections and/or the recollections of others around them.

The same is true of any thoughts ascribed to these people. When we ascribe an incidental action to any character, such as the nodding of a head or the smoothing out of a tablecloth, that action took place. It is recorded in a transcript or on videotape, or the person involved recalled it for us. Whenever we discuss the reasons for a person's action, such as the invoking of a particular stratagem, we have confirmed those reasons with that person or with someone close to that person. Where this was not possible and we had to deduce the reasons from the words and actions involved, we so qualify the reasoning in the text.

In the early part of the book, we tell the story of the birth-control device itself. Here we make use of the documentary evidence and testimony that has been put out over the last twelve years. In so doing, we may at times come to our own judgments and conclusions regarding events. However, we always have "support" in the judgments and conclusions that had already been made by many judges and jurors based on the facts as they saw them and as you will see them in this book.

We have also given the drug company involved, the A. H. Robins Company, and its lead attorneys, Alexander H. Slaughter and Griffin Bell, the opportunity of providing their side of all that is contained herein. They have declined on various grounds.

Finally, while we have great respect for the law, its methods, and its institutions, there are times when Justice must peer out from under her blindfold to see the truth. The story you are about to read tells of such a time.

ACKNOWLEDGMENTS

We wish to acknowledge the help of a number of individuals without whom this book would have been an impossible task to complete.

In Wichita, attorney Bradley Post has spent the last decade trying to obtain justice for the victims of the Dalkon Shield as lead counsel in what are known as the multidistrict litigation (MDL) proceedings of the federal court system. He opened his files to us and was always available to answer questions or clear up problems, ever mindful of the fact that he represents one side in the dispute and never neglecting to remind us to take what he says are "facts" with a grain of salt. Senior U.S. District Court Judge Emeritus Frank Theis has overseen the MDL proceedings for nearly nine years now. Approximately one thousand Dalkon Shield cases are still part of the MDL, and this represents only a portion of his workload. Nevertheless, he generously gave of his time to describe the MDL proceedings within the bounds of judicial propriety.

In Minneapolis, where the main story in this book takes place, we are indebted in great part to the law firm of Robins, Zelle, Larson & Kaplan in general, and to a number of very kind, hard-working individuals within that firm who nevertheless gave selflessly of their time to assist us. That they did so at a time when their offices were being moved to a new building and their files were in complete disarray makes their contributions even more noteworthy. Special thanks go to attorneys Dale Larson and Mike Ciresi, who opened all the doors and made us privy to their thoughts; Ann Barcelow, who was so diligent in our behalf at a time when she was swamped with more important things; and paralegal Barbara Phillips, who could put her finger on an obscure line of testimony or locate the right section of a videotape at a moment's notice and often did.

In New York, we acknowledge the assistance of our agent, Diana Price, and our editors at Doubleday, James Raimes (who has since left) and Paul Aron, who had the foresight to know a good book when they saw one and who gave the time necessary to put it into shape. We also thank their able assistant, Alice Fasano, for her aid. And we thank Jacob Jorgensen, M.D., for his technical assistance—and especially for accepting the many post-midnight telephone calls with queries.

And finally, to Susan, Carol Ann, Jennifer, Malki, Bob, Patricia, Juda, J.J., and Molly, who had to put up with a great deal of neglect during a holiday season so this book could be written on time. We owe them the greatest debt of all.

Sheldon Engelmayer
and Robert Wagman
New York City
June 1985

Contents

1 *Judging the Judge* 1

2 *The A. H. Robins Company* 6

3 *The Case Against the Dalkon Shield* 15

4 *The Dalkon Shield Cover-up* 39

5 *Defending the Dalkon Shield* 63

6 *The Warrior Judge* 103

7 *Breaking the Logjam* 131

8 *The Judge Takes Command* 165

9 *A Matter of Discovery* 194

10 *The Judge Has His Say* 227

11 *The Judge on Trial* 264

12 *Aftermath* 288

"Justice, justice, shall you pursue, that you may live . . ."

Deuteronomy 16:20

1

JUDGING THE JUDGE

It was 9:30 A.M., Monday, July 9, 1984.

In the marble hallway outside the St. Paul courtroom, the television cameras were setting up. Reporters were milling around about the double doors, talking to each other mostly and trying to snatch comments from the notables who would enter. Two courtroom artists were checking their supplies one last time and preparing some preliminary sketches. There would be no cameras allowed in the courtroom and they were there to record the event for posterity and the evening news.

A steady stream of people had begun to gather an hour earlier. They included lawyers, court employees, and the curious. They had read that forty seats would be devoted to the nation's press and they knew that even though extra folding chairs had been set up in the courtroom, there would be no more than seventy seats for the public, and they all wanted seats.

Toward the front of the room at two long conference tables, attorneys sat and conferred among themselves.

At one counsel table, as they are called, was the familiar lanky figure of Ramsey Clark, the sixty-sixth attorney general of the United States, a disposable ball-point pen playing nervously under and over the fingers of one hand, his grim face reminding one of his public days of battle against the Vietnam War and for the rights of minorities and of the poor. He was conferring with another man,

Joe Walters, whose face was unfamiliar to the many out-of-state media people and even some of the locals among the spectators, but who is a senior partner of one of Minneapolis's largest law firms, O'Connor and Hannan.

At the other table sat Griffin Bell, the seventy-second attorney general of the United States, talking with his associate, Charles Kirbo, close personal friend and former personal attorney of Jimmy Carter, the moralist President. Their presence evoked memories of the Carter presidency, and a time when the nation put human rights and human dignity ahead of political pragmatism and expediency.

These were men who should have been on the same side—especially now, especially here—but on this day they were not. On this day, which some in the media had dubbed "the Battle of the Attorneys General," Clark and Bell would confront each other over issues of due process and judicial independence.

Suddenly, the words "All rise" were heard and everyone's attention turned to the front of the courtroom as five men in long black pleated robes entered through a door near the right-hand corner of the far wall of dark mahogany wood. The men ascended the two steps to the bench and took their seats beneath the Great Seal of the United States.

Pursuant to the Judicial Discipline and Conduct Act, Title 28, United States Code, Section 372, the spectators were told, the Judicial Council of the Eighth Circuit U.S. Court of Appeals had convened "a special investigative committee" to investigate a complaint filed against Miles W. Lord, chief judge of the U.S. District Court for the District of Minnesota, a complaint that had charged the judge with "gross abuse of judicial discretion and power."

"The legal issue for consideration by the committee," Griffin Bell argued, "is whether Chief Judge Miles W. Lord has engaged in 'conduct prejudicial to the effective and expeditious administration of the business of the courts.' . . . The gravamen of the complaints is that Judge Lord required [my clients] to appear in his court as a precondition of the settlement of two . . . cases pending before him. When [they] appeared in court on February 29[, 1984], they executed the settlement agreement, and then Judge Lord harshly denounced them . . . from the bench.

"Despite [the Federal Rules of Civil Procedure], which explicitly permits the parties to settle and dismiss a lawsuit without the court's involvement . . . , Judge Lord interfered with a private settlement . . . ," Bell's complaint continued.

"Judge Lord said, 'You don't have to argue that I am prejudiced at this point. I am.' . . . Judge Lord, by his own admission, [thus had] allowed himself to remain as judge of a case in which he knew he was biased against the defendant . . . .

"Judge Lord denounced [my clients] from the bench without affording them any of their rights under the Due Process Clause of the Fifth Amendment. . . . Since [my clients] were not parties to any litigation, and since in any event the . . . cases before Judge Lord had been settled, they had no remedy by way of appeal or otherwise. Thus, Judge Lord abused the judicial immunity of his office [and he did all this] in a manner prejudicial to the effective and expeditious administration of the business of the courts."

If people had not died, if lives had not been ruined, if there had not been so much tragedy, it almost would have been a funny scene.

There was a grim-faced Miles Lord—"the people's judge," his close friend Hubert Humphrey once called him—sitting in the front row of the courtroom, on a bench immediately before the bar, the mahogany barrier that separated the spectators' seats from those of the actors in the drama, flanked by his two sons and two daughters, as the five-judge committee heard the arguments and the witnesses and sat in judgment on him.

Lord had sat through so many trials over the years and had heard so many arguments. However, he had always sat there as the judge, the man with the final word, the decider of the fates of others. Now he was the "defendant" in the dock, so to speak. Griffin Bell was his "prosecutor"; Ramsey Clark, one of the men responsible for Lord's having been made a judge (as deputy attorney general, it was his job to process judicial nominations), was his defense counsel.

At specific issue was a courtroom "reprimand" Judge Lord had delivered on February 29, 1984, to three top officers of a major drug manufacturer, the A. H. Robins Company—president E. Claiborne Robins, Jr., vice-president and general counsel William A. "Skip" Forrest, Jr., and senior vice-president Carl D. Lunsford, Ph.D., the company's director of research and development, with supervisory control over the Robins medical staff.

A. H. Robins is the maker of, among other things, Chap Stick lip balm, the Robitussin line of cough suppressants, and Sergeant's pet products. Over the course of eighty-one days of involvement, but with no trial ever held, Judge Lord had come to believe that the company, its officers and its executives had deliberately and willfully sold to women a contraceptive intrauterine device (IUD) known as the Dalkon Shield that was nothing less than "a deadly depth charge in their wombs ready to explode at any time." Five million of those devices had been sold worldwide and, as Lord had contended that Leap Day, they had turned into "instruments of death, of mutilation [and] of disease."

Now, it was the company's turn to have its say and, it hoped, to have its way: punishment for Judge Lord and vindication for itself. That, Griffin Bell explained to the committee, was the reason he had evoked a 1980 statute he had himself helped create while he headed the Justice Department.

"The heart of our case is that Judge Lord made findings of fact [on February 29], in what he now calls a reprimand, without notice, without an opportunity to be heard, without an opportunity to offer witnesses, without an opportunity to cross-examine witnesses, and altogether a denial, a *gross* denial, of due process of law," Bell explained in the deep Southern tones that had become so familiar during the Carter years.

"This is a case that [had] been settled . . . ," Bell told the investigative committee, "a case which [had] never been tried. . . . [I]f we had had a hearing, [Lord's] charges could have been contested, [we could have shown] that there's two sides . . . ; we would have been able to show some countervailing evidence. . . . We never got a hearing on these things. We didn't have charges . . . , [no] time to get up and [give] our defense."

Through all of this, Lord sat with his sons and daughters and tried to look unconcerned, although he was anything but. He had walked into the courtroom smiling and joking and shaking hands. He would walk out grim and reflective and uncertain.

Throughout the proceedings, however, he would never waver in his conviction that what he did that Leap Day was right. "My job as a judge is to see that justice is done," he has said. "The whole object is to get at the truth. . . . I worship the truth," and the truth—or, at least, the truth as he believed it—was being denied in his courtroom.

The system was being abused, Lord felt; the evidence supporting this was legion. And attempts to prevent him from trying the case on the facts were so frequent and even predictable as to be laughable. He had to do what he did, Lord believed; he had to say what he said. Justice demanded it. Truth demanded it. To hell with the consequences.

To hell with the consequences, that is, unless the end result was a judiciary incapable of meting out justice for fear of having to face a hearing such as this one.

And yet, Lord told himself as Griffin Bell presented the case against him, it had been more than fourteen years since the debut of the Dalkon Shield; it had been twelve years since the first suit was filed against its manufacturer, the A. H. Robins Company. Since then, more than a score of women had died because of the Dalkon Shield, one as recently as March 1984, a month after he had pleaded with the Robins executives to recall the IUD; thousands of women had lost their ability ever to have children; at least hundreds of children had been born malformed and handicapped; countless others were unborn because their would-have-been mothers miscarried owing to infection.

Lord's mind replayed the faces of a number of the victims who had been in his courtroom that Leap Day, the tears streaming from their eyes as he spoke, their sometimes uncontrollable sobs breaking the otherwise thick silence around them.

Someone had to speak for the victims, he felt, whatever the price. And that someone, fate had dictated, was Miles W. Lord.

2

THE A. H. ROBINS COMPANY

In one sense, the story of the A. H. Robins Company is a quintessential American success story: In 1866, just after the close of the Civil War, Albert Hanley Robins opened a small apothecary shop in downtown Richmond, Virginia. Less than a century later his tiny shop had emerged as a major multinational pharmaceutical manufacturer on the Fortune 500 list.

The first half century of the company's history is anything but inspiring. In the beginning, the tiny apothecary operated much as any such venture of its day. Twelve years after the shop opened, however, the business expanded into a "manufacturing" enterprise of sorts: While A. H. Robins tended to the walk-in business at the counter, his son and daughter-in-law carried on a small "pill-rolling" operation above the store. In addition, the newly "expanded" business began selling the patent medicines of the day—such hard-to-do-without products as Brain Food, sarsaparilla (in those days a popular curative for chronic rheumatism, various skin diseases, and syphilis), Cascara Compound (a not too pleasant purgative), and iron and wine pills.

The A. H. Robins Company traces its history to that 1878 expansion. Its actual growth, however, did not begin until 1933. In that year, as Franklin Delano Roosevelt assumed the national reigns of power with the promise of pulling the nation out of the Great Depression by its bootstraps, Edwin Claiborne Robins, Sr., grandson of A.H., took over the reigns of the company with dreams of doing the same thing for his family's business. His company had only four employees and annual sales of $4,800. Profits were almost nonexistent.

E. Claiborne Robins, Sr., was not a pharmacist, but he was a salesman par excellence. He knew what had to be done to fulfill his dream and he immediately set about doing it, eschewing the sentimental links to the past that so often keep companies from becoming anything more than mom-and-pop concerns. There was no room in his plan for the "that's the way my father did it and his father before him" kind of thinking.

One of his first decisions was to stop doing business "the old-fashioned way," selling medicines directly to the public, and to concentrate instead on selling "ethical" (prescription) drugs to physicians and pharmacists. The company, however, had nothing to sell to these health professionals; medical science had moved far away from plant roots and tree bark, the staple ingredients of patent medicines. Robins thus turned to the medical literature of the day to find out what physicians and pharmacists were clamoring for most. He found that there was a need for an effective antispasmodic remedy to relieve distress in the stomach and intestinal tract. The A. H. Robins Company soon began marketing a drug called Donnatal; over fifty years later, it remains a preeminent drug in its field and a major Robins item.

With Donnatal leading the way and helped on by a few other products, the company experienced moderate growth through the end of World War II. It was at this point that the company embarked on the road that would make it a major manufacturer of mass-marketed ethical and nonprescription drugs. Robins knew that Donnatal alone could not forever carry his company, much less allow it to grow in the manner he desired, so he returned to the medical literature in search of new ideas.

As a result of that search, the A. H. Robins Company added several new drugs to its sales line in the immediate years after the war: Entozyme and Donnazyme, essentially twin products designed to help relieve stomach distress and fill out the successful Donnatal line; Pabolate, a weak aspirinlike analgesic used mainly to help relieve mild arthritic pain; and, in 1948, a prescription cough remedy known as Robitussin. These products are still being sold today;

the Robitussin line of "cough suppressants" is now sold over the counter.

The year 1948 saw more important changes at the A. H. Robins Company than the birth of Robitussin. The company had been operating as a partnership of various Robins family members and their heirs; that year, the business was finally incorporated.

Also in 1948, the company for the first time began to underwrite its own research program. Four years later, it added its own manufacturing operation. (Until then, Robins had farmed out both its research and its manufacturing—having long ago given up pill-rolling above the store—to other drug companies.) It would be several more years, however, before any product which it developed from scratch was brought to market; in the interim, Robins continued to add to its product line by licensing products developed by other drug companies, including overseas manufacturers. Finally, in 1957, Robaxin, a muscle relaxant, the first true A. H. Robins–researched and developed product, was brought to market.

The next major milestone in the company's history was reached in 1963. Thirty years after E. Claiborne Robins, Sr., had taken over the family-owned company with its four employees, the A. H. Robins Company saw net sales of $47 million and after-tax profits in excess of $5 million. The company's net worth would soon exceed $28 million. Robins was now a multinational, too; 14 percent of its sales came from foreign operations in Canada, Mexico, England and South America. In the process of turning a tiny apothecary shop into a force to be reckoned with in the drug industry, E. Claiborne Robins, Sr., had also turned his family into one of the wealthiest in the state of Virginia.

Now it was time to go public. Robins family members offered 425,000 of their shares for sale and the company went public with the stock traded over-the-counter, even as its products could not be because of the ethical nature of the business at this time.

Having become a public company in a strong cash position, Robins was quickly bitten by the acquisition bug that was affecting so many U.S. companies at that time. Its first major acquisition was, indeed, an inspired one: Robins took over the Morton Manufacturing Company, which had hit it big with a lip balm called Chap Stick. The product had quickly captured the lion's share of the market and, in fact, was the fastest-moving over-the-counter item in drugstores. Yet the Morton acquisition was important for more than Chap Stick, for it reversed the company's decision made thirty years earlier to sell only ethical products through health professionals. The acquisition of Morton, Chap Stick and Chap-ans, a medicated hand cream, thus represented Robins's reentry into the proprietary (over-the-counter) drug field.

Over the next several years the company continued to prosper, so much so that in 1965 it listed itself on the New York Stock Exchange, with the family offering for sale another 375,000 of its more than 2.7 million shares. Even with the sale, the family continued to own 82.2 percent of the outstanding stock with a paper value of $141 million. (Currently, the Robins family ownership continues in excess of 52 percent.)

From the day it went public, the A. H. Robins Company, Inc., never looked back. Almost every year, it bought or sold some company. Among its other major acquisitions was the Polk Miller Products Corporation, a manufacturer of flea collars and other pet-care products, including the Sergeant's line of pet and flea collars; the American Drug Corporation; the VioBin Corporation, a maker of nutritional supplements; U.S. Clinical Products; Scientific Laboratories, Inc., a major producer of animal pharmaceutical products; and Parfums Caron, a Paris-based fragrance manufacturer. The company also acquired drug companies in West Germany, Brazil, Italy, Colombia, Mexico, and South Africa.

With all of the acquisitions, Robins in the early 1970s seemed to lose sight of what it truly was: a manufacturer of ethical drug products. Its research and development of new prescription drugs, for more than two decades the backbone of the company, now began to falter and, finally, seemed to collapse. Since 1970, the company has filed with the U.S. Food and Drug Administration (FDA) over thirty investigational new drug applications (INDs), the first step in developing a drug product for marketing. But of these INDs, only three actually made it to market and none of them have been "successful." In fact, as of this writing no successful new prescription drug has come out of Robins since 1968, although the company has high hopes for a new antihypertensive drug called Tenex.

Nevertheless, by 1973, backed by the acquisitions, company sales had risen to $189 million, though its share of the drug market had not budged in a decade. In 1962, it had ranked eighteenth among drug manufacturers with its 1.9 percent market share of ethical drugs; it was still ranked eighteenth in 1972, with a 2 percent share, a statistically insignificant increase.

Other problems began to set in during the 1970s. Some of Robins's acquisitions were going sour and these failures were beginning to hurt. Among these were a poultry-breeding venture and two small cosmetic lines that would eventually lose the company $4.7 million.

In 1978, E. Claiborne Robins, Jr., who years before had unsuccessfully sought to play baseball for the Pittsburgh Pirates, took over as president and chief executive officer of the company his great-grandfather had begun over a century earlier, his grandfather had kept going, and his father had built into a huge business.

His answer to the problems facing his company was to unload the unprofitable ventures (such as the poultry-breeding and the heavily advertised but poorly received Quencher line of cosmetics) and to further branch out into fields totally unrelated to the drug and health-care products business.

Under the young Robins's leadership, the company has purchased, among other things, two radio stations in Greensboro, North Carolina, and the Quinton Medical Company, a manufacturer of medical instruments. It also announced that it intended to make other significant investments in both broadcasting and medical instrumentation.

Young Robins also shook up the company's management team, began a major worldwide capital improvements effort, and, in a bid to put new life into the company's ethical drug business, boosted the bare-bones drug research and development budget which by that time had sunken well below the industry norm, raided the competition for experts in drug metabolism and clinical pharmacology, and actively pursued new licensing agreements with European pharmaceutical firms to market certain of their drugs in the United States.

Young Robins apparently inherited his father's magic touch. Under normal circumstances, the company's present financial picture would have to be considered very healthy indeed. In 1983, for example, net sales had grown to $563 million, an increase of almost $200 million in the first five years of E. Claiborne Robins, Jr.'s, reign. Operating profits had almost doubled in the same period from $53 million to $100 million and the annual cash dividend had doubled.

Things, however, are far from normal at the A. H. Robins headquarters in Richmond, Virginia. As E. Claiborne Robins, Sr., noted in his 1982 message to company stockholders, there is a "dark side" to the company's financial picture. That dark side is the Dalkon Shield intrauterine device that the A. H. Robins Company purchased almost overnight in June 1970.

Because of the Dalkon Shield, several thousand women have suffered from pelvic inflammatory disease (PID), a generic term for a variety of pelvic infections that can attack the uterus, fallopian tubes, or ovaries, and many of them were made sterile as a result. At least twenty-two women have died from the infections it caused. The Dalkon Shield has been blamed for causing septic abortions (badly infected miscarriages), for children's having been born malformed or handicapped, and for the deaths of some of those children.

The Dalkon Shield was never much of a profit maker, at least according to the figures Robins chooses to make public. When Robins was forced to withdraw the product in June 1974, a scant three and a half years after it had debuted the IUD nationally, net profits from the device (or so it says) had amounted to only about $500,000 on total sales of about $11 million. In fact, the Dalkon Shield had played such a small role in the company's growth that when production was discontinued not one employee had to be let go.

Against this reported half-million-dollar profit, Robins and its insurance carrier, Aetna Life and Casualty Company, have paid out well over $100 million in legal expenses alone defending the deluge of product liability suits caused by the Dalkon Shield, and they have already paid out or owe more than $245 million in judgments and settlements in approximately 8,700 of these cases. (To demonstrate the heavy financial toll continuing from the Dalkon Shield debacle, in the record-setting year of 1983 when total company profits increased to $105.7 million, Dalkon Shield expenses borne directly by the company amounted to almost 20 percent of that profit, $18.7 million, a big chunk by anyone's calculations. Things only got worse in the first half of 1984: while revenues rose an additional 33 percent, Dalkon Shield expenses claimed $42.3 million, and the year was only half over.)

At least 4,500 cases still remain unresolved and more are being added at what sometimes seems a furious pace—on average, there was one suit being filed every two and a half hours in the first quarter of 1985 alone. These figures, therefore, will continue to climb; some highly respected financial analysts believe that, in the end, the total bill to Robins in claims and judgments alone (not counting legal expenses) will come to between $800 million and $1.2 billion.

To meet this obligation, Robins on April 2, 1985, announced that it was creating a $615 million reserve fund from which it would pay all awards and settlements for damages actually suffered by a victim or her heirs (known as compensatory damages) in pending and future Dalkon Shield cases through the year 2002, along with legal expenses. What the fund does not cover, however, are foreign claims filed against the company and, more important, money awards that juries might impose in order to punish Robins. These awards, known as punitive damage awards, could run into the millions of dollars per case. (On May 3, 1985, for example, a Kansas jury awarded a Topeka woman $9.2 million for her Dalkon Shield injuries; $7.5 million of that award was for punitive damages.)

Robins and its officers downplay the possibility of punitive damage awards, although they do concede that such awards have the potential to wreak havoc on the company and its future. "There is a risk with punitive damages," admits G. E. R. Stiles, Robins's chief financial officer, adding that repeated punitive judgments "could put the company in a very bad position financially."

Financial analysts would have preferred Robins to provide for punitive damage awards. "There's no question about it," analyst Joseph Riccardo of Bear, Stearns and Company has said. "If they get hit with some big punitive damage awards, that's going to do them a lot of harm. They're clearly not out of the woods yet."

Worse, at least from a purely accounting standpoint, Robins is now deep in the red financially. To begin with, Robins claims that the $615 million reserve fund is much higher than the company's net worth—the value of assets over liabilities—which Robins puts at $370 million. This means that Robins's net worth is now in the minus column, to the tune of $128 million.

Furthermore, the money for the fund will be charged against 1984 revenues. Thus, on paper at least, Robins will have suffered a deficit in 1984 of $461.6 million, its first loss since incorporating and, as Stiles believes, perhaps "one of the largest losses ever booked" by any company in a single year.

Stiles, however, insists that the on-paper loss does not mean the company is in any real trouble. "We are not [bankrupt] and we are not in danger of that," Stiles told the press conference announcing the reserve fund. "We are operating today just as we did yesterday and as we will be next September. It's business as usual."

The paper loss again points up the high price Robins has been paying because of the Dalkon Shield debacle. Actually, 1984 produced record earnings for Robins. Its operating earnings for 1984 had gone over the $128 million mark, a 21 percent increase over the previous high recorded in 1983. Sales were nearly $632 million —a 12 percent gain over the high of $563.5 million set in 1983. Such numbers offer great promise to stockholders and investors. Because of the Dalkon Shield, however, Robins's books now show a loss. Under Virginia law, this means that the company cannot pay dividends to its stockholders until it is back in the black—and that is not expected to happen at least before 1987. This can hurt the price of Robins's stock as well, which in turn could make the stock less interesting to investors.

Adding to Robins's woes was a five-year dispute with Aetna (since 1979) over how the insurer assigned claims and what insurance applied to those claims. The two companies had decided years ago that Robins would pick up the punitive damage awards and that Aetna would pay a share of the compensatory damage awards up to policy limits for all claims through February 1977, when Robins stopped insuring the Dalkon Shield, plus most legal expenses. Robins, however, sued Aetna because, or so Robins said, the carrier was improperly assigning cases to specific years and was deducting legal expenses from the liability limits, thus virtually exhausting the liability coverage. The Robins suit against Aetna was dropped in November 1984, a week before the trial was to have begun, when Aetna agreed to an additional $70 million in insurance coverage, bringing to about $153 million the total amount of insurance coverage Robins had left at the start of 1985. However, Robins is still solely liable for any claims arising from Dalkon Shield use after February 1977.

The decision to purchase the Dalkon Shield thus is potentially one of the costliest mistakes made by any drug firm in the last thirty years. The heavy financial price Robins must eventually pay for this mistake, however, cannot compare with the price that has been paid by the women who were fitted by the "superior IUD" from the A. H. Robins Company.

To this day, however, Robins has adamantly refused to accept any responsibility for the damage done to women and children by the Dalkon Shield, insisting despite all the evidence that there was never anything wrong with the product. On the contrary, officials and employees of the company—even in the latter part of 1984, when little doubt remained in anyone's mind (except, perhaps, those at the A. H. Robins Company) as to the dangers of the Dalkon Shield—continued to deny that those dangers existed.

This stubborn refusal to recall the Dalkon Shield no matter what scientific facts presented themselves pales, however, beside another fact: as Denver, Colorado, District Court Judge Robert P. Fullerton so bluntly stated it, the A. H. Robins Company, in "a conscious decision" based on the desire for profit, decided "to market an inadequately tested, dangerous product by unethical and improper means, using known false and misleading advertising. . . . [O]nce the company was made specifically aware of the numerous dangerous side effects of the device . . . , it suppressed that information . . . , made additional false claims, and then resorted to an effort to cover up the facts."

Judge Fullerton made these findings of fact on June 13, 1980, in upholding a jury's at that time extraordinary punitive damage award against Robins of $6.2 million. But Judge Fullerton and the jurors barely knew the half of it.

3

THE CASE AGAINST THE DALKON SHIELD

"This is the worst case of intentional disregard for people's rights that I have ever seen," Mike Ciresi told the jurors.

It was December 15, 1983, and the young plaintiff's attorney was standing sideways at a lectern in a U.S. district courtroom in St. Paul, Minnesota. He was summing up his side of the case of *Martha E. Hahn* v. *A. H. Robins Company* and he wanted the jurors to imagine themselves to be Martha Hahn.

"At some indeterminate time in the future," Ciresi told the jurors that day, "you're going to have a slow, insidious development of infection within the uterus, your tubes and ovaries. You won't know it's happening, but it will be a ticking time bomb, because there will be a constant flow of bacteria from your vagina to your uterus which will eventually . . . [overwhelm] your defense mechanisms . . . , and it's going to develop into an abscess. . . . [Y]ou're going to be sicker than you've ever been in your life, and you're going to go into the hospital for nine days. . . .

"[T]hey're going to stick needles into your arms, and your arms will be bleeding, and you're going to have fear as to if you're ever going to have a child. And then you're going to get a little better, and you're going to have hope, but you'll still not know what's coming down the road.

"Then you're going to go home and they're going to continue to treat you for that infection. It's not going to get better [though], and you're going to wake up one morning and you're going to be so sick that you can't move. You're going to be crying, and you're going to ask your husband to [take you] to the hospital. . . .

"When you're in the hospital, first of all, they're going to give you antibiotics, and they're going to drain the abscess, and they're going to get two cups of that pus out of the inside of you that's caused by this device [the Dalkon Shield], and then you're going to sit for two days and wonder and hope and pray that you're going to get better.

"You're going to hope that you can have children when you leave this hospital. But it's not going to happen because your doctor is going to tell you that the threat of that abscess rupturing is a threat to your life. He's going to tell you he has to operate, and he's going to tell you that 'I can't tell you if I'm going to take all of the reproductive organs or only some; I can't tell you whether you're going to live. But we're going to operate.'

"So you spend that last night before the operation, which is on Christmas Eve day, and you wake up in the morning and you wonder whether you're going to see Christmas and whether you're going to see New Year's. You wonder if you're ever going to be a full, complete woman. . . .

"Then you're going to be operated on and you're going to wake up, and the first thing you're going to be is grateful to be alive. . . . [Y]ou're going to hear a noise and you're not going to know what that noise is. You'll discover it's a heart monitor, and it increases its beat as you move, and you're going to wonder how long you're going to hear that.

"Then you're told [on this Christmas Eve that] you lost all [your] reproductive organs. You are going to be told [on Christmas Eve] . . . that you can never have children.

"You will never have those pudgy arms around you. You will never come home at night to see the face of your father or mother in your children. They will never see your face, or the face[s] of your parents, or the face[s] of your children's children.

"You will never have the ability to expand your own horizons by having your own children to take care of. You may never be able to completely love anyone but yourself, because you have never loved your own child. You will never see them grow. You will never go through the PTA meetings. You will never have any of those joys which make life worthwhile. . . .

"[Martha Hahn] has suffered. She has suffered at the hands of this company, and I detest them, and there is no question in my mind I detest them.

"I have borne her cause as well as I can. I pass it on to you."

Martha Hahn's story is the story of at least eleven thousand American women. It is a story that actually began in the late 1960s.

The Sexual Revolution was under way. However, the biggest weapon in its armory, the oral contraceptive (i.e., the Pill), was under attack.

"At that time, there was a growing body of evidence suggesting that oral contraception may cause problems in some women who were using them," according to Emanuel A. Friedman, M.D., professor of obstetrics and gynecology at Harvard Medical School, and chairman of the Department of Obstetrics and Gynecology at Boston's Beth Israel Hospital. "Specifically," the physician testified in the Hahn case, "the oral contraception in those days had rather high dosages of estrogen . . . [that] were thought and subsequently found to be associated with clotting problems in women, so that some women . . . developed very serious . . . complications, like stroke, or coronary artery occlusion, myocardial infarctions, very serious kinds of problems. Rare, but nonetheless serious."

That is why the Dalkon Shield was invented. It was supposed to have given women a way to prevent pregnancy that was as effective as the Pill, but much safer to use. Instead, the Dalkon Shield gave women like Martha Hahn permanent and unwanted protection against pregnancy by making them sterile, took some lives and ruined others, and otherwise provided much pain and suffering that could have been avoided.

"Robins did not have a single obstetrician or gynecologist on its medical staff," attorney Roger L. Tuttle wrote in the *Oklahoma Bar Journal* in 1983. "Still, Robins was generally recognized as having the best and most aggressive . . . sales force in the country. Upon seeing the financial opportunity presented with the Dalkon Shield, it vigorously pursued an aggressive marketing campaign. . . . Probably as a sophisticated pharmaceutical manufacturer, Robins should have known better, but the temptation to rush to market for financial gain was too great to resist."

Tuttle's comments cannot be taken lightly or dismissed out of hand as plaintiff counsel's rhetoric, for the only client Roger Tuttle ever represented in the Dalkon Shield case was the A. H. Robins Company. From 1972 through 1975, Tuttle was the Robins staff attorney who had direct responsibility for managing the Dalkon Shield cases being brought against his employers.

Thus, by the admission of its own onetime counsel, whom Robins now attacks as a disgruntled former employee, the story of the Dalkon Shield is one of greed and corporate recklessness of nearly unparalleled dimensions on the part of the A. H. Robins Company.

The Dalkon Shield is an egg-shaped plastic intrauterine device that looks very much like a modern artist's conception of a crab, with five "fins" of varying sizes protruding from either side to make expulsion from the uterus difficult. Attached to the device is a nylon tailstring designed as a marker to provide physicians and the women using it with a way to determine whether the device is in place.

For no reason in particular, it seems, the tailstring is multifilamented, which means that it is actually made up of several thinner strings (filaments) combined. Most other intrauterine devices use monofilamented strings; in 1970, this type of string was considered state-of-the-art and it still is today. Encasing the Dalkon Shield's unique tailstring is a nylon sheath, presumably placed there to protect the tailstring from "wicking," gathering fluid containing bacteria from the vagina and carrying the bacteria-contaminated fluid up the tailstring to the otherwise sterile environment of the uterus.

"[T]he vagina contains a great many bacteria," Dr. Friedman explained to the Hahn jury. ". . . [I]t's perfectly normal for the vagina to have bacteria . . . , but it's not normal for the body of the uterus . . . to contain any bacteria, and the reason it's not normal is because of the cervical mucus which prevents bacteria from gaining access from the vagina through the cervical canal into the cavity of the uterus. So, that cervical mucus [under normal circumstances] prevents bacteria from ascending."

The Dalkon Shield's unique tailstring is the *ab*normal circumstance. Over the years, studies have shown that the multifilamented nylon tailstring traps vaginal bacteria and allows them to fester and multiply, eventually causing serious infections of the type that Martha Hahn suffered—sometimes leading to death and often leading to sterility.

The longer the Dalkon Shield remains in a woman's uterus, the greater the danger to that woman because of the deterioration of the IUD's components, especially the nylon used in the tailstring and the sheath covering it. Of this, there is little doubt today. According to one study of over eight hundred Dalkon Shields conducted on behalf of the National Women's Health Network, sheath cracks or ruptures were found in 68 percent of the devices that had been in place for one to six months; in 70 percent of Shields in place for thirteen to eighteen months; in 80 percent of the IUDs in place for twenty-five to thirty-six months; and in 100 percent of Dalkon Shields in place for more than forty-nine months.

In and of themselves, however, the ruptures in the sheaths are minor. It is only when the ruptures are combined with the tailstring's own design flaws that the situation becomes critical. A related study also commissioned by the National Women's Health Network showed that the nylon tailstring becomes more of a magnet for vaginal bacteria as time goes on. The bacteria gather around the tailstring and, when mixed with body fluids, work their way up the filaments, past the protective "wall" of the cervical mucus, and into the sterile uterus. This is the wicking effect, so named because it resembles the way a wick draws up fluids into a lamp. The nylon sheaths were supposed to protect the tailstrings from being contaminated; ruptured sheaths, however, leave the tailstrings exposed to the very contamination from which they were supposed to have been protected. Even if the sheaths did not rupture, however, the tailstrings would become contaminated because the two ends are already exposed.

What all this means, as the U.S. Food and Drug Administration has pointed out, is that women wearing the Dalkon Shield stand a much higher chance of contracting pelvic inflammatory disease than women wearing other IUDs, or who use some other form of contraception. Says the FDA:

"An analysis of data from the Women's Health Study of 622 women hospitalized with initial episodes of PID and 2,369 hospitalized controls with no PID showed that women wearing the Dalkon Shield have a fivefold increased risk for PID compared with women using other types of IUDs [such as the Copper-7, Progestasert, Saf-T-Coil, and Lippes Loop]. In the study, although only a small proportion of IUD users were wearing the Dalkon Shield, the device accounted for almost 20 percent of the excess risk of PID among all IUD users."

Pelvic inflammatory disease is not something to be taken lightly, as Martha Hahn learned the hard way and as Mike Ciresi so graphically described it to the jury. "Pelvic inflammatory disease is a general catch-basket term for a series of . . . disorders, all of which pertain to infection of the fallopian tubes; the tubes and the ovaries, specifically," Dr. Friedman explained. "But in terms of the various kinds of pelvic inflammatory disease, it refers to a sequence beginning usually with an acute infection, meaning sudden, very . . . severe infection with fever and inflammation . . . , hot inflammation I guess would be the best word from the lay point of view, which then over time may recur, become more chronic in nature. . . .

"If the disease is recurrent, as it often is under circumstances of a repetitive infection, one can also see abscess formation—that is, pockets of pus—develop within the tube and involve the tube and the ovaries simultaneously, destroying their function and structure; and pelvic inflammatory disease can also involve structures adjacent to the fallopian tubes and ovaries. . . .

"[The principal clinical sign of an acute pelvic infection is pain,] generally located . . . in the lower pelvis on either side of the uterus; the lower abdomen's generally quite painful to the patient and, when examination is made, quite tender to touch. . . . In addition, the patient will experience fever as a consequence of the body's reaction to the infection which is taking place in her tubes."

Another problem area for the Dalkon Shield is its effectiveness in preventing pregnancies. According to product literature prepared by Robins in late 1970, "Protection against pregnancy has approximated 99% which is comparable to that obtained with the sequential oral contraceptive method." This was a lie, although the company continues to vigorously insist that, when properly inserted, the device lives up to that claim. Numerous studies have shown that the Dalkon Shield had pregnancy rates ranging from anywhere between 5 percent and 10 percent; whichever study one prefers, therefore, the pregnancy rate is still far greater than with other

IUDs, with rates ranging from 1.5 percent to 3 percent, and certainly far greater than Robins's claim of 1.1 percent.

The unwanted pregnancies, however, are only a part of the problem. Of greater concern is what happens because the Dalkon Shield is in place as the fetus grows. Often, the Dalkon Shield will offer resistance to the amniotic cavity encasing the fetus (the so-called water bag that breaks shortly before birth), either rupturing the thin membrane or irritating it sufficiently to bring on premature births of children, many of whom suffer from such problems as cerebral palsy, hydrocephalus, and mental retardation.

The A. H. Robins Company denies all this, of course. It insists that the Dalkon Shield is safe and effective if properly inserted and properly used. The studies are wrong; the FDA is wrong; the women who have been victimized by the Dalkon Shield are wrong.

A. H. Robins has maintained this attitude from the very first with the Dalkon Shield, when it purchased the device from the Dalkon Corporation and its four investors. No matter what it knew or discovered about the device, Robins chose to act as though it had never even heard the information. Its marketing of the IUD moved inexorably forward, until nearly 5 million women worldwide had been fitted with the device and tens of thousands had been injured by it and some of them had died. Even then, Robins continued to insist that nothing was wrong with the product.

These denials even came at a time when the company was readying a face-saving plan proposed by Robins attorney Griffin Bell to warn women of the dangers posed by the Dalkon Shield. For example, on August 23, 1984, Robins's director of medical services since 1970, Fletcher B. Owen, Jr., M.D., Ph.D., testified that, if the Dalkon Shield were still being marketed, he would recommend that women be fitted with the device despite the seemingly irrefutable evidence that shows the device to be dangerous. A seemingly astonished Mike Ciresi, who has been a major thorn in Robins's side, then asked Dr. Owen whether he would also advise those women of the at least twenty-one known or suspected Dalkon Shield-related deaths reported up to that time and of the many thousands of lawsuits by women such as Martha Hahn alleging that the Dalkon Shield had destroyed their ability to ever have children or caused them to give birth to brain-damaged children. "I wouldn't have any reason to tell them," Dr. Owen replied.

At the same time as Dr. Owen was insisting that he would still recommend his company's IUD to women—a time when Robins itself was preparing what even Bell admits was a recall of the device —the *FDA Drug Bulletin* was urging physicians to remove the Dalkon Shield "from any woman still wearing one." The FDA advisory added that "the risk of PID in women wearing the Dalkon Shield, even if the woman is asymptomatic [meaning that she has shown no signs of any problems because of the device], is of such significance that the benefits of removal outweigh the risks associated with insertion of another type of IUD."

This kind of testimonial attitude on the part of Dr. Owen and other Robins officials, including company president and chief executive officer E. Claiborne Robins, Jr., can be put down to posturing and courtroom tactics, but things actually run deeper than merely expressing doubts about the studies or confidence in the product: A. H. Robins has been and still is covering up for the fact that it knew all about the Dalkon Shield's potential for inflicting harm even before it began marketing the device.

Robins, quite naturally, insists that such allegations are false, no matter how the evidence may appear. "Why doesn't the American public realize," E. C. Robins, Jr., has said, "that a company that is over 100 years old wouldn't make a decision that could destroy it in a matter of minutes? Yet the people, the courts, the newspapers are trying to destroy it."

However, it is difficult to believe the company's protestations in light of two facts: (1) the nature of the evidence that has been amassed against Robins over the last twelve years; and (2) how hard Robins has worked to keep relevant evidence from its own files on the Dalkon Shield from the courts. The company has done all it could do to prevent legitimate discovery.

There is also considerable evidence, thanks to the involvement of Chief Judge Miles W. Lord, that Robins misled the courts for nearly nine years into believing that it had turned over all the documents, studies, reports, and memoranda it had on the Dalkon Shield when it knew that it had not done so. There is even evidence, some of which Robins confirms, that potentially sensitive documents were destroyed after two judges had issued nondestruct orders protecting those documents.

Robins also insists that it conducted rigid tests on the Dalkon

Shield before marketing the product, although it has not produced much proof of those tests, claiming for the most part that the information is "privileged" because the tests had been commissioned by its attorneys, not its scientists. In truth, however, there can be only one logical reason why Robins resists publishing those studies. As onetime Robins attorney Tuttle has written, "Had Robins been willing to wait for the results of its own testing . . . , it likely would not be in the difficult position it faces today."

There is even evidence that Robins in 1971 went so far as to misstate to the FDA the nature of the copper used in the device in order to avoid having to properly test the Dalkon Shield. Minute amounts of copper released into the uterus can improve contraception, although no one is certain why this is so, just as no one is certain why IUDs prevent conception. However, if a "medical device" does release copper, that device must be classified as a drug, according to FDA rules which were announced in early 1971, because it is presumably having a biological effect on the body. Also according to the FDA rules, no new drug may be marketed without first filing a new drug application, followed by a rigorous three-stage testing program to prove both safety and effectiveness, and then by a review by an expert panel—a process that takes several years.

In fact, within months of Robins's Dalkon Shield being introduced to the marketplace, two manufacturers—the Population Council and G. D. Searle and Company—had been informed that they would have to file NDAs on the copper-based IUDs they were then preparing to market, and that the IUDs would have to be put through the rigorous testing program required for new drugs. The Population Council's IUD had been developed in 1969; it was still awaiting approval in June 1974 when Robins suspended domestic sales of its device. The Searle IUD had been ready for marketing at about the same time as the Dalkon Shield; it won approval less than three months before sales of the Dalkon Shield were suspended.

To avoid the lengthy process required for approval of new drugs (Robins, as Tuttle himself has stated, was eager to cash in on the fears women then had of the Pill), the company informed the FDA that the copper in its device did not enhance contraception in any way and thus the IUD was still a "device," not a "drug." However, the evidence indicates that Robins knew otherwise or, at the very least, suspected otherwise.

Prior to the FDA's ruling that required devices with biologically active copper to be classified as drugs, for example, an internal Robins memorandum dated June 10, 1970, specifically referred to the "drug effect" of the copper sulfate in the Dalkon Shield. The memorandum, written by Robins's then director of product planning, W. Roy Smith, to the company's vice-president and general manager, Charles E. Morton, states clearly that copper sulfate had been added to the Dalkon Shield "for the express purpose of getting an added 'drug effect' . . . [and for] the express purpose of improving effectiveness."

Robins was even claiming in its printed material that the copper in the Dalkon Shield had a biological effect. In a detailed monograph prepared for its sales force, Robins noted that "certain metal ions, specifically copper ions, will enhance the effectiveness of the device," adding that "copper sulfate has been incorporated into the plastic mix from which the Shield is molded." The added copper, Robins claimed in the monograph, was one of the "features of the Dalkon Shield which make this unquestionably a superior IUD." After the FDA's ruling, Robins revised the monograph, deleting these references to copper.

Plaintiffs' attorneys such as Mike Ciresi have suggested that Robins also sought to avoid the NDA process because it feared that the Dalkon Shield would not survive the testing. This, too, has evidentiary support. A suggestive statement found in the minutes of a Robins Research Committee meeting held on November 11, 1971, for example, states that "[the copper] may represent a threat to the product if the FDA declares it a new drug."

To understand the extent of this corporate cover-up on the part of the A. H. Robins Company, a brief history of the Dalkon Shield is in order.

In the early 1960s, Hugh J. Davis, M.D., then an assistant professor of obstetrics and gynecology at Johns Hopkins University, began experimenting with intrauterine birth-control devices. Davis had no experience in obstetrics and only limited experience in gynecology, despite his position. He was not even board-certified in obstetrics and gynecology. His field was cytopathology, or the study of cells and how they function. Nevertheless, together with

Edmund Jones, an employee of the Ortho Pharmaceutical Company which specialized in contraceptive products and devices, Dr. Davis in 1964 began work on the development of an IUD that was alternately called the Incon and the Shield. In 1967, he and Jones applied for a patent on a device they called the Incon Ring. Dr. Davis, as an employee of Johns Hopkins, then had to assign his right and interest in the patent to his employer; similarly, Jones assigned his interest to Ortho Pharmaceuticals.

Dr. Davis apparently had little confidence in the Incon Ring as a marketable device (or, perhaps, had little interest in it because he would not stand to profit from it). In December 1967, therefore, he and an acquaintance of his, Irwin Lerner, an electrical engineer from Stamford, Connecticut, began discussing ways of improving on the Incon Ring's design. Lerner agreed to take over the project and Dr. Davis, for his part in designing and testing the device, was to receive a percentage of the profits from the eventual sale of the product.

By mid-1968, "Win" Lerner had redesigned the Incon Ring, adding a central membrane and fins along the side, giving the device its crablike appearance. Dr. Davis then began testing the device in September 1968, mainly using patients at the Johns Hopkins Pregnancy Clinic but including, as well, some of his private patients. Two months later, Irwin Lerner, by himself, filed for a patent on the device. Nowhere on that patent application could the name Hugh J. Davis be found.

This was no oversight, nor was it an attempt by Lerner to freeze out his partner from any future income. Rather, it appears to have been a deliberate attempt by Lerner and Dr. Davis to hide the physician's financial interest in the device. (Curiously, even today the A. H. Robins Company continues to foster the notion that Dr. Davis operated at arm's length from Lerner. In a mid-1984 court filing, for example, Robins gave the following brief history of the Dalkon Shield: "[The] Dalkon Shield had been invented between January and August 1968 by Irwin Lerner and was clinically tested by Dr. Hugh J. Davis of the Johns Hopkins Department of Obstetrics and Gynecology starting in September 1968.")

There may have been a second motive, as well, for the deception. Dr. Davis was then in the process of studying the device's effectiveness and the results of that study would be used to market the IUD.

Proper study protocol, however, requires that the investigating scientist have no interest in the object of the study, or the results would be automatically suspect.

Whatever the reason for Lerner's applying for the patent in his own name alone, it clearly was not that Dr. Davis had nobly removed himself from any financial gain in the device. On the contrary, on January 7, 1969, a scant three months after the patent application was filed, a new corporation was formed—the Dalkon Corporation, either an apparently loose acronym for its three investors, *Da*vis, *L*erner and *Cohn* (Hartford, Connecticut, attorney Robert E. Cohn, Lerner's counsel), or an acronym for the *Da*vis, *L*erner, *con*traceptive device, although no one has admitted to either explanation. According to the incorporation papers, Lerner, who was to handle production and distribution, received a 55 percent share of the new corporation and its product; Dr. Davis received 35 percent, and attorney Cohn 10 percent.

Adding weight to the argument that Dr. Davis deliberately sought to conceal his interest in the Dalkon Shield is testimony he gave a year later, in January 1970. Dr. Davis was appearing as the lead witness before Senator Gaylord Nelson's Subcommittee on Monopoly of the Senate Select Committee on Small Business, which was then investigating the "present status of competition in the pharmaceutical industry." The brunt of Dr. Davis's testimony was that the contraceptive pill was as dangerous as everyone was then saying it was, but that there was hope on the horizon: work was being done on new, safe, and effective intrauterine devices and one or more would soon be available to consumers. As Dr. Davis concluded his testimony, there followed this exchange with the committee's counsel:

MR. DUFFY: Doctor, while we are on the subject of intrauterine devices, in preparation for these hearings we became aware of the report that indicated that you had recently patented such a device. Is there any truth or substance to that report?

DR. DAVIS: I hold no recent patent on any intrauterine device. The Johns Hopkins University holds a patent on an intrauterine device that was developed in 1964 in a joint development venture together with the Ortho Research Foundation. That particular device was a ring which was used for experimental purposes and has never been marketed, and I doubt ever will be marketed.

MR. DUFFY: You say you have—

DR. DAVIS: My name appears on a joint patent together with a Mr. Jones, and this patent is held jointly by the Johns Hopkins University, for whom I am an employee, and by the Ortho company. In the public interest, this device was developed in 1964 and was the object of a patent application. This is not a marketed item and I doubt ever will be.

MR. DUFFY: Then you have no particular commercial interest in any of the intrauterine devices?

DR. DAVIS: That is correct.

Dr. Davis had also withheld knowledge of his interest in the Dalkon Shield when, two months before his testimony to Senator Nelson's committee, he submitted the results of his "twelve-month" study of the new device for publication in *The American Journal of Obstetrics and Gynecology.* "The Shield Intrauterine Device: A Superior Modern Contraceptive" was published by the journal on February 1, 1970. In it, Dr. Davis stated:

"Recent experience with a shield design approaches the ideal of combining very low pregnancy rates with minimal side effects. These modern devices are demonstrating such excellence as to justify a revision of current [negative] attitudes toward the efficacy of intrauterine devices."

Dr. Davis then went on to describe the Dalkon Shield:

"Several features distinguish the Dalkon Shield device (Dalkon Shield, 341 Shore Road, Greenwich, Connecticut 06830) as compared with the old ring, bow, loop, and spiral type of IUD. The shield contour conforms to the mid-range of uterine cavity, as determined by silicone casts prepared from normal uteri. The device is light and flexible to minimize cramping. Small lateral fins promote retention and permit accommodation to uterine contractions and variations in uterine shape. A central membrane increases endometrial surface contact [contact with the mucous membrane lining the uterus], as well as precluding bowel strangulation in the event of perforation, a rare complication observed with closed loop design IUD's. Relative to the generally available plastic IUD's, the shield is less bulky, simple to insert and exceptionally well tolerated" by the women wearing it.

Next, Dr. Davis provided the results of the "twelve-month" study and then summed up his report:

"In our experience, both the protection against pregnancy (99 per cent) and the tolerance (96 per cent) achieved by this modern shield type of IUD is superior to sequential oral contraceptives. . . . Pregnancy rates listed for the combined orals are 0.7 per cent, for the sequentials 1.4 per cent, for the loop 2.7 per cent, and for the double coil 2.8 per cent. Only the combined type of oral contraceptive offers a slightly greater protection (0.4 per cent) than our results with the shield intrauterine device. . . . Taken altogether, the superior performance of the shield intrauterine device makes this technic a first choice method of conception control."

Aside from deliberately leaving out his financial interests in the device he called "a first choice method" of contraception, Dr. Davis neglected to provide the dates for his "twelve-month" study: September 1968 to September 1969. This is important considering the date of the published study, February 1970. Dr. Davis submitted his study to the journal in October. (In fact, the manuscript was received by the journal on October 24, 1969.) The only way he could have done so was if he began writing up his findings immediately at the end of the twelfth month, sometime in mid-September. Pregnancy, however, can take as long as two to three months to show up, as any physician should know. A true twelve-month study, therefore, would require at least two or three months of follow-up beyond the test period in order for the one-year results to be valid. Dr. Davis's published results showed a 1.1 percent pregnancy rate. However, had he waited for a minimum of fourteen months, he would have found (as, indeed, he did find) that the Dalkon Shield's pregnancy rate was much higher than he claimed—above 5 percent —thus making it quite *inferior* to the other devices to which he compared the Dalkon Shield in his study.

Dr. Davis also neglected to mention that only eight women out of the 640 women he reported on had been fitted with the Dalkon Shield in the first month of the study or that women were being added to the study almost until the very end. If he had so advised physicians, then they would have known that his "twelve-month" data covered the experience of only eight women, one of whom soon became pregnant.

It is instructive to see how Dr. Davis today explains away his attempts to hide his financial involvement in the Dalkon Shield. Testifying in 1984 in the case of *Peggy Joan Mample, et al.,* v. *A. H. Robins Company, et al.,* Davis was asked by attorney John Davids:

Q. [I]sn't it true, Dr. Davis, that during the entire time that the Dalkon Shield was marketed, you made a conscious effort to conceal your financial interest in the device?

A. No, I don't think that is true.

Q. Well, Dr. Davis, in February [sic] of 1970 you told a committee of the United States Senate that you had no commercial interest in any IUD, did you not?

A. No interest in a *commercial* IUD, which was absolutely true. [Emphasis ours.]

Q. Well, in February of 1970 the Dalkon Shield was being marketed by the Dalkon Corporation, wasn't it?

A. I think that hearing was in January and I don't—

Q. Late January?

A. Yes. I don't think there had even been any publication about the Shield, much less advertising or anything of the sort.

Q. You knew it was going to be commercially marketed?

A. Yes, I knew that it was going to be.

Q. And you at the time were a signatory to a document indicating you had stock in the Dalkon Corporation?

A. I didn't physically have any stock. I was a shareholder, yes.

Q. And this was Senator Nelson's committee and you testified in front of that committee and were asked by counsel for the committee if you had any interest in any commercially marketed device and you said no?

A. That is correct.

Q. You also in February 1974, when you were asked the question about owning stock in the Dalkon Corporation, you said, no, you didn't own any stock?

A. That is correct.

Q. That was the deposition under oath?

A. That is correct. . . .

Q. Dr. Davis, at that time did you make the statement that you had made a decision not to hold stock in the Dalkon Corporation because you felt there would be a conflict of interest? Did you make that statement?

A. Yes, at one time I had made that statement and that decision.

Q. And did you say that you felt it would be a conflict of interest because you did not feel that you should be in a position of testing and evaluating a device in which on one side you were functioning as an evaluator and on the other side you were in a capacity as a private individual to profit from participating in a corporation?

A. Yes, I had a distinct concern about this.

Q. Okay. Now, Dr. Davis, you were in just such a position during the entire time that the Dalkon Shield was marketed, weren't you?

A. Not really.

Q. Well, you were acting as a tester and evaluator during the entire time the Dalkon Shield was marketed, weren't you?

A. We did the initial testing. I received no payment from the Dalkon Corporation or Mr. Lerner or anybody else for carrying this out. . . .

Q. And you were receiving royalties from Robins?

A. I received some payments from Mr. Cohn which I think in part were derived from royalty payments that Robins was making. . . .

Q. You would agree, Dr. Davis, would you not, when the Shield was sold to Robins [in June 1970], the rights to the Dalkon Shield, you received over $240,000 as part of that initial payment?

A. Yes, I think that is correct.

Q. And you received during the period of time the Shield was marketed in excess of $300,000 in royalties?

A. Yes.

Q. Now, would you agree that it would constitute a conflict of interest for a doctor to be in a position of testing and evaluating a device in which that doctor had a financial interest and could gain a profit?

A. Potentially, yes.

Q. Well, you say "potentially," doctor. Wouldn't you agree that that was, in fact, a conflict of interest?

A. No.

Quite naturally, considering the efficacy claims, Dr. Davis's February 1970 study with its two important omissions evoked considerable interest in the Dalkon Shield, which had gone on the market in a limited way in November. Indeed, a handwritten internal memorandum from the Robins files dated June 8, 1970, states, "Davis' paper was [the] main reason for interest" in the Dalkon Shield. More than that, there were no other studies to support these findings and the company knew it (just as it knew of Davis's financial interest), so again only Davis's study could be responsible for any interest in the device. As a June 11, 1970, Robins memorandum states, "Definitive information on the Dalkon Shield is available primarily from Dr. Hugh Davis' studies."

Once the fourteen-month totals were in, Dr. Davis and engineer Lerner set about modifying the Dalkon Shield. They made some physical changes to the device and added metallic copper and a copper salt in the hope of improving the effectiveness of the IUD against pregnancy. They also developed a second size, this one specifically for nulliparous women—that is, women who had never borne children. (Dr. Davis's published study, written before the new size was even designed, noted that the new IUD was particularly effective for such women because its unique design made it difficult to expel. This meant that it was the first device that could be effectively worn by nulliparous patients, for whom expulsion was then a common problem. Yet, after stressing the nulliparous use, they found they had to design a special size for the nulliparas.)

One thing Dr. Davis and Lerner did not do was tell anyone (except the A. H. Robins Company, that is) that the Davis study was no longer valid in any respect: the fourteen-month totals showed a much higher pregnancy rate and, in any case, the device studied was not the device being sold.

On April 9, 1970, for example, Dr. Davis appeared at the eighth annual Association of Planned Parenthood Physicians meeting in Boston, in which he again stated that the Dalkon Shield was "superior" to all other IUDs and most other contraceptive methods as far as pregnancy was concerned and as far as the nulliparous patient was concerned.

The following week, the Dalkon Corporation took on another investor, Thad J. Earl, M.D., a general practitioner from Defiance, Ohio. Dr. Earl paid fifty thousand dollars for a 7.5 percent share of the company and its Dalkon Shield patent. This changed the financial interests of the three original partners, but only slightly. Dr. Davis's share, for example, was reduced from 35 percent to 32.38 percent.

Dr. Earl promptly became "the most aggressive promoter of the product," according to an internal A. H. Robins memorandum, and it was through him that the Dalkon Shield came to the attention of the drug firm. (Dr. Davis apparently did not like Dr. Earl, which is ironic given subsequent events. A Robins memorandum quotes Dr. Davis as calling his new partner a "Johnny-come-lately" to the contraception field and disparaging Dr. Earl's "snake oil approach" to promoting the product.) John E. McClure, a Robins "detail man," the title given to drug salesmen, met Dr. Earl in mid-May when the physician was promoting the Dalkon Shield at the New Jersey General Practice Association's meeting at Host Farms, Pennsylvania. McClure was impressed enough with Dr. Earl's presentation to telephone company vice-president and general manager Charles E. Morton on May 18 to suggest that this was a product A. H. Robins might want to take over.

Robins was indeed interested. McClure was instructed to forward information on the Dalkon Shield to W. Roy Smith, the company's director of product planning. The packet of information—including a reprint of Dr. Davis's study, a physician's file card containing instructions on use and other relevant details, and a Dalkon Corporation order card—arrived on May 21 and Smith immediately passed it on to medical director Fred A. Clark, Jr., M.D., for review.

On May 25, Smith telephoned Dr. Earl. During the course of that conversation, Dr. Earl informed him that Upjohn Pharmaceuticals was negotiating with the Dalkon Corporation for the IUD. Three days later, Smith, Dr. Clark and an outside consultant, S. E. Davis III, M.D., of the Department of Obstetrics and Gynecology at the Medical College of Virginia, visited Dr. Earl in Defiance. During lunch at a private club and a subsequent visit to Dr. Earl's farm, the Robins team was told that the Upjohn deal would likely be completed the following day, May 29. The men from Richmond suggested that the A. H. Robins Company would better the offer if it decided it wanted the device.

Soon after the May 28 visit to Defiance, the decision was taken to purchase the rights to the Dalkon Shield. Robins, however, did not purchase the device blindly despite the speed with which the deal was consummated. As negotiations for the purchase of the Dalkon Shield went on, Robins's people were learning everything they could about the IUD—and some of what they were learning was disturbing, or at least it should have been.

There is, for example, a June 8, 1970, memorandum from Oscar Klioze, Ph.D., the company's director of pharmaceutical research and analytical services. In it, Dr. Klioze reported on the lack of proper scientific testing of the device. "The only quality control tests run are tensile strength measurements of the extruded plastic prior to molding, the shield membrane and the marker string . . . ," Dr. Klioze wrote. "The device has not been subjected to any formal stability testing. . . . No accelerated aging tests were conducted in developing the device nor was there any study of the 'leeching' effects of the *in vivo* environment on the device."

On the same day Dr. Klioze wrote his memorandum, medical director Dr. Fred Clark visited Dr. Davis in Baltimore to look over the raw data of his published study. The next day, Dr. Clark reported his findings in a three-page memorandum that was sent to Ernest L. Bender, then an A. H. Robins vice-president; Jack Freund, M.D., then vice-president in charge of the medical department (he would soon be put in charge of research); and product planning director Roy Smith.

In that memorandum, Dr. Clark noted that the Dalkon Shield was not the same device studied by Dr. Davis. "Model in use for [the] first year was less flexible, thicker, harder than present, and contained no metallic salts. Changes have been made in the plastic and a copper salt added, the latter beginning around November, 1969 [two months after the Davis study was completed]."

Dr. Clark also noted the inconsistencies between the published results of Dr. Davis's study and the actual fourteen-month totals. Dr. Davis's study "mentions 640 insertions with five pregnancies," Dr. Clark's memorandum states. "However, data given me for the first 14 months (Sept. '68–Nov. '69) covers 832 insertions with 26 pregnancies," or a rate of more than 3 percent.

On that same day, June 9, there was a luncheon meeting held at the Rotunda in Richmond at which this very point was discussed. In attendance were president and chief operating officer William L.

Zimmer III, vice-president Bender, vice-president and general counsel William A. Forrest, Jr., Roy Smith, Dr. Freund, Dr. Clark, general manager Charles Morton, and Dr. Earl. That meeting was memorialized in a June 10 memorandum from Roy Smith to Morton. The memorandum leaves little doubt that Robins's executives knew full well what they were doing (although, obviously, even some of the Robins executives at that luncheon were not being told the entire truth about the pregnancy rates).

"I am concerned over the possibility that we may not have given sufficient consideration to all the problems involved in marketing the Dalkon Shield with the composition presently being distributed by Dalkon," Smith wrote. "At the luncheon yesterday we discussed the possible implications of utilizing the Davis paper for promotional purposes, while marketing a device not identical in composition to that on which the paper was based. I understand the conclusion that was reached and the reasons therefor, i.e., that the composition is not mentioned either in the paper or on the product package, and that the effectiveness rate is even better than that cited by Dr. Davis, but I am not sure that these are the principal considerations."

Two days later, on June 11, vice-president Dr. Freund wrote his own memorandum in which he indicated that he, at least, had gotten the message.

"The follow-up period for the published pregnancy rate [in the Davis study] is not long enough (1 year) to project with confidence to the population as a whole. More recent conversation with Mr. Lerner indicates that the pregnancy rate of the group published by Dr. Davis has increased from 1.1% to 2.3% with a longer follow-up period. Dr. Davis used an earlier version of the Dalkon Shield (without copper) in this reported study. . . . The need for continuing the research effort initiated by Dr. Davis and Mr. Lerner and added studies to support the effectiveness and safety of this device should be emphasized."

Dr. Clark in his June 9 memorandum had also advised his superiors of something Dr. Davis had said, something they obviously took more seriously than the memorandums of Drs. Freund, Clark, and Klioze and Roy Smith. In his memorandum, Dr. Clark mentioned Dr. Davis's belief that speed was of the essence in marketing the Dalkon Shield. "Davis stated that the company which takes the

Dalkon Shield must move fast and distribute much merchandise and really make an inroad 'in the next 8 months,'" Dr. Clark wrote. "My feeling was that others may be working on similar improvements for IUDs."

And speed there was. The day after Dr. Freund's memorandum reiterating the Dalkon Shield's faults—and only fifteen days after its executives first visited Dr. Earl in Defiance—the A. H. Robins Company purchased all rights to the IUD for $750,000 cash plus royalties of 10 percent payable to the Dalkon Corporation (meaning Lerner, Cohn, and Drs. Davis and Earl). In addition, Irwin Lerner and Drs. Davis and Earl were retained by Robins as consultants. Dr. Earl was to be paid $30,000 a year, making him the highest-paid consultant then on the Robins roster; Dr. Davis was to receive $20,000 a year. On June 15, 1970, all income from the sale of Dalkon Shields began to accrue to the A. H. Robins Company.

Fourteen days later, on June 29, in a "Dalkon Shield Orientation Report" that was designed "to alert all concerned persons of the early status of this project and of tentative plans to bring it to market under the Robins label," the following advisory appears in the "Summary" portion: "The string or 'tail' situation needs a careful review since the present 'tail' is reported (by Mr. Lerner) to have a 'wicking' tendency." Among those to whom this memorandum was addressed were E. Claiborne Robins, Sr., the company's chairman and chief executive officer, William L. Zimmer III, and Drs. Freund and Clark.

In September, Robins began putting the finishing touches on its marketing plan. One aspect of that plan was to compare the 1.1 percent pregnancy rate of the Dalkon Shield to that of established IUDs, including the Lippes Loop (2.7 percent) and the Saf-T-Coil (2.8 percent). The rates for these other IUDs had come from a July 1970 report in "Studies in Family Planning—A Publication of the Population Council."

During the week of September 28, 1970, Robins "test-marketed" its comparison at the American Academy of General Practice meeting being held in San Francisco. This so infuriated the maker of the Saf-T-Coil, the Julia Schmidt Company, that its president shot off an angry letter to E. Claiborne Robins, Sr. "The data your company produced at the meeting was taken out of context from the [Population Council] report," the October 8, 1970, letter stated. "Your company's IUD data used for comparison purposes is based on a single study run under totally different conditions and different times from the data reported in the Population Council report." Robins's chairman and chief executive officer had thus been made aware of the means being employed to promote the Dalkon Shield. Apparently he saw nothing wrong with it because the comparison subsequently turned up many times in literature promoting the Dalkon Shield over the next four years.

Also that September, the company prepared the file cards to be sent to physicians along with the Dalkon Shield. The file cards were just that: a series of cards to be kept in a physician's desk file that contained pertinent information about the product. In this case, the cards were quite specific in announcing that the pregnancy rate was a mere 1.1 percent, with no mention of the potential of the tail to wick bacteria into the uterus.

What the cards did say (or at least imply), however, was that if anything went wrong with the patient once the Dalkon Shield was in place, it would be the fault of the inserting physician. "Sepsis may result from unclean technic," one of the cards in the promotional series read, adding that "[p]erforation may result from traumatic insertions."

One caution on these early physicians' file cards is worthy of note. It read: "At the end of two years, replacement with a fresh Dalkon Shield is recommended." As events have now proven, this was a warning well made. Had Robins stuck to this position, it is unlikely the IUD would have caused as much harm as it did, given the fact that it becomes more of a hazard the longer it is worn. Unfortunately, that sentence was replaced the following year by one promoting open-ended use of the Dalkon Shield. The original sentence, a November 11, 1971, marketing memorandum explains, was "creating problems and sales resistance from some physicians."

The company in December 1970 also prepared a very detailed background monograph for its sales staff that ended with the comment that "the Dalkon Shield is an effective, medically safe intrauterine device which produces few significant side effects." This line was to be used by the detail people to promote the product to the physicians in their territories.

That there was still no data other than Dr. Davis's is clear from a

November 20, 1970, memorandum from A. N. Chremos, M.D., the company's director of clinical pharmacology. Dr. Chremos states that Robins was about to begin long-range clinical studies in order to obtain "detailed information on efficacy, safety and toleration" regarding the very product the monograph claimed was "effective, medically safe . . . , [with] few significant side effects." The reason Robins had to go to the expense of such a study, Dr. Chremos said, was "the dearth of publishable data on the Dalkan Shield. . . ."

Of course, it could be argued that the contraception people on the Robins staff could, based on their knowledge and expertise alone, make such a judgment with at least a fair degree of accuracy. Only, as former Robins attorney Roger Tuttle pointed out, the A. H. Robins Company had no such experts on its staff. In fact, contraception was an entirely new area for the company; there was not even one research project under way at Robins in the area of contraception at the time it purchased the Dalkon Shield, nor, apparently, had there ever been such a project. In other words, everyone at the A. H. Robins Company was getting on-the-job training in the field.

This is made clear in at least one memorandum from that period. It was written by George E. Thomas, vice-president of Robins's international division, to president Zimmer on September 10. "I worry," Thomas wrote, "that we seem to have no present or past [research and development] effort on contraception and contraceptive methods . . . , we have no market knowledge or experience in our company, and we are prepared to learn on the job."

The situation was compounded during the pre–market-testing period when a Detroit, Michigan, physician named W. L. Floyd informed a Robins detail man that the device was not superior, that the Davis study was biased, and that the pregnancy rate was probably closer to 5 percent than 1.1 percent (how Dr. Floyd knew all this is unclear; the physician eventually went on the Robins payroll as a member of its Dalkon Shield Advisory Committee). The detail man hurried off a memorandum on the discussion to his superiors in Richmond. Dr. Floyd's warning was ignored, however, when Robins launched its massive advertising and promotional blitz in January 1971.

There was one other serious omission from the Robins literature on the Dalkon Shield that had appeared in the Dalkon Corporation's literature: a suggestion to physicians that patients fitted with the Dalkon Shield use an added form of contraception during the first few months with the IUD. "Recent reports from clinical investigators," the Dalkon Corporation had written, "strongly recommend adjunctive use of spermicide foam, jelly, or cream to enhance contraceptive effectiveness during the first three months after insertion of the Dalkon Shield." Dr. Davis has testified under oath that he very likely discussed this caveat with people at Robins.

The entire history of the Dalkon Shield from the time of its purchase by the A. H. Robins Company in June 1970 until its national roll-out campaign in January 1971 thus appears to be one of "damn the caution, full speed ahead." Dr. Davis had told Dr. Clark on June 8 that the product had to be on the market within eight months; Robins got it out in under seven.

There was more to the speed by which the Dalkon Shield was brought to the consumer, however, than merely heeding the advice of one of its inventors. Clearly, the company did not really believe the product would be around for very long. In George Thomas's memorandum to William Zimmer, for example, the international vice-president stated that "we must assume that there is at least a possibility that someone will come out with an improved I.U.D. that could make our DALKON SHIELD obsolescent quickly," and that "it would be a mistake for us to consider this as a long-range product."

This thought was echoed in the November 20, 1970, memorandum written by Dr. Chremos that discussed the undertaking of clinical studies. "It is very probably correct to say," Dr. Chremos wrote, "that in five years all the presently used means of contraception will be at or near obsolescence."

That obvious pressure was put on by management to push the product can nowhere be better seen than in a telegram sent by E. D. Hood, apparently a divisional sales manager for Robins, to detail man John S. Campana on February 26, 1971: "Northern division will not be humiliated by a lack of Dalkon sales. If you have not sold at least 25 packages of 8 then you are instructed to call me. Be prepared to give me your callback figures. No excuses or hedging will be tolerated, or look for another occupation."

4

THE DALKON SHIELD COVER-UP

Almost from the outset, skeptical physicians such as Dr. Floyd criticized the pregnancy study done by Dr. Davis. Eventually, there would even be suggestions (apparently based on off-the-cuff remarks made by Dr. Davis at a meeting with colleagues as well as the Dalkon Corporation's caveat in its literature which Robins ignored) that the unusually low pregnancy rate he achieved had been helped along by the use of an additional contraceptive. Dr. Davis, while admitting that he often suggested to his private patients that they use a foam or jelly together with the Dalkon Shield, vehemently denied that any additional contraceptive was used by the women subjects of his study, most of whom were patients at the Johns Hopkins Pregnancy Clinic.

The pregnancy-rate controversy aside, many physicians were reluctant to prescribe the device for other reasons, including their belief that the unusual shape made it difficult to insert and remove and painful to wear.

Even the competition was having a go at the new product. On March 26, 1971, a Robins detail man, Walt Schoenberger, handwrote a memorandum to the Robins medical department: "What is our Dalkon 'string' made of?" he asked. "Competition (Ortho) is telling my doctors that it will break, it will fray easily, and that it is 'multi-layered' so that the inner core acts as a wick to induce infection into the uterus."

Competitors bad-mouthing another company's product is not unusual and ordinarily it would not be worth worrying about. Ortho Pharmaceuticals, however, was no mere competitor; unlike Robins, it had a track record in the contraceptive field. More important, perhaps, what the Ortho people were saying about the Dalkon Shield were not general comments but very specific ones that required someone at Ortho to have carefully examined the product. Especially considering that the Robins people had heard it all before, this was one time that a competitor's bad-mouthing should have received some serious consideration. Instead, Robins decided to deny that any problem existed, even to its own salesmen, and to cavalierly put down the criticism as little more than sour grapes.

On April 22, 1971, Anne W. Board, M.D., a Robins medical staffer, responded to Schoenberger. The string, she wrote the detail man, "is nonabsorbable and 'wicking' has not been a problem. True, I suppose the string may break if sudden jerking motions are applied, but then, steel cables have been known to snap on occasion, too."

In early April 1971, while Dr. Board was preparing her letter to Schoenberger, Elderin Wayne Crowder, quality-control supervisor at the Chap Stick Company, the Robins subsidiary responsible for manufacturing the Dalkon Shield, returned from a visit to Irwin Lerner. What he had learned about the potential wicking problem had concerned him greatly. Lerner had told him of the wicking tendency, for one thing. He had also discovered abrasions on the nylon sheathing and holes in a number of Dalkon Shield tailstrings. Even though, as Robins has since pointed out derogatorily, Crowder never formally graduated from high school, he knew what it all added up to in terms of the women using the device. He wanted to pursue the matter further and so went to the office of his immediate superior, a Mr. Ross, to discuss what could be done.

"I told him that . . . I was concerned that water—fluids—would wet out the inside of the [tail]string and that bacteria would grow and progress through the string, resulting in a uterine infection," Crowder recalled under oath several years later. "His response was that the design of the device wasn't my responsibility and to leave it alone."

Crowder, however, could not leave it alone. "I felt that the design in combination with the damage to the [tail]string sheathing very definitely did make it fall within my area of responsibility," he later said. Having been warned against doing so, however, Crowder put the matter aside for a while; he would first talk to some people and see whether he was making too much out of nothing.

By late June, Crowder had learned enough to know that the problem was serious and that he had to do something. He designed a simple test to see whether he could demonstrate the tailstring's wicking tendency. "I clipped the string off below the attachment knot and immersed a portion of the string in water, but left the top portion of the string out of the water," he recalled. The string was allowed to sit in the beaker of water overnight. "Then, under the microscope, taking the string end and 'milking' it between my finger and thumbnail . . . , you would see a drop of water come out of the core of the string."

Crowder invited Ross to come to the laboratory, where he demonstrated the wicking under the microscope. "His response eventually in that conversation was to become extremely angry . . . ," Crowder said. "[He] reminded me that he had told me before that it wasn't my responsibility and to leave it alone. . . . I told him that I couldn't, in good conscience, not say something about something that I felt could cause infections. And he said that my conscience didn't pay my salary. . . . He referred to my persistent 'insubordination,' [that] was the word he used, and not doing as I had been told to do and forgetting about it, and if I valued my job I would do as I was told."

In early July, Crowder was called to Ross's office to discuss another problem with the tailstring—male sensitivity to it. The string, apparently, had a tendency to harden from the fluid it was absorbing. That caused injury to the penis. The complaints of men who had suffered such injury apparently was something with which the company wanted to deal.

In the office, he found Chap Stick president Daniel E. French. Since they were discussing the tailstring anyway, Crowder decided to tell French about the wicking problem. French seemed concerned and asked what could be done. Crowder suggested at the very least heat-sealing the two ends of the string so they would no longer be exposed, but French said Robins would never go for the idea; it would cut into profits.

The conversation then returned to the problem of male sensitivity to the string during intercourse. French, Crowder recalled under oath, crassly joked "that maybe I could get some of the girls in the factory to help me with the testing." With that, French left. Ross then told Crowder that he hoped Crowder had gotten the tailstring problem out of his system.

Crowder had not gotten it out of his system, however. On July 28, 1971, he formalized his simple wicking study in a memorandum. On August 5, 1971, French, no longer able to ignore Crowder's findings, notified project coordinator Ellen J. "Kitty" Preston, M.D., that problems existed with the tailstring. According to a memorandum Dr. Preston wrote to Dr. Clark on August 9, "Mr. French suggested that alternate types of materials should be looked into. . . . Mr. French says the reason given for the sheath is that it provides protection against bacterial invasion. He points out, however, that both ends of the string are cut and left open. It has been shown that the open ends will wick water. It seems to him that if this is so that the ends will wick body fluids containing bacteria."

Clearly, from the evidence, the tailstring problem was now being taken seriously enough by Robins for the company to consider replacing it, if for no other reason than that Crowder's memorandum made it impossible to ignore. This much was made clear in a memorandum to Dr. Oscar Klioze dated September 2, 1971. "I have resisted changes in the past," one David A. Mefford told the pharmaceutical research director, explaining that his main concern was keeping productivity high, "but I believe the time to make changes is rapidly approaching." Mefford then went on to recommend a number of possible changes for the tailstring.

Some physicians, meanwhile, were beginning to voice their own concerns and this, too, may have had a role in getting Robins to reevaluate its position regarding the tailstring. One in particular, Kermit Krantz, M.D., of Kansas University Medical Center, had been so vociferous in detailing his complaints about the Dalkon Shield that E. J. Smith, Robins's Midwest hospital divisional manager, suggested in a letter to Dr. Fletcher Owen, the company's medical services director, "if you are able to neutralize this man, it will certainly help our sales in that area." The letter was dated November 12, 1971.

At about this time, Robins named Kenneth E. Moore project

director for the Dalkon Shield. On November 5, 1971, Moore reported to a special high-level management committee that problems with the tailstring did indeed exist. The recommendation was made by the committee that a substitute be found. A memorandum written by Moore to Crowder on November 12 shows clearly that the company was by then investigating new materials with which to replace the tailstring.

At least for some at Robins, the tailstring situation was approaching the critical stage. On February 15, 1972, an internal meeting regarding the Dalkon Shield was told that Robins "should be very concerned" about the strength of the nylon string. "[A] report was quoted by Ken Moore which showed that after a period of 17 months in situ an 80% loss of strength of nylon cord was experienced."

That same meeting heard other problems relating to the Dalkon Shield discussed. A toxicology study involving baboons was apparently going sour; "in recent weeks, three have died," according to the minutes. (The baboon study was begun in August 1971 and lasted for two years. The final results showed that one out of eight baboons died and that 30 percent suffered uterine perforations. Robins has never released the results of that study.) "Increased pregnancy rates have been received—no specific figures were mentioned but generalized as 4–5 in 80–90 insertions," which works out to a raw pregnancy rate of between 5 and 6 percent. "Perforations, difficulty of removal, string breaking on removal (3 instances one physician), were other problems reported," the meeting also was told.

Moore's next step in determining how to handle the tailstring problem was to bring in an outside expert, John Autian, Ph.D., "one of the leading plastics toxicologists in the country and a faculty member at both the Pharmacy and Dental Schools at the University of Tennessee," according to Moore's April 18 memorandum of the visit.

"When asked about establishing time periods beyond which the Dalkon Shield should no longer be used," Moore wrote, "Dr. Autian indicated that we should be thinking in terms of establishing definite limitations" similar to the two-year limit discontinued several months earlier because it was interfering with sales. As far as the nylon tailstring was concerned, Dr. Autian "feels we have a definite problem with this because historically it has been shown that nylon does deteriorate in situ over a period of time."

By April 25, Moore in a handwritten memorandum noted that the company was now "desperately searching" for a tailstring replacement. At no time, however, did Robins inform physicians that a potential problem existed and that, at the very least, women using the Dalkon Shield should be closely monitored.

Around this time, the company decided that it had to counter the growing adverse publicity regarding the Dalkon Shield. Robins had earlier—and quietly—hired a New York public relations firm, Wilcox and Company, to help promote the Dalkon Shield to women. The campaign violated the drug industry's own code of practice because the Dalkon Shield was considered an ethical device. As such, advertising and promotion should have been directed exclusively at physicians. However, marketing studies indicated that by far the majority of birth-control devices had been prescribed to patients who had specifically requested those devices. Hence, the public relations effort was directed at getting women to discount all of the negative things they had been hearing about the device and to get them to specifically ask their physicians for the Dalkon Shield.

In one letter to Richard L. Wilcox, dated June 30, 1972, Ken Moore enclosed an article on contraception from a Detroit newspaper quoting Dr. Joan Stryker, "an arch enemy of Dr. Hugh Davis." Reading the article, Moore noted, "you would never know the Dalkon Shield exists." He then concluded by saying that "a positively written, well-placed article would go a long way toward neutralizing the bombardments of the enemy and the claims of our competitors who are too frightened to acknowledge the existence of the Dalkon Shield."

Some of those "bombardments," however, were not coming from critics or the media but from lawsuits and threatened lawsuits against the company. There were enough of them, in fact, for Robins to assign attorney Roger Tuttle to deal with them and to begin to issue a monthly litigation status report.

Those "bombardments" also were coming from friends at this point, such as a five-page letter on June 23, 1972, from Dr. Thad Earl to John L. Burke, Robins's general sales manager at the time. In the letter, Dr. Earl, the man who had done the original selling of the Dalkon Shield to Robins and who was Robins's highest-paid outside consultant, discussed various problems he had been told about by physicians using the Dalkon Shield and how he had attempted to resolve them. The letter was basically an upbeat one, but there was one critical paragraph:

"The next situation I have found is with women becoming pregnant and if the Shield is left in place the women abort at 3½ to 5 months and become septic. I am advising physicians that the device should be removed as soon as diagnosis of pregnancy is made. Numerous physicians have noted this. In my six pregnancies, I removed one and she carried full term, the rest all aborted and became septic. I therefore feel it is hazardous to leave the device in and I advised that it be removed. I realize that this is a small statistic and that we should correlate this data with other investigators across the country, because most men are experiencing the same problem."

On June 29, Ken Moore prepared a long memorandum commenting on Dr. Earl's letter. In it, the Dalkon Shield project manager did indeed take Dr. Earl seriously. He pointed out that the opinion of Dr. Earl regarding removal during pregnancy "is completely in reverse of what we have been recommending since it was felt that the pregnancy would have a better chance of continuing to term if the Dalkon Shield were left in place," a position taken by Robins's nonexperts in contraception without benefit of a single test. Moore then urged that "every effort should be made to arrive at some definite conclusion as soon as possible which will enable us to make a positive statement one way or the other as to whether the Dalkon Shield should be left in place or removed if the patient becomes pregnant."

In October 1972, Robins made clear just how much attention it had paid to Dr. Earl's letter. The company issued revised product literature in which it addressed the pregnancy problem head-on. "When pregnancy does occur," the company claimed in a brochure meant for patients, "the bag of water [the amniotic sac] pushes the IUD to one side and the developing baby is not really touching the device at all." The data supplied by Dr. Earl had thus been discounted, seemingly out of hand, and not even a reference to it was made. Instead, Robins made a bald statement about pregnancy for which it apparently had no supporting evidence.

Increasingly as the months went by, Tuttle's monthly litigation status reports were painting an ever-bleaker picture of the Dalkon Shield problem. On September 11, research vice-president Dr. Jack Freund issued a memorandum to senior staffers involved with the IUD, such as Drs. Clark and Owen and Ken Moore. In that memorandum, Dr. Freund urged them to "place any requests for data to support our position in these cases at the top of your list of priorities."

By November, Tuttle's litigation reports had become alarming. There was no longer any question; something had to be done about the Dalkon Shield. On November 9, 1972, a companywide committee meeting was held to discuss just that. Considering everything that was supposed to be wrong with the product, not to mention the allegations being made against the Dalkon Shield in the ever-growing number of lawsuits, one might have expected that the committee's deliberations would center on ways of determining once and for all what the problems were and what steps should be taken to rectify those problems. Judging from the minutes of that meeting, however, very little thought seems to have been given to the possibility that the device itself was at fault. Rather, the committee tried to blame everything on outside forces.

There were many such outside forces the committee had to choose from, the minutes reveal, including "adverse publicity in the form of unsubstantiated 'pot shots' " by physicians with probable interests in other forms of contraception; "adverse publicity as a result of unsuccessful use of the Dalkon Shield by a minority but vociferous group of physicians" who were "in large part [ignorant] of the proper insertion protocol or [indifferent] to adhering to it"; and "lack of physician support for the Dalkon Shield at the major fertility meetings." One internal force the committee faulted was "the company's failure to get the 'good word' out about the Dalkon Shield," which really meant Robins's inability to find physicians and independent data to support the product.

The solution offered centered on the establishment of a Dalkon Shield Advisory Program, to include a committee of seven consultant obstetrician-gynecologists "strategically located around the country." Each physician would receive up to $10,000 a year and would "be called upon to assist physicians/clinics experiencing serious problems . . . via correspondence or a personal visit." They were also "to render support to our sales representatives at key national and regional meetings." The qualifications for these people included solid credentials, personable appearance and, above all, a successful history with the Dalkon Shield.

The committee also recommended that greater use be made of Dr. Davis, who would "troubleshoot in particularly difficult situations," and called for "at least ten retrospective studies . . . for the purposes of obtaining favorable Dalkon Shield data." There is nothing in the minutes to suggest that anyone felt even the slightest bit uneasy about using Dr. Davis in this way considering his past history of producing questionable data and his royalty interest in the IUD, not to mention their own comments regarding critics of the Dalkon Shield who had known financial interests in other devices.

The only action the committee took regarding any of the real problems with the Dalkon Shield was a decision to test a product called Gore-Tex, a polytetrafluoroethylene (Teflon) material, as a substitute for the tailstring. This decision, however, was preceded by a discussion of whether the new, presumably safer material made sense from the standpoint of cost. The current string cost considerably less than a penny a Shield (0.63 cents), whereas the new Teflon material cost 6.1 cents per Shield. The decision to go ahead with the tests was made after it was noted that, as the minutes explained, "Chap Stick [the Robins subsidiary that actually manufactured the Dalkon Shield] has observed a great deal of variation in the nylon string from reel to reel. There has been considerable breakage with some reels and very little with others. Therefore, in all likelihood, the cost per shield for the nylon string is greater than 0.63 cents when one considers the material wasted due to breakage."

(Apparently, there was still enough of a cost differential between the nylon string and Gore-Tex because no substitution was ever made, even though the company was forever telling the media over the next two years that a substitution was imminent. "Nothing better illustrates the corporate greed of Robins and its strategy to place corporate profits above human safety" than the eventual decision not to replace the tailstring, according to court papers filed by plaintiffs' attorney Bradley Post, through whose efforts much of the early evidence against Robins was amassed.)

Robins also decided to launch a massive advertising campaign in medical journals to overcome the increasingly bad publicity the Dalkon Shield was getting, publicity that had resulted in a serious sales slump. There was at least an element of bad taste in one advertisement, which has been referred to as "the flying uterus ad." It included a full-page photograph of a number of uteri that had been removed from women during the course of hysterectomies; three of the uteri were small and were placed randomly in the upper-left-hand corner of the page, along with silicone casts of the uterine cavity similar to the ones Dr. Davis had used to design the Dalkon Shield in the first place. One uterus, however, was blown up to six and a half inches in length and, at one point, eight inches wide. In the uterine cavity itself was placed a Dalkon Shield with its circular "eye" at the top. The deep red giant uterus, together with the ovaries, was placed in a diagonal position, its upper part leaning to the left of the reader. The overall effect reminds one of a headless Mighty Mouse puffing up his chest and flexing his muscles as he flies off after saving the day. "The 'second generation' IUD is here," the advertisement proclaimed.

The campaign also included an apparently unprecedented eight-page advertisement. This advertisement, among other things, reported the "results" of studies done by four researchers—Drs. Davis and Earl, Donald Ostergard, M.D., and Mary Gabrielson, M.D. —on the effectiveness of the Dalkon Shield. This prompted at least one physician to write a sharp letter of protest to Robins. He was Russel J. Thomsen, M.D., a U.S. Army major stationed at the military hospital at Fort Polk, Louisiana.

"The four studies quoted (Davis, Earl, Ostergard, Gabrielson) are probably the best you could find for your advertisement," Dr. Thomsen quite perceptively noted in his letter to Robins's Professional Services Department on December 15, 1972. "But these are pathetically inadequate studies in evaluating the effectiveness and complications of an intrauterine device. And the presentation of data in the advertisement is typically deceptive in nature.

"Need I illustrate[? The] Davis study covered a time period of 12 months with 640 insertions and 3,549 woman-months of use. This simply means that the study covered 640 insertions with the average of time used by each insertion being only 5.5 months. Earl's study covers a little more time (8.6 months average insertion time), but Ostergard and Gabrielson give pathetic average insertion study times of only 4.3 and 4.9 months respectively. Need I point out that the grand average of your four quoted studies involving 3,174 insertions covering 17,222 woman-months gives an equally pathetic average insertion study time of 5.4 months[?]

"In your own ad you suggest 'A supplemental contraceptive method . . . during a 2–3 month post-insertion adjustment phase.' If that three month period is subtracted from the 5.4 months average insertion study time one comes to the startling conclusion that you are selling this product with an ad that really makes claims based on a partial guarantee covering only about 2.4 months of average time during which the Dalkon Shield is the only form of contraception recommended."

Dr. Thomsen went on to say that he had been keen on the Dalkon Shield when it was first introduced, but that he no longer prescribed it to patients. His experience and that of his colleagues, he wrote, indicated a pregnancy rate of nearly 10 percent and a high incidence of such serious complications as pelvic inflammatory disease.

"Actually," he added, "the only complication of this apparently dangerous intrauterine device which is seemingly low is spontaneous expulsion. This is undoubtedly related to the other observed fact that the usual medical removal of a Dalkon Shield is a painful experience indeed for a woman."

Dr. Thomsen also told Robins he was sending a similar complaint to the FDA.

Dr. Thomsen did not know the half of it as far as the studies quoted in the advertisement were concerned. He knew, of course, that Dr. Davis's study was faulty, although he did not know about Dr. Davis's financial interest in the device, or the fact that only seven women out of the 640 had used the device for the full twelve months. Dr. Thomsen had no way of knowing that use of Dr. Earl's study, published in 1971, should have obligated Robins (at least morally and ethically) to mention the physician's June 23, 1972, warning about the dangers of leaving the Dalkon Shield in once pregnancy is established. (For that matter, he did not even know of Dr. Earl's letter or of Dr. Earl's financial interest in the Dalkon Shield.)

Dr. Thomsen also did not know that the study conducted by Dr.

Mary Gabrielson was based on preliminary data assembled from the first nine months of an eighteen-month study and that Robins knew that the data was misleading before it published the advertisement. Approximately four months before the advertisement appeared, Dr. Gabrielson completed her study and passed her results on to Robins. Rather than the 1.9 percent rate cited in the advertisement, Dr. Gabrielson informed Robins that the twelve-month results showed a pregnancy rate of 4.2 percent, while the eighteen-month rate was 5.1 percent.

And then there was the Ostergard study. Dr. Ostergard, who has described himself as "contraceptive expert," traveled to defend the Dalkon Shield wherever Robins would send him—at a fee of $500 a day plus expenses. On February 4, 1972, the director of Robins's Biometry Department, Lester W. Preston, Jr., Ph.D., wrote a memorandum to Dr. Fred Clark explaining why he had ordered "that *all* Data Management and Analysis activities should be immediately suspended on both prospective and retrospective Dalkon Shield data from Dr. Donald Ostergard." The problems with Ostergard's data, Preston wrote, included "such facets as multiple data sheets not agreeing in content, from the same patient; many, many obvious 'errors' in completing the forms (i.e. obvious inconsistencies)—as well as ambiguities; gross deviations from protocol instructions . . . ; questionable patient selection; administrative aspects (e.g. designating re-insertion patients as a new patient); etc." Ostergard's retrospective data, Preston added, was "fraught with the *most obvious* errors. . . . I dislike the expression, but [Ostergard's work] could well turn out to be a clear-cut case of GIGO [computerese for "garbage in, garbage out"]." (Note: We have deliberately avoided appending "Dr." to Preston's name in order to distinguish him from his physician wife, Dr. Ellen J. Preston, and not out of any disregard for his academic credentials.)

Apparently, Dr. Clark's superior, Dr. Jack Freund, disagreed with Preston's assessment that the Ostergard data had created a "dismal situation" for Robins's data analysts; Preston was overruled and the questionable data continued to be used—after being worked over by Robins's own staffers to make it more acceptable.

There was one other fact Dr. Thomsen was not aware of when he wrote his letter that December: Robins's ten-investigator study of the Dalkon Shield had found that, out of 2,160 insertions in place for less than a year, on average, there were more than sixty cases of pelvic inflammatory disease. Rather than publish the study, Robins suppressed it; it would take several years and very persistent attorneys to discover the data. When Robins finally did publish the results; these too were questionable. A clinic in Defiance, Ohio, was one of the ten investigators used. According to the Robins "results," that clinic showed only one case of PID in 149 insertions. However, a 1984 review of that data by the clinic showed 18 cases of PID in 120 insertions. (Twenty-nine files could not be found.) This indicated a rate that was fifteen to twenty times higher than Robins's rate for the clinic, assuming that the twenty-nine missing cases showed no instances of PID.

And then came January 1973. The product had been launched a scant two years earlier and it was already highly controversial, to say the least. Matters, however, were about to take a decided turn for the worse in this anniversary month: A physician named Marshal reported the death in 1971 of a woman who had suffered from pelvic inflammatory disease.

The Dalkon Shield had claimed its first life.

On January 4, 1973, Robins notified the FDA of the potential problems, a point Robins inevitably cites as in its favor. However, Robins had little choice; the FDA requires such notification after a certain number of complaints have been lodged against a product under its regulatory control. Moreover, FDA investigators had to make five visits to Robins before they were given permission to review the complaint files. Even then, the files were opened only to FDA field investigators, not the agency's medical officers.

A month later, Robins's search for a Dalkon Shield advisory committee was well under way. However, a second death had been reported by then and a bunker mentality appears to have set in at the A. H. Robins Company, with critics now being openly referred to as "enemies."

In a lengthy memorandum dated February 13, 1973, to "regional managers only," the company called for their help in finding physicians for the panel. However, the regional managers were cautioned that the project was to be kept secret even, if possible, from their own people. "Publicity regarding this program would be highly undesirable at this point," the memorandum stated; "therefore, we leave it to your good judgment as to how much information you should share with your divisional and/or district managers in obtaining their suggestions. Under no circumstances should any prospective physician panelists be contacted at this juncture."

The situation continued to deteriorate throughout 1973 as the negative statistics—and the lawsuits—mounted. In April, an article appeared in the *Journal of Reproductive Medicine* written by obstetrician-gynecologist Jerome Abrams, M.D., of Plainfield, New Jersey. Dr. Abrams was then a consultant to the Union County Area branch of the Planned Parenthood Foundation of America (PPF). "After two years and 110 Shield insertions with only 4 expulsions and 10 removals," Dr. Abrams wrote, "six pregnancies were accumulated. At approximately this time, a memorandum . . . was received from Planned Parenthood reporting 6 pregnancies after only 52 insertions. Our confidence in the Shield has been seriously undermined. We are now investigating [another] type of IUD."

There was nothing new in the article from Robins's point of view; the memorandum Dr. Abrams referred to had been distributed in the latter part of 1972 and had been one of the subjects discussed during the November 6 interdepartmental meeting that had recommended creation of an advisory board. Nevertheless, the article now made public the information that had been disseminated only to PPF chapters and that only sent Robins retreating further into its bunker. The problem was exacerbated even further when, later in the year, the *National Review* included an excerpt from Dr. Abrams's article in one it was doing on IUDs. By September, the *National Review* article, which had been syndicated, was appearing in newspapers across the country. To everyone reading it, the message was clear: the nation's leading promoter of contraception, Planned Parenthood, disapproved of the Dalkon Shield.

Still, the A. H. Robins Company continued to do everything that it could to promote the Dalkon Shield, including continuing to deny that design flaws existed. In a September 5, 1973, letter, for example, project coordinator Ellen J. Preston, M.D., wrote in answer to a letter from Robins's medical director in England, who had reported on several PID cases and the theory being suggested that the wicking tailstring was at fault:

"You bring up the question of a possible wicking effect due to the multifilament nature of our string material. This question has been posed before, but it is the opinion of Hugh Davis and others that whatever wicking the multifilament may provide is overcome entirely by having the filaments enclosed in the sheath. . . . [Of] course, if the sheath is destroyed in someway [sic], then perhaps a problem might exist. We know this can happen, but I do not believe it is very frequent."

(It is impossible to determine who wrote that paragraph, or whether Robins's attorneys participated in its preparation. That it was a "boiler plate" paragraph that would be used almost verbatim in other letters above signatures other than Dr. Preston's is almost certain, however. It is duplicated practically word for word, for example, in a letter sent by another Robins physician, A. O. McMichael, M.D., on May 21, 1974.)

Attorney Tuttle explained the lengths to which the company went in late 1973 to compound the cover-up and counter the increasingly negative reports regarding its embattled IUD. The company, Tuttle testified in August 1984, reacted primarily with a disinformation campaign—by launching a series of newspaper advertisements quoting letters from satisfied Dalkon Shield users. The letters, Tuttle insisted, were written by A. H. Robins Company employees.

The company also did other things to bolster its corporate image during this period, including allowing a number of its executives to appear in full-page advertisements in 1974 for the Dale Carnegie Management Seminar. The Dalkon Shield was not the sole reason Robins was desirous of promoting a more positive image at that time, although it was the major one. The company had run into a streak of bad fortune in a number of areas. A new appetite suppressant, Pondimin, was not gaining acceptance in the marketplace; the FDA had questioned the validity of the company's claims for some of its ethical drugs; and its ninety-day flea collars, which reports at the time described as having been made from a substance akin to Nazi nerve gas, were reportedly killing pets as well as fleas.

While Robins sought to improve its image, the Dalkon Shield toll mounted inexorably higher. By late 1973, Robins had information on thirty-six users of the Dalkon Shield who had suffered septic abortions, five of whom had died; a sixth death involved a nonpregnant woman who had died of septicemia.

Robins at this time issued revised product literature and urged its sales representatives "at the *first opportunity* to call [the changes in the literature] to the attention of all appropriate physicians." The new literature warned physicians that "[s]evere sepsis with fatal outcome, most often associated with spontaneous abortion following pregnancy with a Dalkon Shield *in situ* has been reported," warning them that "serious consideration should be given to removing the device when the diagnosis of pregnancy is made. . . ."

The new literature also warned physicians that the "proportion of pregnancies which terminate in spontaneous abortion is considerably higher in the presence of IUD's," thus softening the blow to the Dalkon Shield by accentuating the generic nature of the problem. Finally, it cautioned the physicians that the "risk of accidental pregnancy with IUD's may be higher during the first two or three menstrual cycles following insertion." Therefore, physicians should prescribe a supplemental contraceptive method for that period, or alternatively "during the ovulatory period of the menstrual cycle on a continuing basis. . . ."

Here, again, however, Robins was only doing what it had to do; there were too many reports in the general and professional media for it to remain silent. Nevertheless, it continued the cover-up by couching the new warnings in generic terms as often as possible in order to present the Dalkon Shield as no more dangerous than any other IUD. The facts, however, are different. Robins, for example, told the physicians that the probability of septic abortions was considerably higher "in the presence of IUD's," but as the FDA would reveal later on in the year, of 287 reported cases of septic abortions associated with IUD use, more than 75 percent related to the Dalkon Shield.

The following month, February 1974, saw the convening of a conference sponsored by Robins on septic abortions. The conference, held at the company's headquarters in Richmond, was characterized more by what Robins failed to report to the physicians present than by anything else. For example, Robins did not mention Dr. Thad Earl's letter of June 23, 1972, which warned of septic abortions and recommended removal of the Dalkon Shield once pregnancy was established. (Dr. Earl was not even invited to the conference.) It did not mention any of the data it had amassed relating to the wicking tendencies of the tailstring, either, or that an expert of the company's own choosing had determined that the nylon material would deteriorate in time. The conference ended with no definitive result one way or the other.

Several months later, on May 8, 1974, Robins sent a mildly worded letter to 120,000 physicians informing them about the problems that had been reported to it. According to the letter, which has become known as "Dear Doctor I," women considering using a Dalkon Shield should "be advised prior to the procedure [of fitting the device] that a therapeutic abortion may be recommended in the event of accidental pregnancy." The letter, however, made no suggestion that women already fitted with the Dalkon Shield be contacted and the device removed, except in cases where pregnancy had already occurred. It also did not discuss the problem of pelvic inflammatory disease.

Just in case any physicians failed to get the letter, Planned Parenthood reproduced it and mailed copies to each of its seven hundred affiliated clinics with orders to stop prescribing the Dalkon Shield until the federation could meet to discuss what further action to take. Planned Parenthood also sent out press releases announcing what it had done. The releases included copies of Robins's letter. The next day, the PPF's National Medical Committee went one step further: It instructed all affiliated clinics to call in their patients who had been fitted with a Dalkon Shield, warn them of the risks, and offer them a substitute.

At this point, there was no question at Robins's headquarters that the Dalkon Shield was finished as a viable product. An April 30, 1974, status report on the Dalkon Shield prepared by Allen Polon, Ken Moore's successor as project manager, had already made it clear that the product was doomed domestically and probably eventually would be dead internationally (although, at that point, it was still doing quite well outside the United States). Net domestic sales in 1972 had amounted to $2,739,885. In 1973, that figure had dropped to $1,901,997. First-quarter sales for 1974 were down by nearly 50 percent and that trend was expected to continue; the sales estimate for 1975, for example, was $175,000; it was $125,000 for 1976; $90,000 for 1977; and $50,000 for 1978.

Some would argue, just using good business sense, that the Dalkon Shield should have been dropped from the product line. The status report, however, stated that this was not possible for a reason that had nothing to do with marketing: "It is the opinion of

Mr. Tuttle that if this product is taken off the market it will be a 'confession of liability' and Robins would lose many of the pending law suits [sic]."

A way had to be found to let go of the Dalkon Shield while not appearing to do so. That way quickly presented itself:

In late June 1974, the acting director of the FDA's Bureau of Medical Devices wrote an "Action Memo" to Food and Drug commissioner Alex M. Schmidt, M.D., recommending in part that Robins, "because of the health hazard" presented by the Dalkon Shield, be requested "to cease distribution of the Shield and [to] recall all stocks of the device that have not been implanted. . . . If firm refuses to recall, we are prepared to request an injunction and to institute multiple seizures." On June 26, the FDA sent a letter to Robins requesting that the company voluntarily withdraw the Dalkon Shield from the marketplace.

It was an ideal situation for Robins. By appearing to bow to FDA pressure in "temporarily" suspending the Dalkon Shield (although it would not recall the unused devices at this point), the company could still argue that it had faith in the product and that the controversial IUD would be back—with a new tailstring, no less. At the same time, the company would continue international sales of the product, which were in any case a lot stronger than domestic sales at that point. In that way, the company would even be able to demonstrate its confidence in the IUD.

On June 28, therefore, Robins "gave in" to the FDA pressure and "temporarily" stopped shipping the Dalkon Shield to the domestic market pending a safety study by the federal agency. Outside the United States, meanwhile, Robins continued to sell Dalkon Shields in seventy-nine foreign countries, including Canada, before altogether halting shipments of the contraceptive device nine months later. In all, Robins sold 2.2 million of the devices in foreign countries.

By the beginning of July, the numbers had dramatically increased again. Now there were over one hundred cases reported of uterine infections, with seven deaths. The U.S. Department of Health, Education and Welfare (HEW) wasted no time in contacting more than three thousand federally supported family planning clinics, ordering them to stop prescribing the Dalkon Shield. At the same time, HEW urged private physicians not to prescribe the device because of doubts about its safety and effectiveness.

On July 3, deputy assistant HEW secretary for population affairs Louis M. Hellman, M.D., who also chaired the FDA's Advisory Committee on Obstetrics and Gynecology, stated that, "pending final action by the Food and Drug Administration, it is unnecessary at this time to recall patients for removal of the device. If patients come in, however, to consult with their physicians or for routine appointments, the device should be removed at that time."

As the summer continued, Dr. Schmidt pondered the choices he had to make regarding the Dalkon Shield. Finally, on August 21, he appointed a special advisory panel of distinguished obstetrician-gynecologists in clinical practice to review the situation. At the panel's first meeting, the agency announced that the Dalkon Shield toll had climbed yet again. There were now eleven deaths associated with the Dalkon Shield and 209 septic abortions. By contrast, the FDA stated, the Lippes Loop device had five deaths associated with it and only twenty-one septic abortions—and it had been on the market much longer than the Dalkon Shield. The Saf-T-Coil, yet another device that had been on the market for a number of years, had only one death and eight septic abortions connected with it.

On October 30, the advisory panel decided that the moratorium on the commercial distribution of the Dalkon Shield should remain in effect pending accumulation of definitive data on its safety and efficacy.

Robins by this time was aggressively selling the Dalkon Shield in international markets. The type of advertising it used as part of its campaign is worth noting for two reasons: (1) The nature of the exaggerated claims made suggests that Robins was attempting to "dump" the Dalkon Shield on foreign markets before the bottom fell out for the IUD internationally; and (2) the lack of any reference in those advertisements to the situation in the United States suggests that Robins was continuing to ignore the dangers of its product even as the toll of injuries and deaths mounted.

In a full-page advertisement in the November 1974 issue of the *Australian and New Zealand Journal of Obstetrics and Gynaecology,* for example, Robins claimed that the "pregnancy rate . . . of the Dalkon Shield is lower than that of oral contraceptives," and supported this claim with a study purporting to show that the Pill had a 7.7 percent pregnancy rate—which is approximately 700 percent higher than the commonly accepted rates for oral contraceptives at the time. In a very small-print footnote, Robins qualified this by pointing out that, according to the study from which the data was taken, the absurd pregnancy rate was "probably due to improper use of the pill, and not to a defect in its theoretical effectiveness. . . ."

The advertisement also stated that the Dalkon Shield "affords exceptional patient tolerance, comfort and convenience"; that it "is light and flexible to minimise cramping, and anatomically engineered for optimum uterine placement, fit, tolerance and retention"; and that it "has the highest continuation rate and the lowest medical and personal removal rate of all presently available devices."

Five days before Christmas 1974, the FDA released updated figures. The death toll now stood at fourteen. As for septic abortions, out of 287 cases reported relating to IUD use, 219 involved the Dalkon Shield.

And then something strange happened. At the same time as these figures were released, the FDA gave the A. H. Robins Company a totally unexpected (and basically unwanted) Christmas present. "I am today announcing the following actions," Food and Drug commissioner Schmidt said at a December 20 press conference.

"One: In order to develop the type of definitive data the Advisory Committee has requested, distribution of the Dalkon Shield will be resumed under a formal registry and reporting system. The manufacturer, A. H. Robins Company, has agreed to distribute the device directly to those physicians who agree to register patients at the time of insertion and keep detailed records of patient experience with the device.

"Two: Physicians are now being advised of the registry program. . . ."

There was a catch, however: Robins would be allowed to market the Dalkon Shield only if it replaced the multifilamented tailstring with a monofilamented one.

Within hours of Dr. Schmidt's press conference, Planned Parenthood announced that it would nevertheless continue its ban on the Dalkon Shield. Robins, meanwhile, immediately announced "plans" to begin distribution of the Dalkon Shield under the FDA's guidelines. The company never had any intention of again marketing the Dalkon Shield, but the publicity value of the FDA's surprise decision was too good an opportunity to waste.

That publicity, however, was short-lived. Many members of the advisory committee simply could not abide the action Commissioner Schmidt had taken and made their private complaints public. On December 23, panel member Emanuel A. Friedman, M.D., of Harvard Medical School, wrote to Horace Thompson, M.D., chairman of the committee: "I wish to tender my resignation immediately. . . . In our long deliberations we felt almost unanimously that continuing the moratorium was the appropriate course of action. I cannot understand how it is possible for Dr. Schmidt to justify reversing this recommendation. . . . In essence I feel the committee has been emasculated by the action of the commissioner. . . . I feel very strongly that the Dalkon Shield puts women at risk."

Dr. Thompson himself wrote Dr. Schmidt in protest, saying, "I disagree strongly with your action."

Yet another committee member fired off a shocked letter to Dr. Schmidt on New Year's Eve. "The action taken by the FDA in effect circumvents the recommendations of the committee . . . ," wrote Richard Dickey, M.D., a professor at Louisiana State University Medical School. "The precipitous action in releasing the Dalkon Shield for commercial distribution at this time . . . may needlessly endanger more women. . . . It is now imperative that the FDA announce its position on the recall of the Dalkon Shields already distributed but not inserted because of the contradictory statements being published in both the lay press and medical newspapers."

Robins took no public notice of the growing debate over the FDA's ruling. That debate, however, brought new pressure to bear on the company, this time from physicians and clinics with Dalkon Shields in stock that they no longer intended using. Understandably, they wanted their money back. On January 20, 1975, Robins gave in to this pressure and offered to purchase back from wholesalers, physicians, hospitals, and family planning clinics the Dalkon Shields they had on hand. The company called the offer a "market withdrawal."

By April 1975, when foreign sales were apparently suspended (exactly when this occurred is hard to document), the numbers of victims had again spurted upward: the toll now stood at 245 septic abortions and fifteen deaths. On August 8, the company announced that the Dalkon Shield was now permanently off the market despite the fact that the A. H. Robins Company "remains firm in its belief that the Dalkon Shield, when properly used, is a safe and effective IUD."

In October, Robins announced that it had by then paid $1,548,000 for the settlement of litigation, legal fees, and other expenses arising out of Dalkon Shield lawsuits. Once again, however, it took the opportunity to reiterate its position that the Dalkon Shield was as safe as any other IUD.

Congress at about this time was considering a bill that would subject companies to criminal penalties if they knowingly produced and marketed unsafe products. Nothing ever came of the legislation, but while it was still pending, attorney Tuttle says he had a conversation about it with Dr. Jack Freund, now the company's research vice-president. "You should be on your knees praying to your God or mine," Tuttle has testified as having told Dr. Freund, because "you'd be doing hard time if the truth [about the Dalkon Shield] were ever known."

At about the same time, too, plaintiffs' attorney Bradley Post formally requested Robins to recall the Dalkon Shield. Sales of the device may have stopped, but many of the nearly 2.5 million women who had been fitted with it were still wearing it and a recall, he argued, was the only way to get to these women. Robins did not even bother to respond to the request. Two years later, as the toll continued to mount, Post joined with another attorney, Aaron M. Levine of Washington, D.C., in petitioning the FDA to issue a recall. It declined.

By March 1980, there had been seventeen deaths and countless uterine infections, septic abortions and emergency hysterectomies connected with the IUD. Robins had lost $21 million in lawsuits over the use of the Dalkon Shield and had 665 more lawsuits pending and 315 claims to settle. Robins's insurance companies had paid out more than $55 million.

During the following spring and summer, following an outpouring of new lawsuits numbering in the thousands, a series of meetings took place at the Robins headquarters about what further action needed to be taken. Attending those meetings, in addition to Robins personnel, were Alexander H. Slaughter, Frank J. Tatum, and/or other attorneys from the law firm of McGuire, Woods & Battle (to which former Robins president William Zimmer had since returned), which had responsibility for coordinating the Dalkon Shield defense.

That a recall of the device was discussed at that time is almost certain. Clearly, however, the decision that resulted from those meetings was tempered by the needs of Robins's defense posture in the many lawsuits. A recall would have been a virtual admission of liability. Some other way had to be found, therefore, to warn physicians to get the Dalkon Shield removed while continuing to maintain that the device was safe.

That way became the letter known as "Dear Doctor II," prepared apparently with the help of Robins's outside counsel. On September 25, 1980, Robins informed physicians that the Dalkon Shield should be removed from all women using it, although it still denied that anything was wrong with the product. "Since any present users of the Dalkon Shield are in the long-term use category," the letter stated, "we now recommend removal of this IUD from any of your patients who continue to use it, even though they may not be experiencing any pelvic symptoms at this time." The letter, Robins stated, was prompted by recent information in the medical literature that now questioned the wisdom of a woman wearing any IUD for too long a time.

The FDA, for one, was not impressed. Lillian Yin, M.D., who headed up the federal agency's obstetric- and gynecological-device division, suggested in a memorandum that the letter "may be [merely] an attempt to reduce [Robins's] liability in the multitude of [law]suits which they continue to be involved in by using this still controversial issue to affect the removal of their product without calling for a recall."

Surprisingly, despite the innocuous nature of the letter, a number of physicians and even some newspaper readers nevertheless saw the letter as a product recall. F. R. Fahrner, M.D., of Joliet, Illinois, for example, wrote to Dr. Fletcher Owen on behalf of his Family Medical Group pointing out that "when any industry sets out a recall they usually pay for the recall," adding that "we feel that this is your obligation to pay for the Dalkon Shield removals."

Janet Nowak, after claiming to have read "in the September 25 (1980) New York Times that The A. H. Robins Company was recalling the Dalkon Shield due to numerous health problems," also demanded of Dr. Owen that the company pick up the tab for the removal. "The replacement cost will be $75.00," the Westport, Connecticut, woman wrote. "In view of the fact that the Robins Company is recalling a defective and potentially life threatening product I feel that the replacement cost should be paid for by you." (The New York *Times* never carried such a story. On September 26, however, it did report that Robins had "recommended to physicians today [September 25] that they recall all of the intrauterine devices regardless of whether women using them have suffered ill effects." That undoubtedly was the article Ms. Nowak was referring to in her letter.)

Owen apparently answered all such letters in much the same manner: by denying that any recall had taken place and by playing down the urgency of the situation. To Ms. Nowak, for example, he wrote on October 13, "Our present recommendation for removal of all remaining Dalkon Shields is as indicated above based upon new and recent information from the medical literature. It is not an urgent matter. . . ."

After ten years of experience, nearly twenty known deaths and thousands of known serious injuries, Robins still insisted that removing the Dalkon Shield "is not an urgent matter." In fact, about the only "urgent matter" relating to the Dalkon Shield in Robins's point of view was successfully defending the thousands of lawsuits that had been filed against it. At times it would seem that Robins and its attorneys would stop at nothing to win those suits.

5

DEFENDING THE DALKON SHIELD

On September 29, 1982, within forty-eight hours of being notified that a Chicago man had died, apparently after ingesting a poisoned Extra Strength Tylenol pain reliever, the McNeil Consumer Products Division of Johnson & Johnson issued a national product recall. Twenty-two million bottles were removed from shelves nationwide, to be returned to McNeil and destroyed. Free exchanges were offered for any of the product already in consumer hands.

This national recall campaign was conducted despite the fact that the problem was clearly a localized one (i.e., in and around the Chicago area) and despite the evidence that Tylenol *in that area only* had been randomly injected with poison by some deranged individual.

The company paid in excess of $100 million for its recall. The product's acceptance in the marketplace also suffered. Before the incident, Tylenol held a commanding 37 percent share of the billion-dollar-a-year over-the-counter painkiller market. After the recall, that share immediately dropped to 7 percent. (Within a year after the introduction of new "triple-sealed" packaging, Tylenol's share had climbed to 30 percent, within striking distance of its old mark.)

The A. H. Robins Company responded very differently to the problems being created by the Dalkon Shield. Its strategy was one of denial, buck-passing, cover-up, questionable testimony, intimidation, obfuscation, distortion, and delay.

At the very least, Robins knew even before it acquired the rights to the Dalkon Shield in 1970 that IUDs generally were a potential legal problem. In February 1968, the FDA's Advisory Committee on Obstetrics and Gynecology issued a "Report on Intrauterine Contraceptive Devices." It provided readers with the current state of knowledge regarding IUDs and information on the testing that would need to be done and on what possible side effects should be anticipated, including various types of injuries the devices were known to cause. Specifically, the report cited statistics of ten deaths and 751 cases of severe infection and perforation of the uterus. IUD users were more likely to get pelvic infections, the report added; if they miscarried, it would probably be a septic abortion.

Given all this, the FDA's Advisory Committee reported, "IUDs provide a fertile field for medicolegal suits."

Thus, from the very beginning, Robins was aware both of the medical complications that were possible in the case of IUDs and of the legal ramifications of those complications. From the outset, therefore, it prepared the groundwork for its future defenses from those complications even as it failed to address the complications themselves.

"The first lawsuits concerning the Dalkon Shield were filed in early 1972 and were relatively unsophisticated product liability suits grounded on the theory of uterine perforation," Roger L. Tuttle, who as in-house counsel directed the company's litigation strategies from 1972 to 1975, wrote in his 1983 article in the *Oklahoma Bar Journal.* "Plaintiffs' attorneys, without a thorough understanding of human anatomy, theorized that the device migrated from the uterus into the abdominal cavity causing two elements of damage. The first was actual invasion of the peritoneum through the uterine wall, and the other was the subsequent pregnancy resulting in an 'unwanted' child because the device was in the stomach, not in the uterus. Other early cases were concerned with pelvic inflammatory disease. . . ."

Its first line of defense, Robins decided, would be to shift any blame for problems to the physicians who inserted the Dalkon Shield.

"Robins defended these early cases on the basis that inasmuch as the device was available only on prescription from a licensed physician who had all the available product information, he was the responsible entity," Tuttle explained in the law journal article. "Robins argued that in perforation cases the physician was too hurried in his insertion technique, pushed on the inserter stick too vigorously, and simply shoved the device through the uterine wall." The argument is a valid one; as such, plaintiffs in perforation cases find it extremely difficult to prove their claims.

"In pelvic inflammatory disease cases," the onetime Robins attorney continued, "Robins argued that the physician did not thoroughly examine the patient to determine pre-existing disease and accommodated his patient by inserting the device in a contaminated field. In both classes of cases, Robins took the legal position that it had no *privity* with the consumer, who was the patient of an intervening factor, the physician, and that if there was an actionable tort for negligence, then it had to be the result of the active participation of the physician.

"Robins argued that with this device the standard should be different from that associated with a drug that was merely ingested by the patient without any activity on the part of the physician. Furthermore, Robins contended that no warranties attached since the device was promoted only to physicians and pharmacists and could not be obtained or used by the consumer directly.

"In those cases in which the attending physician was not jointly sued by the patient, Robins cross-claimed against the physician."

Robins's argument of no *privity*—that is, no legal connection or relationship with the ultimate consumer—was fraudulent. Beginning in December 1971, after all, Robins was involved through the New York public relations firm of Wilcox and Company in a media campaign aimed directly at influencing women to ask their physicians for the Dalkon Shield because an external marketing study had reported that an estimated 60 percent of IUD sales resulted from patient requests rather than physician preference.

The campaign was unethical. The Dalkon Shield could be obtained only through a physician. As such, it was subject to the same industrywide rules for advertising and promotion as are ethical (prescription) drugs—and at the time advertising and promotion of ethical drugs was considered proper only when directed at health professionals in their journals and through the mail. Lay advertising and promotion was seriously frowned upon.

That the A. H. Robins Company anticipated the need for a blame-the-doctor defense even before it began selling the Dalkon Shield is clear from various internal and external Robins documents.

In August 1970, for example, the Marketing Research Department cautioned company officials on the need to establish a positive history of use before the Dalkon Shield could be randomly marketed to all physicians wanting the devices. Noting that "enough problems arise when competent physicians perform [IUD] insertions," the department warned against initially selling the Dalkon Shield to physicians who are "just casually familiar with pelvic anatomy."

Sales to such physicians, the department memorandum explained, "could be very detrimental to the establishment of this product" because their inexperience and poor knowledge would translate into a greater number of Dalkon Shield-related complications. "Complications," the memorandum pointed out, "are sometimes evaluated by number and severity and not why they came about. It would be to our advantage to keep our 'press' as good as possible until use is more widespread and the merits of our device better known. Once proven and accepted, complications with use of the Dalkon Shield would be far less damaging." The report added: "The need for a good initial show is imperative."

Another document indicating a premarketing intent to let physicians take the heat for Dalkon Shield problems is the set of file cards that were sent to physicians warning them that "sepsis may result from unclean technic" and "perforation may result from traumatic insertions." Similar warnings to physicians appear in nearly every piece of literature Robins ever produced relating to the Dalkon Shield.

Once problems did begin to crop up, the preplanned "blame-the-doctor" defense was rolled out. The first complaints Robins received, for example, related to the higher-than-claimed pregnancy rates physicians were finding in their experiences with the Dalkon Shield. Time and again, Robins blamed those higher rates on poor insertions by the physician even though it knew that its published 1.1 percent pregnancy rate was based on the incomplete data supplied by the device's coinventor, Dr. Hugh Davis. Project manager Ken Moore even called this "the most logical explanation for the disparities" in his June 29, 1972, memorandum commenting on Dr. Thad Earl's letter which discussed the problems being encountered with the Dalkon Shield in pregnant women.

From the relative standpoint of problems caused by the Dalkon Shield, the pregnancy rate alone was a minor one. A major one, however, was described in that very same letter by Dr. Earl: the potential for the Dalkon Shield to cause life-threatening infection to the woman who becomes pregnant while the device is in place. Robins could have published new information and warnings, but to do so would have meant a loss in sales. Instead, it chose to point the finger at physicians.

Another part of the Robins blame-the-doctor defense strategy was to locate physicians who had only good experiences with the Dalkon Shield but who were not tainted by any connection with the company. Obviously, if such physicians testified in cases of colleagues who had bad experiences, it would at the least suggest to the juries that the doctor, not the device, was at fault. As Tuttle explained in a November 6, 1972, memorandum to Dr. Fred Clark, Robins's medical director:

"In my judgment, what we need is a number of retrospective studies by clinicians who have had a very favorable experience with the Dalkon Shield but who were not on our 'payroll' at the time they started using the Shield.

"I believe that the prospective studies which you have been undertaking and which are now in process, are most helpful; but, the results of these studies are tainted by the fact that [they] were made at our expressed request and subsidized entirely by us. What we need are studies conducted by physicians who had no 'connection' with Robins and who only after-the-fact were paid to examine their data and make the same available to us. Of course, should this program be undertaken, it should be explained to any physicians selected that we would want them to be available to testify in our behalf concerning the results of their studies, all at our expense, should the occasion warrant."

So important was it to Robins in its early defense of the Dalkon Shield cases to have physicians with apparently no connection to the company testify favorably on behalf of the product that the company was not above using what must be considered at the very least dubious testimony. At the head of the list of its Dalkon Shield defenders was Dr. Hugh Davis. As the man whose study created all of the initial interest in the Dalkon Shield and whose subsequent book on IUDs kept that interest going, not to mention his prestigious connection to Johns Hopkins, Dr. Davis was an ideal witness ("literally the man 'who wrote the book,' " as Tuttle described him in a May 23, 1972, letter), provided that no one knew of Dr. Davis's financial interest in the very product he studied. Even when being deposed, therefore, Dr. Davis would deny under oath any financial connection with the Dalkon Shield, just as he had done before Senator Gaylord Nelson's subcommittee in February 1970.

There is, for example, a deposition Dr. Davis gave in the case of *Connie Deemer* v. *A. H. Robins Company* on February 20, 1974, in the offices of the Robins legal department. Attorney Bradley Post did the questioning:

Q. Did you act as a consultant for the Dalkon Corporation after it was organized?

A. I did. . . .

Q. What pay, if any, did you receive from either Mr. [Irwin] Lerner, or the Dalkon Corporation?

A. I received a reimbursement for my expenses, and I received a royalty . . . payment from [Mr. Lerner] for a number of years concerned with the formulation of a spray that is in use in cytology for the fixing of cells. . . .

Q. Did you receive any pay from Mr. Lerner for work on the Dalkon Shield?

A. I did not.

Q. Did you have any royalty agreement whereby you received money for Dalkon Shields that were sold?

A. I never received any royalty from the Dalkon Corporation for Dalkon Shields. . . .

Q. What does the word Dalkon mean?

A. It doesn't mean anything, as far as I know.

Q. Was that a name contrived from the names Davis, Lerner and Cohn?

A. I think it could be interpreted that way. . . .

Q. Do you know what royalties Mr. Lerner, or the Dalkon Corporation, receives from the Robins Company?

A. . . . I believe from what I recall of what Mr. Lerner told me that they have an agreement with Robins that covers something like five percent of the sales as a royalty to be payable to the Dalkon Corporation. . . .

Q. Do you have an agreement with Mr. Lerner or the Dalkon Corporation whereby you receive any of the royalties he receives from the Robins Company sales of the Dalkon Shield?

A. I do not.

Q. Have you ever?

A. No.

Q. Have you ever owned any stock in the Dalkon Corporation?

A. No, I do not own any stock in the Dalkon Corporation.

Q. I said, have you *ever* owned any stock in the Dalkon Corporation?

A. I was trying to recall the events around 1968. Mr. Lerner offered me some stock in this corporation and my decision at that time was not to hold it because I felt there was a conflict of interest. I did not feel . . . I should be in a position of testing and evaluating a device in which on one side I was functioning as an evaluator and on the other side I was . . . participating in the corporation.

At the time Davis gave this seemingly noble testimony, he had already received nearly $600,000 for his share of the sale of the Dalkon Shield to Robins and in royalties received from Robins for the sale of the IUDs. He knew he was misstating the facts and, he claimed several years later, so did the Robins attorneys present. In fact, as he testified in a series of depositions beginning in November 1976 and ending in March 1977, the Robins attorneys made him do it (something the attorneys vehemently deny).

Q. Did you ever tell Mr. Tuttle that you were reluctant in any way to testify in cases involving the Dalkon Shield because of your financial interest?

A. Yes.

Q. Did Mr. Tuttle indicate to you that he felt that you had an obligation to testify in cases involving the Dalkon Shield because of your consultation agreement for which you were being paid twenty thousand dollars per year by Robins . . . ?

A. Mr. Tuttle indicated to me on numerous occasions that he and the Robins Company were extremely anxious that I should appear and function as an expert witness in connection with some of this litigation and I think that would be an accurate statement with respect to Mr. Tuttle's position.

Q. Did Mr. Tuttle have knowledge of the fact that you held a financial interest in the Dalkon Shield before you gave testimony [in the February 1974 Deemer deposition] . . . ?

A. Yes, I believe he did.

Q. Did you express any reluctance to testify in litigation involving the Dalkon Shield because of your financial interest in the device?

A. I did.

Q. Did you express that reluctance to Mr. Tuttle?

A. I did. . . .

Q. Did you in discussions with Mr. Tuttle discuss how questions would be answered concerning your interest in the Dalkon Shield before you gave deposition testimony?

A. Yes.

Q. Did you ever have discussions with Mr. [William] Forrest, general counsel for Robins, concerning giving testimony in Dalkon Shield litigation?

A. Yes, I've met with Mr. Forrest.

Q. Was Mr. Tuttle present during those times?

A. I believe so. . . .

Tuttle, under oath, has denied knowing that Dr. Davis had a financial interest in the Dalkon Shield when he used the physician as an expert witness. He insisted that he only learned about this situation in late 1974 after speaking with Robert Cohn, the attorney who had set up the Dalkon Corporation and had been one of its three original partners. Cohn, however, was also deposed and he gave a completely different version. Tuttle, he said, never called him to ask whether Dr. Davis had any financial interest in the Dalkon Shield, nor would he have expected Tuttle to make such inquiry since the Robins Company had been fully informed as to the financial interests of all the owners in June 1970.

Even if Tuttle is telling the truth about not knowing, there is no question that the A. H. Robins Company did know of Dr. Davis's involvement; there are countless memoranda indicating this. A memorandum "to files" dated June 10, 1970, and captioned "Dalkon Shield Purchase—Outline," has as its item number two: "Lerner, Davis, Earl and Cohn execute agreement assigning to Robins . . . shield and inserter and all improvements thereto in respect of design, formulation, or otherwise and any patents obtainable therein." And international vice-president George Thomas's September 10, 1970, memorandum to company president William Zimmer twice makes references to it: "The new owners [sic] of AHR (Lerner, Davis and Cohn)" and "I suspect our new friends (Lerner, Davis, and Cohn) are interested only in milking" the Dalkon Shield. Someone, therefore, should have warned Tuttle that Davis's testimony was less than candid if not outright perjurious.

One person who could have so informed Tuttle (and, in fact, should have as an officer of the court) was company president and chief operating officer Zimmer, who before and since his tenure at the A. H. Robins Company was counsel to McGuire, Woods & Battle, the Richmond law firm that serves as Robins's lead defense counsel. Another such officer of the court, William A. Forrest, Jr., Robins's general counsel, also could have told Tuttle. His handwritten notes made on June 5, 1970, clearly show that he indeed did know about Dr. Davis's connection from the very beginning. And, according to Dr. Davis's account, Forrest did sit in on at least one meeting at which Dr. Davis's upcoming Dalkon Shield testimony was discussed.

The use of dubious testimony by physician/experts was not limited to either Davis or the early days of Dalkon Shield litigation. "Dubious," in fact, was too mild a term for the three-judge federal appeals panel that in January 1985 reviewed the testimony of Robins expert Louis Keith, M.D. The court used a much stronger word —"perjury"—to characterize Dr. Keith's testimony in the case of *Linda and William Harre* v. *A. H. Robins Company.* The perjury, the court stated, was committed "with complicity of [Robins's] counsel."

The suit charged that Mrs. Harre, like Martha Hahn, had contracted pelvic inflammatory disease as a result of the Dalkon Shield;

subsequently, she became sterile. The trial began in Tampa, Florida, on March 3, 1983. During the twelve days that followed, experts for the Harres blamed the PID on the wicking of the Dalkon Shield tailstring. Among the witnesses for the Harres was Howard Tatum, M.D., a Dalkon Shield opponent for over a decade.

Against these witnesses came Keith, a board-certified Chicago obstetrician and professor of medicine at Northwestern University, a former director of the Illinois Family Planning Association and a paid Robins consultant since 1977. Keith was the last witness to testify and, in the words of the appellate court, "was the only one [of Robins's witnesses] who purportedly had conducted or directed wicking studies."

The positioning of Keith as the final witness was unquestionably strategic. He was the last person the jury would hear before the attorneys made their final arguments and the jurors decided the case, meaning that his testimony would—it was hoped—be the one the jury would remember best. In the opinion of the three-judge appellate court, that strategy paid off for Robins.

Keith testified that based on his review of Linda Harre's medical records, her PID was the result of chronic cervicitis. Robins attorney Charles E. Osthimer III (whose apparent coaching of E. Claiborne Robins, Sr., ten months later would earn him stern warnings from U.S. District Court Judge Miles W. Lord) then asked Keith whether in his opinion the Dalkon Shield was at fault.

Sid Matthew, the Harres' attorney, objected. Keith, he argued, could not testify on the issue of causation because no foundation had been laid as to his experience with the Dalkon Shield. The objection was sustained and Osthimer dropped that line of questioning for the rest of the afternoon. When Keith resumed the stand the next day, however, Osthimer began to lay that foundation.

"Now, Doctor, have you done or are you doing any studies under your direction on the Dalkon Shield tailstring itself?" Osthimer asked.

"Yes," Keith responded, "studies are being done *under my direction.*" These experiments, Keith said, were designed to "gain information on the allegation that . . . the string wicked bacteria." Osthimer then asked Keith to "describe the design of *your experiment,* first of all, and then I want you to *describe what you did.*" Keith complied and Osthimer followed by asking, "Did *you do any other studies* with Dalkon Shield tailstrings?" (Emphases ours unless otherwise noted.)

"Well, there were a series of experiments," the Robins physician replied, adding, "In some, there were pure bacteriological experiments and then, after these were done, *we did* some with radioactive material."

A few moments later, Osthimer said to Keith:

"You stated that you did some studies with bacteriological implications, and then you started to talk about radioactive materials. Could you explain *what you did* in that portion of the study, please?"

"It was simply taking the same design, *as we had before,* and labeling a bacteria," Keith began his response.

After he concluded, Osthimer asked: "Could you draw a diagram of the way in which *you conducted* these experiments?" Keith said yes and proceeded to do so, explaining the diagram as he went along.

"Now, *in your experiment,* did you reverse the situation?" Osthimer inquired next.

"Yes," replied Keith, *"we also did some* that went like that."

"Now, Dr. Keith," Osthimer asked at length, "in conducting these experiments, did you have somebody working with you who was a microbiologist?"

"I did," Keith answered.

"And did you have someone working with you who was an expert in the use of radioactive labeling of bacteria?" Osthimer inquired next.

"Yes," Keith responded. "These people were experts."

Finally, the proper foundation having been laid, the physician was permitted to testify that, in his opinion, the Dalkon Shield did not contribute to Linda Harre's illness; its tailstring did not wick bacteria; and the device itself was not unreasonably dangerous for use as an IUD during the time period in question.

The next day, Robins used Keith's testimony to refute the studies that had demonstrated the wicking tendency of the Dalkon Shield tailstring.

"The best test that has been done on this subject was done *under the auspices of Dr. Keith,"* said Robins attorney Thomas H. Sloan, Jr. "He testified here yesterday and he described the test that was done by this microbiologist which was a test that more closely duplicated the human situation than any laboratory test done by Dr. Tatum."

Sloan then reiterated this, saying that Keith *"has had that* [test] done" and *"he has done it."* (Emphases appear in 11th Circuit decision.)

Clearly, the Harres' entire case against Robins hinged on whether the jurors believed that the Dalkon Shield tailstring wicked bacteria. Robins itself admitted that wicking was "the crux of the [Harres'] case." This crucial point was even highlighted by U.S. District Judge William J. Castagna, who on the record stated that wicking was "a principal argument" of the case. On March 17, two days after it began its deliberations, the jury returned a verdict in favor of A. H. Robins.

On November 1, 1983, or nearly eight months after he testified in the Harre case (the timing is important), Keith was deposed in San Francisco in the case of *Dembrowsky* v. *A. H. Robins Company.* In that case, plaintiff's attorney Dennis B. Conklin wanted to ask Keith about the experiments that he had testified in the Harre case were being done "under [his] direction." To do so, however, required the laying of a proper foundation. He began this task by inquiring whether Keith had "done any experimental work" on the Dalkon Shield tailstrings.

"No," Keith answered, "other than to look at one, I think, under a microscope."

Conklin, armed with Keith's testimony in Harre, was astonished. "You haven't done *any* wicking experiments?" he asked incredulously.

"I haven't," Keith responded matter-of-factly.

Conklin pursued the point. "Has somebody under your supervision done some?" After all, Keith had stated that he had directed the experiments.

"Not under my supervision," Keith said. *"I didn't supervise anybody."*

Keith went on to testify that he frequently consulted with a Dr. Eric Brown, a professor of microbiology at Chicago Medical School. Dr. Brown, Keith testified, had done some experiments, but Keith's knowledge of those experiments was based solely on talking with Dr. Brown and twice looking over Brown's laboratory notes; he personally had not observed any of the tests.

Conklin then asked Keith when Dr. Brown had conducted these tests. *"Within the last six months,"* came Keith's reply. (Emphasis appears in 11th Circuit decision.)

"Are those the same ones you testified about in Florida?" Conklin asked Keith, referring to the physician's testimony *eight* months earlier.

"Yes," the physician answered.

Thomas Sloan represented Robins in both Harre and Dembrowsky. In their appeal, the Harres argued that the jury might have reached a different verdict if it had not been for Keith's and Sloan's representations that Keith had personally conducted or directed such experiments.

Robins argued that the discrepancies in Keith's testimony were "minor inconsistencies" relating only to whether it was Keith or Brown who had conducted the tests. The important matter was Keith's knowledge of those tests and his testimony in Dembrowsky showed that he did have such knowledge. Thus, Robins claimed, no new trial was warranted.

Judge Castagna agreed with Robins that the inconsistencies were indeed minor and an appeal was carried to the 11th Circuit U.S. Court of Appeals. That court issued its decision on January 21, 1985.

The Hon. John W. Peck (actually the senior circuit judge for the 6th U.S. Circuit but sitting by designation on the appeals court) wrote the unanimous opinion for the three-judge panel. His decision ordering a new trial was a blistering one. Keith, he said, was "a material witness [who had] testified falsely on the ultimate issue in the case," and "the defense attorneys knew or should have known of the falsity of the testimony."

The court disagreed "with the characterization of the discrepancies as 'minor inconsistencies.' Further," it said, "we do not share the opinion of Robins, as asserted in its brief, that the differences are 'incidental' and 'trivial' in nature, nor do we agree that the testimony in question was on a 'tangential matter.' "

The court then detailed the "intractable conflicts . . . apparent in Dr. Keith's testimony in this case and his testimony in the Dembrowsky deposition." He could not have conducted studies if he did not do any studies, the court stated. He could not have had studies done "under [his] direction" if he "didn't supervise anybody." He could not have had somebody working with him on these tests who was a microbiologist, or an expert in the radioactive labeling of bacteria, because he neither made such tests nor supervised them.

It was not Keith's testimony alone, however, that was at issue, Judge Peck's decision stated. Keith's testimony, he said, "was exacerbated by the argument of counsel to the jury"—specifically, Sloan's statements that the "best test" for wicking had been done "under the auspices of Dr. Keith," that Keith "has had that [test] done," and that "he has done it." Said Judge Peck: "These statements of counsel, like Dr. Keith's testimony, squarely conflicted with Dr. Keith's Dembrowsky testimony."

The court next focused on Robins's argument that the inconsistency was only over who conducted the tests, not what Keith knew about them, and that it was Keith's knowledge of those tests that was important.

Noting that Keith had appeared as a witness in the Harre case eight months before being deposed in Dembrowsky and that, in the latter case, he had testified that Brown had conducted his tests "[w]ithin the last six months," the court stated:

"Thus it is established out of Dr. Keith's own mouth that he testified in the trial of the present action [Harre] to experiments that had not yet been conducted. The knowledge gained by Dr. Keith could not have been, as Robins urges, the important issue, since when he testified at trial he obviously could not have possessed any knowledge of Dr. Brown's experiment."

The court then turned to the question of whether Keith's testimony had prevented the Harres from fully and fairly presenting their case. "Of the numerous expert witnesses for the defense," the court found, "Dr. Keith was the only one who purportedly had conducted or directed wicking studies. His testimony went to the ultimate issue of causation. . . . We are convinced that had counsel for [the Harres] been aware that Dr. Keith had not actually directed, participated in, or even observed the experiments he described, it would have made a difference in their approach to the case and particularly in their cross-examination of Dr. Keith." This, the court found, had hurt the Harres' case.

The court then addressed the question of whether Robins's attorneys knew Keith was perjuring himself: "Robins states that appellants' allegations of attorney complicity are baseless. However, in view of the fact that Dr. Keith had acted as a consultant/expert for Robins since 1977, it becomes obvious that Robins's counsel must have been aware that Dr. Keith's testimony in Dembrowsky contradicted his testimony in the trial of this action.

"Further, we are disturbed by the comments of counsel for Robins in closing arguments and the nature of questions asked in direct examination which tend to support the implication that Dr. Keith was actually involved in the tests. This court is deeply disturbed by the fact that a material expert witness, with complicity of counsel, would falsely testify on the ultimate issue of causation."

Robins carried its blame-the-doctor strategy even to the point of agreeing to help plaintiffs' attorneys take on physicians. Robins's cooperation involved supplying expert witnesses and trial exhibits. The only condition: Robins was to be held blameless and kept out of the suit.

On November 21, 1972, for example, Tuttle sent the following items to Wichita, Kansas, attorney Dan S. Garrity:

"(1) A complete Dalkon Shield (standard model) in its sterile package;

"(2) A copy of the 'file card' informational brochure on this product for physicians and a copy of an informational brochure for patients;

"(3) Copies of a pertinent part of Dr. Davis' book concerning I.U.D.'s and an FDA report concerning the same."

Tuttle then went on to offer his company's cooperation "with the understanding that you will not bring us in as a party defendant on any action you may file arising out of the captioned matter. . . ."

In another instance, Tuttle worked out a deal whereby Robins not only worked against a physician in one case but by so doing was relieved of having to defend itself in another suit.

"In line with our conversation of yesterday," Detroit, Michigan, attorney Stanley S. Schwartz wrote to Tuttle on May 9, 1973, "permit me to set forth what I believe to be our understanding in this matter.

"In the case of Beltzman v Salesin, you will make available to me for deposition purposes Dr. Owens [sic] and Dr. Davis. . . . The doctors will be deposed on the basis of concept and ideas, testing, and performance. My line of inquiry will not relate to any possible manufacturing defects in design or otherwise, but will, per contra, relate only to the signal and salient elements necessary to create a *prima facie* case against Dr. Salesin.

"Further, notwithstanding the fact that the statute of limitations has not run against the manufacturer, I will not institute any suit against your company and will devote all efforts and initiative against Dr. Salesin in this case which is now set for trial on July 2, 1973.

"As you know, my office will be substituting in the case of Hauer v. A. H. Robins Company; A. Lewis Hayes, M.D.; Alan C. Lakin, M.D., and Michael S. Salesin, M.D. . . . After we complete the taking of depositions, I will strongly urge Mr. Hauer to authorize me to voluntarily dismiss the action against your company."

The Robins strategy of buck-passing resulted in more than simply getting out from under many of the early suits filed. Another result, or so plaintiffs and their attorneys contend, was to influence malpractice-conscious physicians to tell their patients that there were other "causes" for the problems they may have been experiencing because of the Dalkon Shield. It also dissuaded these physicians from notifying Robins of the problems they were finding; after all, if the blame was going to be put elsewhere, it made no sense to complain to the manufacturer of the device.

This underreporting—even Robins's own expert witnesses admit there was serious underreporting considering the level of the controversy—played to Robins's advantage for years thereafter, in suit after suit. In one 1981 case, for example, Karlis Adamsons, M.D., a professor of obstetrics and gynecology, used the underreporting to score points for Robins. In 1973, the lawyer questioning him said, Robins had received reports of patients using the IUD who had "some sort of a pelvic infection." He was then asked whether he had reviewed summaries of those reports and he said that he had.

Q. Given the numbers of Dalkon Shields that were being used in that period of time, in your opinion was [sic] the numbers of reports in any way comparable to what you would have expected given a random chance of a sexually active woman getting pelvic infection?

A. Well, the numbers were astonishingly low. . . . [We] would expect twenty-thousand patients per year being reported just on the basis that they were female and they were sexually active to end with genital infection. The reports that the Robins Company received—I'm not sure when this was, but it was less than I think one hundred or so over that period. So that the numbers were very much lower than I would have expected. . . .

Q. How would you characterize, with your background and experience, the fact that Robins put [information on pelvic inflammatory disease] in their [sic] labeling, given the low numbers of actual reports of pelvic infections?

A. . . . It certainly cannot be interpreted that they had concluded that the device caused infection or that the observed frequency exceeded that which normally would have occurred in any sexually active female population.

In fact, Dr. Adamsons testified, "my interpretation of this additional [PID] information . . . is that the Robins Company was very cautious. . . ." Dr. Adamsons, who thus far has been paid approximately $112,000 by Robins for his testimony in various Dalkon Shield lawsuits, never prescribed one of the devices for a patient, nor did he ever insert one.

This early strategy was clearly successful. As Tuttle notes in his article, even when Robins was sued, "the special damages per case were well under $10,000. Statistically, by injury, well over 50 percent of the cases were perforations, 35 percent were pelvic inflammatory disease cases, 10 percent were unwanted children, and the balance was a melange of theories, including one exotic dancer who claimed a caesarian section for delivery of a live birth was caused by the device and the resultant scars left her disfigured and lowered her economic value as an exotic dancer."

In the early days, too, Robins believed that it was better to try any suits filed against it than to settle, and to fight any judgments against it all the way up the appeals ladder. This policy had a dual purpose. It was meant to discourage the "nuisance suits" that are inevitably filed when a company is too quick to settle. It was also meant as a form of intimidation: plaintiffs and their attorneys would be put on notice that there was no way they could afford the protracted litigation Robins was prepared to undertake.

"Our posture is that the Company intends to try any case that is actually filed," Tuttle explained to Dr. Davis in a May 23, 1972, letter, "without consideration of settlement short of verdict against us. Even so, it is my present plan to appeal adverse verdicts to the highest appellate court which will be willing to entertain an appeal. Hopefully, by this posture we can both gain experience and also persuade plaintiffs' attorneys that the Robins Company is not a 'patsy' when it comes to the Dalkon Shield."

It was not too long after this strategy was conceived, however, that Robins realized how dangerous a course it had set for itself.

In July 1972, a California attorney named Ronald Mallen wrote Robins a clearly suit-threatening letter alleging that Mallen's wife had become pregnant while wearing the Dalkon Shield. On August 10, 1972, Tuttle responded with the company line. He made every effort to dissuade Mallen from filing suit over the unwanted pregnancy, adding that "if you elect to litigate against us, I assure you that we will be prepared to vigorously defend to the highest appellate court available."

Throughout the letter, Tuttle made it clear how blameless Robins was; in effect, by setting forth the outlines of his company's defense, he hoped that attorney Mallen would have no doubt how solid Robins's case would be. "[A]lthough we regret that your wife became pregnant while wearing a Dalkon Shield," he wrote, "it is evident in your letter that you and your wife were fully informed and aware that this I.U.D. was not 100% effective in preventing pregnancy. All literature on the Dalkon Shield points this out, and statements concerning the contraceptive effectiveness of the Dalkon Shield have been based on available published scientific data (see attached). . . . All statements made in the Dalkon Shield literature are, of course, based on statistical evidence. Unfortunately, it is impossible to predict ahead of time in which women the Dalkon Shield will fail and how long after insertion it might fail."

Tuttle, of course, also attempted to shift the blame to Mrs. Mallen's physician, even as he was trying to convince her husband that no one was to blame except fate. "Obviously," his letter stated, "the best results with any I.U.D. are felt by most authorities to be dependent on proper insertion technique by the attending physician. In the case of the Dalkon Shield this is accomplished by meticulous attention to the recommended procedure for insertion of the Dalkon Shield as outlined in our official labeling (see attached)."

Mallen, however, would not be dissuaded; he asked one of his law firm associates, John B. Hook, to handle the matter. After a bit of legwork, Hook and Mallen drafted a letter letting Tuttle know just how little they thought of Robins's defense. Obviously, they had been doing their homework.

"[D]o you deny that your inventor, Dr. Davis, used supplemental means of contraception in testing and compiling the statistics on the pregnancy rate?" Hook's letter asked pointedly. "Do you deny that he so admitted at a recent meeting of physicians . . . ? Our original sources of information regarding the falsity of these [pregnancy] statements were witnesses who heard your inventor (Dr. Davis) admit that his tests were performed while using supplemental contraceptive methods. Secondly, several physicians (including Dr. Smith [Mrs. Mallen's physician]) had encountered a five to six percent pregnancy rate. . . .

"In preparing for suit we preliminarily surveyed local physicians and discovered two facts. First, *all* of the physicians have encountered a pregnancy rate greater than one percent, estimated to be at least five percent. Second, *none* of the physicians have . . . been advised [by Robins] of the unreliability of the prior representations. We are currently preparing to broaden our survey to exhaustively cover, at a minimum, the Northern California area in anticipation of possible class litigation."

The letter from attorney Hook was just too full of danger signals to be ignored. Of primary concern was the implied threat of discovery. Such discovery would leave Robins much too vulnerable, considering what its files contained regarding the safety and effectiveness of the Dalkon Shield. The Mallen "case," therefore, caused the company to rethink its strategy of going to trial at all costs; hereafter, trials were to be avoided whenever possible. As a result, of the approximately 7,500 cases settled in one form or another from 1972 through February 1985, fewer than forty ever went to a jury—and many of those were the difficult-to-prove perforation cases.

That Robins took the case of *Mallen* v. *Robins* seriously can be seen in a memorandum dated September 11, 1972, from Dr. Jack Freund. In it, Dr. Freund called the case probably "the most important" then pending against the company, adding that "[it] is imperative that this case be successfully defended." (It appears that Aetna also took the case very seriously; based on it, according to references found in the unexpurgated minutes of the Robins board of directors thanks to the intervention of Judge Lord, the insurance company apparently almost withdrew its liability coverage on the Dalkon Shield because of Robins's fraudulent promotional campaign.)

Ironically, Ronald and Penelope Mallen never did file suit against Robins because, as Mallen, a litigation attorney, explained to us recently, the couple gave birth to a beautiful boy named Seth and so had nothing to complain about. Mallen, however, does say that he takes pleasure from the fact that his letter and the one he helped John Hook write to Robins have played important roles in subsequent Dalkon Shield suits where real injuries had taken place.

Despite its shift from the trial-at-all-costs approach, Robins continued its tactic of passing the buck to physicians. This tactic apparently worked well until the spring of 1974, when a combination of factors caught up with the company: the federal government's Center for Disease Control in Atlanta and the FDA itself began circulating Dalkon Shield casualty figures; a plaintiffs' attorneys group, the Association of Trial Lawyers of America, began publicizing the suits against Robins; and attorney Bradley Post did what Robins feared Mallen would do: he uncovered the first "smoking gun":

As Tuttle recalls it in his law journal article, "as a result of pretrial discovery, a plaintiff's attorney [Post] found the famous Dr. Fred Clark memo of June 9, 1970, alluding to [Dr. Davis's] dual sets of [pregnancy] statistics. Although these statistics do not bear on or address safety, plaintiffs' lawyers thereafter argued to judges and juries that Robins could not be trusted, that it was covering up, and that it had misled physicians and consumers and the FDA."

From this point on, simply shifting blame to the physician would not be adequate. Also inadequate at this time was Robins's in-house capability to handle the suits being filed against it. As a consequence, the company in mid-1975 employed one of Virginia's largest law firms—McGuire, Woods & Battle—"to supply the assets required in lawyers, paralegals, research assistants and secretaries," as Tuttle explained it.

The no-trial-at-all-costs strategy first propounded after Mallen and reinforced as a result of Post's discovery now became permanently central to the Robins defense plan. Settlement, however, was also to be the last resort. Intimidation was to be the focus of initial efforts. First, the plaintiff's attorney would be intimidated; if that failed, Robins would intimidate the plaintiff-victim, often using the basest tactics available.

The case of George Gubbins, a sole practitioner just outside of Minneapolis, is representative of how Robins sought to intimidate attorneys. Gubbins, on behalf of a client, was trying to work out a settlement with Robins but was getting nowhere. As he relates it, a defense attorney "told me the reason for [Robins's] failure to negotiate was because I could not afford to go through a trial that would take two or three months because it would take too much out of my practice."

Gubbins knew the attorney was right. Properly prosecuting a case against Robins can be expensive. The Minneapolis law firm of Robins, Zelle, Larson & Kaplan estimates that it spent $850,000 out-of-pocket and $3 million in attorneys' time to try just two Dalkon Shield cases. A sole practitioner such as Gubbins is thus fair game for intimidating tactics.

Robins at one point even attempted—unsuccessfully—to get two Minneapolis attorneys, Bob Appert and Jerry Pyle, disbarred. The purpose of the effort, which was fronted by a Minneapolis law firm hired by Robins and/or Aetna, was twofold: to "pay back" Appert and Pyle for sparking a veritable flood of Dalkon Shield lawsuits; and to delay as long as possible any resolution of the hundreds of such lawsuits on which they were working.

Following the Supreme Court's historic *Bates* decision permitting attorneys to advertise within certain guidelines, the two began to send out mailings to women around the country warning them of the hazards of the Dalkon Shield and offering to handle such cases for any aggrieved parties. Perhaps, as some have suggested, the two were ambulance-chasing, but their promotion conformed with the new guidelines and actually performed a valuable public service. As the judge in the case noted in vindicating the two men, they "made several injured parties aware of their legal position and absent access to the letter and brochure, some of those individuals would not have been made aware of their rights. . . . The litigation that resulted from [the promotion] further publicized the injuries suffered and the dangers associated with the use of the Dalkon Shield."

Nevertheless, Robins's goals in pursuing disbarment were achieved: because of the drawn-out nature of their defense, Appert and Pyle were eventually forced to let go of the several hundred Dalkon Shield cases they had gathered from around the country; and those cases began languishing in Minnesota's state and federal courts.

Ironically, the Robins "success" turned out to be the biggest strategical error the company had ever made in the Dalkon Shield litigation. Had Appert and Pyle been left alone, the cases they were handling would have been settled the way most Dalkon Shield cases had been settled until then: on terms favorable to Robins. Instead, the crowded federal court calendar created by the long delay necessitated spreading the Dalkon Shield cases around to all of the state's U.S. district court judges, including Chief Judge Miles W. Lord. As for Appert and Pyle's Dalkon Shield cases, those were taken over by Robins, Zelle, Larson & Kaplan—bringing attorneys Dale Larson and Mike Ciresi into the case for the first time. The triple-threat combination thus formed would prove to be too great even for the mighty Robins litigation machine. As an attorney involved in the disbarment effort eventually told Larson sarcastically, "Appert and Pyle was the smartest thing we ever did, ha, ha."

That Robins would play hardball no matter how small an amount of money involved was seen in yet another Minnesota case brought by Dorothy Rasche. As a result of a pelvic infection she got from wearing the Dalkon Shield, she had suffered permanent tubal damage, a charge that two doctors were prepared to support under oath. Rasche wanted a mere $12,500 to settle the case. Robins offered $7,500. When Rasche's attorneys requested a court date, Robins withdrew its settlement offer and informed the court that it believed it would take two months to try the case. Judge Harry McLaughlin, to whom the case was assigned, rightly thought this was absurd. He, therefore, forced a settlement whereby Robins paid $8,000 to Rasche and her attorneys agreed to waive their fees.

Another tactic is to bar plaintiffs' attorneys from future Dalkon Shield litigation, thus insuring that the knowledge and expertise they may have gained would never again be put to use again against Robins.

Two California attorneys, Rodney Klein of Sacramento and Anthony Klein of Bakersfield (they are not related), represented several plaintiffs in a consolidated proceeding before U.S. district judge Spencer Williams in San Francisco. Because they were getting nowhere in settlement efforts, they contacted Larson and Ciresi to ask for assistance and to share information.

One thing the California lawyers had to offer their Minnesota colleagues in return was a film made by the Chemical Engineering and Microbiology Department of Stanford University which demonstrated the critical wicking effect of the Dalkon Shield tailstring.

Shortly after Larson and Ciresi appeared at a pretrial hearing in the case, Robins's attorneys suddenly offered a substantial settlement provided that the Stanford evidence was destroyed, the experts agreed never to testify, and the two attorneys agreed not to aid any other attorneys in Dalkon Shield cases and to not accept any further cases for themselves. Rod Klein says he agreed to the severe restrictions regretfully, because the settlement "was in the best interests of my clients."

Minneapolis lawyer Kenneth Green says he received much the same kind of demand, and so does Dale Larson.

". . . Judge [Donald K.] Alsop had five cases sent out for simultaneous trial last fall before five judges," Green explained to Judge Lord at an *in camera* meeting held in the judge's chambers on February 2, 1984. "I had one of those cases, which was Cynthia Lodin. . . . [I]t was shortly before trial—my best recollection would be about a week before trial, and I could be wrong on that—that [a Robins attorney] did call and did say that he would make an offer, and the offer, after a little more negotiation, ultimately did settle the case. . . . But [the attorney] did say that he would not make the offer unless I consented—and I have a lot of background in these cases, as they know, that goes clear back to 1977—they would not make the offer to me unless I would commit to not taking on any of the other five cases, including George Gubbins's case, which was [specifically] mentioned. . . ."

Larson says his offer came when in August 1983 he met in Chicago to discuss a possible settlement in a case he was handling with a number of Robins's attorneys, including Alexander H. Slaughter and Frank J. Tatum, the McGuire, Woods attorneys whom Larson and Ciresi describe as the architects of the company's national trial strategy. At the meeting Clifford "Kip" Perrin, of another Richmond firm also representing Robins, said that an absolute condition to any settlement would be an agreement on the part of Larson's firm not to accept any additional Dalkon Shield cases (they had approximately three hundred at the time, 80 percent of which had come from Appert and Pyle). Then, at a November 1983 meeting, William P. Kogar, a more senior partner of Perrin's firm, restated the condition and told Larson it was nonnegotiable and a "deal breaker." Larson refused, telling the attorneys that he thought such an agreement would be a violation of the code of ethics.

(Section DR 2-108b of the Code of Professional Responsibility states that, "in connection with the settlement of a controversy or suit, counsel shall not enter into any agreement that restricts his right to practice law." It is also a violation of the code for one attorney to force or entice another to violate the code.)

When Robins could not intimidate a plaintiff's attorney out of pressing a lawsuit, it tried to intimidate the plaintiff herself. This tactic is part of a much broader one known as the Three-Dog Defense, which is common in product-liability suits: "I don't own a dog, but if I do, my dog didn't bite you. And if it did, it was your own fault."

The case of Margaret Worsham, a Florida nurse who won a $3.5 million verdict against Robins (later reduced by the court to $1.45 million) is typical of the Three-Dog Defense. Mrs. Worsham suffered a very serious pelvic infection resulting in a major abscess which necessitated a complete hysterectomy. Robins argued (1) that as a matter of law the Dalkon Shield per se could not be shown to be defective, that it was no more dangerous than any other IUD; (2) that it could not be shown that Mrs. Worsham's specific injury was caused by the Shield (in part because her Shield had been removed during the hysterectomy and discarded by the hospital and was thus unavailable for inspection); and (3) that even if (1) and (2) were proven, it was her own fault because of Mrs. Worsham's life-style or the fact that she did not immediately go to the hospital when the infection was diagnosed.

Part two of Robins's Three-Dog Defense in *Worsham* is known as a "causation defense." In trial after trial, Robins argues that 85 percent of all pelvic infections occur in women who have never worn an IUD. They argue that pelvic infections can be brought on by a wide range of causes, from gonorrhea to gunshots. It makes plaintiffs prove that none of these conditions existed in them. In Margaret Worsham's case, for example, Robins argued that exposure to gonorrhea or appendicitis had caused her infection. Fortunately, she was able to provide medical testimony that she had never had either condition; she was further able to show that the most likely cause of her injury was the Dalkon Shield. The jury in this case believed Mrs. Worsham; for that matter, so did the appellate court, although it lowered the jury award because of Mrs. Worsham's delayed hospitalization.

Sometimes this causation defense becomes even more exotic. In one case, Robins's attorneys argued that a vaginal infection called chlamydia had caused thirty-one-year-old Mary Gunther's subsequent pelvic infection. True, they could not show that Ms. Gunther ever had chlamydia (which can be transmitted sexually), but then, she could not show that she had not had the disease. "When I had my infection," she said, "no one was testing for chlamydia, so of course I had to have had chlamydia."

At the heart of Robins's Three-Dog Defense is the intimidation of the plaintiffs in the hopes of forcing them to drop their suits. The central feature of this tactic is the humiliating of plaintiff-victims by prying into their sex lives and personal habits, including demanding to know the names of all sex partners; their hygienic habits before and after intercourse and in general; their habits during menstruation, etc.; and all in as personal and graphic a manner as the presiding judge will allow.

Robins's attorneys insist that such information is vital to their cases because the more often intercourse occurs, and the more partners a woman has, the greater her risk of infection. "There are other causes of infection and one of them is the sexual life-style," is how general counsel Skip Forrest puts it.

A textbook example of the "dirty-questions" tactic can be found in a deposition taken by Robins attorneys Stephen D. Bell and Mary Trippler of the Minneapolis firm of Faegre and Benson. In deference to the plaintiff-victim and her right to privacy, we are withholding only her name and certain identifying information.

Q. [By Mr. Bell] At what age did you first have intercourse?

A. . . . Must have been twenty, twenty-one.

Q. After you had the Dalkon Shield inserted up until the time that it was removed, what was the frequency with which you were engaging in intercourse?

A. During most of that time, I, I had a steady boyfriend; maybe two steady boyfriends.

Q. Who were they?

A. In 1972—[At this point, the woman's counsel objects to the line of questioning; at length, however, she answered the question.]

Q. What is the last known address, or where did they reside the last time you knew of their whereabouts?

A. [Answer deleted]

Q. Did any of your sexual partners ever tell you that they had had gonorrhea?

A. No.

Q. Any sexual[ly] transmissible diseases?

A. No.

Q. Were they ever treated for a sexual[ly] transmissible disease?

A. Not to my knowledge, no, sir.

Q. Did you ever notice anything unusual about their appearance which might lead you to believe—

A. No, sir.

Q. —they had a sexually transmissible disease?

A. No, sir. . . .

Q. Do you douche?

A. Periodically.

Q. How often?

A. After [sex].

Q. Is that the only time?

A. Yes, basically. . . .

Q. [By Ms. Trippler] From the time that you first became sexually active until the time the Dalkon Shield was inserted, how many sexual partners did you have . . . ?

A. Two.

Q. Within that time period, with what frequency were you engaging in sexual relations; that is, from the time you first became sexually active until the time the Dalkon Shield was inserted?

A. Well, during [my first] marriage, three times, four times a week. . . . Perhaps three.

Q. And with a different—let's see, you were married to [your first husband] from [dates given], is that correct?

A. That is correct.

Q. And you separated after [a matter of time]?
A. Yes.
Q. So, when you are talking about three times a week, that would be approximately from [your wedding] to [your separation]?
A. Correct.
Q. Was it different during other times, during the time from which you first became sexually active until the time the Dalkon Shield was inserted?
A. No.
Q. Three times a week was during that time period?
A. Correct.
Q. Before the Dalkon Shield was inserted, did you have any sexual problems like pain on intercourse, or bleeding?
A. No.
Q. Or after intercourse, things like that?
A. No.
Q. During the time you used the Dalkon Shield, how many sexual parters did you have?
A. Four, five, including my . . . current husband.
Q. And during the time you used the Dalkon Shield, how frequently were you engaging in sexual intercourse?
A. Three times a week.
Q. Did you have any sexual problems during the time period that you were using the Dalkon Shield?
A. No. . . .
Q. After the Dalkon Shield was removed, has your husband been your only sexual partner?
A. Yes. . . .
Q. How frequently have you been engaging in sexual relations after the Dalkon Shield was removed?
A. Okay, for approximately a year and a half two times a week. After my marriage, three to four times a week.
Q. And since the Dalkon Shield has been removed, have you had any problems with pain or bleeding or things of that nature during intercourse or after intercourse?
A. No.
Q. Up until the Dalkon Shield was removed, when you went to the bathroom, did you wipe from front to back, or back to front?
A. Front to back.

Q. Up until the time the Dalkon Shield was removed, did you engage in anal intercourse?

A. No.

Q. During that same period, did you use marital aids, such as artificial penises or vibrators.

A. No.

Q. During that same period, did you engage in oral intercourse?

A. Yes.

Q. With what frequency . . . ?

A. Twenty times.

Q. Altogether?

A. Altogether, approximate.

Q. Sure. Were those twenty times, approximate times, during the time you used the Dalkon Shield or before or both?

A. Both. . . .

Q. Can you tell me how many times you engaged in oral intercourse during that first period from the time you first became sexually active until the time the Dalkon Shield was inserted?

A. Three times.

Q. So, approximately seventeen times would have been during the time you used the Dalkon Shield?

A. Approximately.

Not only did Robins insist on answers to all these questions, its attorneys made a special trip back to court to demand that the plaintiff answer each and every question fully. During an initial deposition session, on advice of counsel, a plaintiff refused to answer questions relating to types of sexual activity and personal hygiene. The Robins attorneys then threatened to return to court to demand that she answer those questions, adding that they would also seek to have her pay their fees for the time all this would take. She still refused; the court granted the motion to compel answers and she was forced to sit through the questioning again.

In a way, this plaintiff was better off than an Iowa woman who was instructed to have her husband present at her deposition. Included in her questioning were such queries as:

"Between the date of your marriage and 1973, did you have sexual relations with anybody other than your husband?"

"After the date of your marriage . . . , did you have sexual relations with any man other than your husband?"

"Have you had sexual relations with more than one person since the date of your marriage to your husband?"

"With what frequency did you have sex with any other man other than your husband after the date of your marriage on February 9, 1963?"

"What type of sex did you have with those men between February 9, 1963, and 1973?"

She was also asked the other "dirty questions" relating to the kinds of sex she and her husband engaged in and matters of personal hygiene. Next her husband was questioned in her presence. He, too, was asked under oath to supply a complete list of all sexual partners, including those he may have slept with after his marriage to his wife. (None of these questions were answered at the time because the woman's attorney vigorously objected.)

Two other frequent "dirty questions" Robins's attorneys attempt to get answered are:

"Did you have any sexual problems, including pain, inability to achieve orgasm or things of that nature prior to the time the Dalkon Shield was inserted?" and,

"Do you engage in intercourse during the time you are menstruating?"

One thirty-three-year-old New England woman was even asked whether the pantyhose she wore had a cotton crotch, or whether it was made completely of nylon. "I'll answer that question," she responded, "but this sounds more like an obscene phone call than anything else."

The "dirty questions" would be understandable if they had a relevance to the Dalkon Shield injuries suffered by the plaintiff-victims, but they do not, no matter what Forrest and other Robins attorneys claim. For example, one of Robins's own experts, Gerald Zatuchni, M.D., testifying in *Hahn* v. *Robins* in Minneapolis, admitted under oath that sexual intercourse, multiple sexual partners, and sexual frequency in and of themselves have nothing to do with causing pelvic inflammatory disease. Similarly, Robins's medical staffers Drs. Ellen Preston and Fred Clark have testified in depositions that Robins never warned women to limit their sexual activities because that would have defeated the purpose of having the device inserted in the first place.

In Dr. Clark's most recent deposition, for example, attorney Mike Ciresi asked the former Robins medical director, "Doctor, during the time that the Dalkon Shield was marketed by the A. H. Robins Company . . . you didn't ever warn that a woman should not have more than one sex partner while using the device?"

"No," Dr. Clark said, "that would have been beyond the bounds of expectation, I think."

"Sure," Ciresi agreed, "and you knew that women who used this device might have oral sex?"

"I don't know . . . that anybody thought about it."

"You knew that women who might use this device might have anal sex?" Ciresi continued.

"Well, my response is the same," Dr. Clark said.

"Did you ever warn that women who use the device should not have oral or anal sex?"

"No, we didn't."

"Did you ever warn that women who used the device should wipe from front to back, as opposed to back to front?"

"No," Clark said, obviously a bit perturbed by the line of questioning, "those types of things, Mr. Attorney, would have been totally and completely beyond the bounds of medical device product labeling not only in 1984 but certainly in 1970. Those were not considered and were not included in product labeling. . . ."

"[A]ll these things that I have asked you about," Ciresi finally said, "would have been in the expected environment of use, if you will, of that device during its marketing period, correct?"

"Yes," Dr. Clark said.

Dr. Ellen J. Preston was even more telling in her answer to Ciresi's question of whether Robins's Dalkon Shield product literature warned women to only have one sex partner. "Why would it do that?" she asked.

The point that the plaintiffs' attorney was trying to make was that Robins knew the Dalkon Shield was going to be used in a sexually active environment. If the company thought that certain kinds of sexual activity increased the risk of infection, it was duty-bound to print a clear and precise warning on the packaging. Since it did not, the questions are not relevant and should not be allowed to be asked.

"When they sold this product, did they tell people not to have sex?" Ciresi asks rhetorically. "Did they sell it to nuns? It was intended for people that were going to have sex, and [then Robins and its attorneys] come [into court] and attack them for it. I can't believe it, but that's what they do."

There is only one reason for such questions: to intimidate plaintiff-victims into either not suing or dropping their suits once begun. Attorney Green's daughter suffered twice from PID while using the Dalkon Shield; the second time, she nearly died. Nevertheless, he counseled her not to bring suit "because of the intimidating and demeaning questioning to which other women had been subjected." She followed his advice. In Oregon, when U.S. district judge Robert Belloni gave Robins carte blanche to ask its "dirty questions," two women dropped their claims rather than face public humiliation.

Another tactic Robins uses is the "Pinto Defense," as one attorney described it, wherein Robins argues that the only evidence admissible by the court is that which relates to the specific injury claimed, or one exactly like it in every detail. Evidence of similar, but not identical, injuries is irrelevant. (Ford Motor Company, in the various product-liability suits arising from design flaws in its Pinto automobile, often sought to bar evidence of crash tests and other documents unless they related to the same make, model, and year as the car involved in the crash.)

When all else fails, however, the Robins strategy becomes, in the words of Judge Lord, a "policy of delay and obfuscation" in matters relating to discovery. Robins long ago determined to withhold the appearance of witnesses requested by the plaintiffs and to prevent or frustrate any plaintiff's attempt to rummage through its corporate files in search of damaging memoranda, reports, correspondence, studies, or any other relevant evidence and it has stuck to that policy ever since.

The experience of Washington State attorney Jane Fantel is typical. She was part of a team of attorneys who represented a mother and daughter, Peg and Melissa Mample, against the A. H. Robins Company. The allegation in this case was that the Dalkon Shield had caused Peg Mample to give birth prematurely and that, as a result, Melissa was born with cerebral palsy.

"In the first trial, the defense essentially argued before the jury that this child's damages could not have been caused by the Dalkon Shield because, if so, there would be many other suits for the same kind of damages," Fantel said. "This implied that there weren't any. They never said there weren't any, but they implied it. So, the jury hung as to the cause of Melissa's injuries." It did decide in Peg Mample's favor, however.

A second trial was ordered for twelve-year-old Melissa and her attorneys promptly requested Robins to produce a list of all similar birth-defect suits. "We defined what a similar case was—a premature birth, a child with birth injuries, a child with birth defects, a child who did not survive but had birth injuries," attorney Fantel said. "They never said they didn't have any. They simply delayed answering the questions and we went through the usual court rigmarole asking that they be made to answer the questions. Well, eventually they [represented] to the court that there was no computerized listing from which they could pull these answers. In fact, there is a computerized listing."

As long ago as May 1981, Robins had filed with the MDL clerk's office a seventy-eight-page computerized listing of cases ranging from Aascen, Linda, to Zimmerman, Paulette. The list includes information on the nature of the case, who the plaintiff's attorney is, who the local counsel for Robins is, and who is sitting on the case, among other facts.

According to Fantel, Robins's attorneys delayed "up to the last minute" delivery of the requested information. At one point, they did turn over a brief list of birth-defect cases, but left off any case involving cerebral palsy. Mample's attorneys, however, demanded a listing of cerebral palsy cases and the court backed them up. Finally, the Robins attorneys amended the listing to include several cerebral palsy cases.

"Once they gave us the relevant information," Fantel recalled, "the court ordered them to produce medical records and through the entire course of the trial, which lasted two months, every day they would trickle in with one set of medical records—and they were woefully inadequate. They would come in, for example, with a set of the mother's medical records, but no child's records. And they moved repeatedly throughout the trial to end discovery."

The reason for the obfuscation was to delay the trial as long as possible in hopes that a plaintiff would take a low settlement (or no settlement) and drop the suit. In Melissa Mample's case, the jury found for her; as a result of a preverdict agreement which has been sealed by the court, the company reportedly paid the girl approximately $2 million.

Robins is able to get away with this by making use of its army of attorneys. As Larson, Ciresi, and Judge Lord were to discover, Robins can draw an individual from its litigation army practically at a moment's notice and bring him or her into court to discuss an issue that, as Ciresi points out, he or she knows little or nothing about. That way, the attorney can make representations to the court that he or she most likely believes to be true, although the representations are nowhere near true.

Another typical experience was the one faced by plaintiff-victim LaVonne Anderson and her attorney, Kenneth Green. Ms. Anderson's suit was filed in 1980 and immediately Robins requested that she answer its lengthy interrogatories, which she did in full on November 19, 1980. For the next three years, Robins made no attempt toward further discovery, did not request to take her deposition or those of her attending physicians. Then at a mid-December 1983 pretrial conference before Judge Lord, Robins argued that it could not possibly be ready by the January 1984 trial date because it did not have adequate time for discovery. (Judge Lord suggested that the Robins litigation army be enlisted to get the job done on time.)

Green had served Robins with interrogatories of his own on January 20, 1984. On February 3, after three days of hearings on Robins's objections not only to Green's discovery but several other cases before him, Judge Lord ordered Robins to reply by February 6. On February 7, Robins filed new objections to the questions asked. On February 10, Alexander Slaughter, Robins's lead counsel, pleaded with Green for a few more days. Finally on February 17, Slaughter had hand-delivered to Green a letter which said, in part, that because "the scope of information and material which must be reviewed in complying with this order is so voluminous . . . it will take us another two or three weeks to have this information, to the extent it is available, ready for the Court and plaintiff's counsel."

It is hard to give Robins the benefit of the doubt in this case. The discovery papers Green had served on Robins were identical to those which had been served on the company in several other Minnesota cases; the information sought was the same as had been sought in numerous cases nationally going back several years. Moreover, essentially all the information being sought was already the subject of long evidentiary hearings by two Minnesota judges, U.S. district judge Donald K. Alsop in June 1983 and Hennepin County district judge Jonathan Lebedoff in November 1983. Both judges had thrown out all of Robins's objections to answering the questions.

In those cases where discovery did go forward and plaintiffs' attorneys did get their hands on incriminating documents, the Robins strategy would shift to an all-out effort to prevent the documents from actually being introduced into the trial. For instance, in *Strempke* v. *Robins,* the company formally objected to almost every one of the 570 documents that were introduced into evidence. Several days were sometimes spent by the trial judge and a federal magistrate hearing the objections, although almost every document either originated with Robins or was found in its files and had been previously used in other Dalkon Shield cases. One hearing lasting three full days resolved only eight documents. Then, even though the judge had thrown out most of Robins's objections, in the next trial in the same jurisdiction, the Martha Hahn case, the company filed six volumes of the same objections and required another lengthy trial, of which half was consumed by ruling yet again on the same objections.

This carefully planned policy of "delay and obfuscation" is yet another form of intimidation: pitting the seemingly bottomless purse of the A. H. Robins Company and its insurer, Aetna, which has been footing the bulk of the legal expenses, against the limited purse of the plaintiff-victim, in the hopes of outlasting the woman who was injured.

It is also a policy that has angered many judges over the years. Senior U.S. district judge emeritus Frank Theis, who has dealt with the Dalkon Shield for nearly nine years, refers to these endless Robins objections as "useless lumber and wreckage."

In a recent interview, Judge Theis elaborated on his characterization. "I have personally always gotten on well with most of the attorneys who have represented Robins," he told us. "Their lead counsel, Alexander Slaughter, is a gentleman at all times. But his purpose has been to delay and to obfuscate, which of course is his privilege and right—if the judge he is before and the counsel he is against let him get away with it. Getting documents from them has been like pulling teeth."

Dade County (Miami), Florida, circuit court judge John I. Gordon, who presided in the case of *Marjorie Devereaux* v. *A. H. Robins Company,* made Robins pay dearly for this tactic.

The suit commenced in March 1981; attorneys for Devereaux filed sixty-seven interrogatories which by July were still unanswered. On July 17, Judge Gordon issued an order compelling answers. After a subsequent hearing, he ordered Robins to come up with its answers by September 17.

When Robins failed to answer by that date, he issued yet another order compelling an immediate reply. Robins then filed an incomplete response. On September 28, Gordon ordered complete answers to all questions by October 9. New, but still incomplete, answers were filed on October 7. On October 22, Gordon heard the plaintiff's motion to compel better answers. Robins's local counsel argued that the answers had to come from the Richmond, Virginia, offices of national lead counsel McGuire, Woods & Battle and, since the national firm had to juggle so many cases at once as well as conduct its other business, it presented him with the answers as best it could as fast as it could.

The judge had finally had enough. He threw the book at Robins, striking its defenses and giving the plaintiff a directed verdict. He then ordered a trial on the sole issue of how much money the plaintiff should get for her damages.

"These people have not complied with discovery," the judge said angrily. "They have not complied with two court orders and I just don't have time for it." He was upheld on appeal. In a majority opinion, the District Court of Appeals of Florida, Third District, said in part that Robins "in effect was playing games with the court and good faith was absent. . . . The trial court has by its order declined to be the victim of any such shell game tactics. . . . The only abuse that appears from this record is the abuse inflicted by [the A. H. Robins Company] upon the trial court, the Plaintiffs, and the . . . Rules of Civil Procedure."

U.S. district judge C. Weston Houck was sitting on the case of *Dianne S. Pate* v. *A. H. Robins Company* when he came up against a similar problem in obtaining answers to interrogatories. After yet another hearing on the matter, the judge decided to call Robins's bluff. "I'm going to give you fifteen days to answer those interrogatories," he told the local counsel for Robins, "and I want the person [in Richmond] who prepares the answers to sign them. . . . [A]nybody with any intelligence at all that reads these [poorly answered] interrogatories and doesn't know what this guy is trying to do . . . isn't being objective. [This as yet nameless person] is trying to keep from producing any information he can to get out of [discovery]. I don't think that is right. . . . I want him to sign it." The judge even threatened to impose sanctions if necessary.

Yet another staple in Robins's legal arsenal is the divide-and-conquer strategy. The company and its attorneys resist with everything at their command the consolidating of similar Dalkon Shield suits into a single trial. Consolidation, after all, would obviate their tactics of delay, harassment and intimidation. The burden of a months-long trial would be shared by a number of individual plaintiffs and their attorneys, including its costs, the physical wear and tear, and the psychological burdens of going up against the Robins litigation machine. The sole practitioner now has a team of attorneys to help ease the work load and is no longer subject to threats such as those made to George Gubbins. Discovery becomes easier, too; judges are more inclined to allow major discovery when it is for a host of plaintiffs as opposed to one lone litigant.

There is, in fact, only one time when Robins favors joining cases together: when it is to the company's advantage. Then it will push as hard for the joint action as it does to prevent such action at other times.

Such is the case with the issue of punitive damages. Compensatory damages normally run in the tens of thousands of dollars or hundreds of thousands of dollars. Punitive damages, on the other hand, often run into the millions of dollars as juries seek to punish the company for its misdeeds. Six and a half million dollars here and a million and a half dollars there can quickly add up to hundreds of millions of dollars of potential exposure should thousands of juries be allowed to address the punitive damages issue individually.

Robins, therefore, would like nothing better than to consolidate the punitive-damages issue into a single class action suit involving all of the thousands of plaintiffs who have filed against the company. Inevitably, a class action suit would limit punitive damages to a single award that eventually would be divided up between those plaintiffs who are later successful in proving that the Dalkon Shield caused their specific injuries.

Conceivably, if the individual pieces of the punitive pie are small enough, a number of plaintiffs would even be forced to drop their suits because it would not be worth pursuing any longer. In one case, for example, a woman is suing the A. H. Robins Company for the mental anguish she suffered while waiting for her baby to be born. That anguish was very real, but juries often find it difficult to award a verdict to a plaintiff on the basis of mental anguish alone. If she loses the case, she cannot share in the punitive pie. If she wins, but the jury only awards her a minimum amount for compensatory damages because her "injury" was not too serious in its opinion, then her share of the punitive pie will be even smaller. In either case, she would be likely to drop her suit.

In 1981, Robins had a class action proceeding handed to it on a platter and it ran with it all the way to the U.S. Supreme Court. U.S. district judge Spencer Williams, sitting in San Francisco, had just completed a ten-week Dalkon Shield trial. He noted that there were an additional 166 similar cases pending in his district alone and 1,573 suits nationwide seeking a total of $2.3 billion in punitive damages. He, therefore, issued a conditional order certifying all Dalkon Shield suits nationally for a single class action on the question of punitive damages; he also certified a second class action for all suits within his district on issues of liability.

Robins was not happy with Williams's second class designation, but it was overjoyed with his class designation on punitive damages. Plaintiffs' attorneys, on the other hand, were unanimous in their opposition to the certification of a class. They appealed to the Ninth U.S. Circuit Court of Appeals.

The case was heard on March 10, 1982. Arguing for Robins was one of the nation's leading experts in constitutional law, Professor Charles Allen Wright of the University of Texas. For the plaintiffs, there was a group of attorneys led by Thomas Brandi of San Francisco and Brad Post.

The Ninth Circuit vacated Judge Williams's order. Robins appealed that ruling to the U.S. Supreme Court, but it refused to hear the case. Robins has not given up, however; in late 1984, it filed a motion in the U.S. District Court for the District of Eastern Virginia (headquartered, as Robins is, in Richmond, a city in which the A. H. Robins Company seemingly can do no wrong) once again requesting that all the Dalkon Shield lawsuits currently outstanding be certified into a class for the purposes of deciding on punitive damages.

Robins, in the early days of the litigation, also favored the joining of all Dalkon Shield suits before the federal courts into a single case for the purposes of discovery.

Under federal court procedure, whenever suits sharing common questions of fact have been filed in a number of different federal jurisdictions, all pretrial procedures can take place in a single "multidistrict litigation" action under the jurisdiction of a single judge. This eliminates duplicative discovery efforts and the possibility of conflicting pretrial rulings. The actual trials, however, continue to take place in the individual jurisdictions where the suit was filed. The judge in each case may order additional discovery where there are questions unique to an individual case, but on all common questions discovery is normally limited to what has been developed in the MDL.

In May 1975, the Judicial Panel on Multi-District Litigation noted that Dalkon Shield suits were then pending in the federal districts of more than a third of the states. These suits seemed to have common questions of fact and causation, so the panel on its own motion issued a show cause order on why the actions should not be consolidated for pretrial purposes into a single district.

A series of hearings were held on the question. Robins supported the move because it would mean that it could limit its major activities to one court and one judge. The company even argued where the MDL should be located: the Eastern District of Virginia. By and large, plaintiffs' counsel objected to the MDL but argued that if it was inevitable, the supervising court should at least be one that was generally convenient to the thousands of plaintiffs, such as the Northern District of Illinois, based in Chicago.

On December 8, 1975, the panel created MDL Docket No. 211 and placed it in the District of Kansas, partly because Kansas is the geographic center of the United States. Also, the district already had the largest number of cases then pending (thirteen), had tried the only Dalkon Shield case to completion until that time *(Connie Deemer* v. *A. H. Robins Company),* and did not suffer from such an overcrowded calendar that it could not undertake what was certain to be a time-consuming procedure.

Judge Theis was put in charge of the MDL. As a starting point, he called for a meeting of all plaintiffs' attorneys. At that meeting, the attorneys elected Bradley Post as lead counsel because he lived in Wichita and had successfully tried the *Deemer* case.

With the designation of the District of Kansas for the MDL, many attorneys sought to transfer their cases to Wichita for trial, arguing that the MDL and the trial site should be the same. Here, Robins reverted to its old divide-and-conquer strategy. It vigorously opposed each and every transfer motion.

Beginning in 1976, the MDL moved forward. Depositions were taken of most key Robins officials and thousands of pages of documents were turned over by the company. Under Judge Theis's supervision, and through the relentless efforts of lead attorney Brad Post, most of the early smoking guns against Robins were uncovered. By 1980, the initial discovery was completed with Robins assuring one and all that it had turned over all relevant documents in its possession that were not covered by claims of privilege. Twice, in August 1981 and September 1982, Judge Theis ordered discovery reopened when it appeared that Robins might still have previously unrevealed documents in its files. In both instances, discovery was terminated when Robins insisted that it had now turned over everything relevant.

Because of the MDL, most judges (including Theis) accepted Robins's word and assumed that discovery was complete. Most plaintiffs' attorneys agreed that the MDL material was sufficient to prove that the Dalkon Shield was defective. Many of them were not satisfied, however. They argued that there was not sufficient evidence arising from the MDL to demonstrate that knowledge of the defect was held by those at the very highest levels of the company, something necessary to claims for substantial punitive damages.

Most of the plaintiffs' attorneys were convinced that such evidence existed and had been secreted away in either Robins's files or those of its main counsel, McGuire, Woods & Battle. "It was inconceivable that in all those years, nobody ever told E. C. [Robins] Sr. or Jr. that there were problems with the Dalkon Shield and what should we do about it," says Mike Ciresi. "It was inconceivable [as the edited minutes in the MDL suggested] that Robins's board of directors never even discussed the Dalkon Shield when the FDA told 'em to take it off the market and when they sent out the 'Dear Doctor' letters."

Therefore, repeated requests were made by individual plaintiffs for additional discovery. As one attorney has described it, however, "Most judges' eyes would just blur over at the idea of undertaking [additional] major discovery for just one single case." Instead, they pointed to the MDL and said discovery was complete.

And then Miles W. Lord entered the scene. He was a judge whose eyes never blurred over at the idea of major discovery in cases involving what he considered to be life-and-death issues. And he was a judge who had little use for tactics of delay, obfuscation, and intimidation. He would consolidate the Dalkon Shield cases before him. He would bar the "dirty questions" unless he could be shown that they were relevant and necessary. He would demand that key Robins executives, including the company chairman and president, submit to exhaustive questioning by the plaintiffs. He would allow additional discovery. And Robins's painstakingly built defensive tactics would crumble one after the other.

For the women who had been injured by the Dalkon Shield and those who, in ignorance of the danger, were still wearing the device, that would make all the difference.

6

THE WARRIOR JUDGE

In mid-April 1974, Robins executives were agonizing over a most difficult problem. Federal agencies had begun circulating Dalkon Shield casualty figures; plaintiffs' attorneys were now receiving a steady flow of information regarding the various suits being filed; and attorney Bradley Post had uncovered the first smoking gun from Robins's own files.

There was too much publicity resulting from all this for the company to continue withholding formal comment to the physicians and other health professionals prescribing and fitting the device. The problem thus facing the Robins executives at the company's Richmond, Virginia, headquarters was how to word the May 8 letter that was to become known as "Dear Doctor I" without admitting that there really were any problems with the Dalkon Shield. The officials did not want that letter—which urged physicians to remove the IUD in the event that a patient became pregnant—to come back later to haunt Robins because of some inadvertent "admission" in its text.

At the same time, a U.S. district judge was sitting in his chambers in a Minneapolis federal courthouse twelve hundred miles to the northwest. He, too, was agonizing over a difficult decision, one he would later call the most difficult he ever had to face while on the federal bench: whether to continue endangering many lives so that others can continue working.

It would be nearly ten years before the men in Richmond met up with the judge from Minneapolis, but when they did, the seemingly unconnected decision they made regarding "Dear Doctor I" and the decision Judge Miles W. Lord made would have profound effects on that confrontation.

Lord's decision that April day had nothing to do with the Dalkon Shield, but it was at least as serious. The Reserve Mining Company of Silver Bay, Minnesota, jointly owned by the Armco and Republic steel companies, mined iron ore on the shores of Lake Superior. As part of its mining process, Reserve dumped 67,000 pounds of taconite tailings into Lake Superior daily. Enraged environmentalists, as well as state and federal pollution experts, charged that the tailings were contaminating the waters of the Great Lake and the thousands of streams that fed from it. In April 1971, the Environmental Protection Agency (EPA) gave Reserve ninety days to comply with the Water Pollution Control Act. When Reserve failed to comply, suit was filed. It was assigned to Judge Lord in February 1972.

The United States of America v. *Reserve Mining Company* was one of the biggest, most important, and most politically sensitive federal lawsuits ever to be filed in Minnesota, an Indian name that literally means "milky blue water." Reserve Mining was one of the state's largest and most powerful employers; its operations were key to the financial health of the entire northeastern portion of the state. Moreover, environmentalists nationwide looked to the complicated legal battle as a benchmark, a test of the effectiveness of the new antipollution laws.

It was the kind of case Judge Lord dreaded; going in, he says, he knew he would end up in trouble. "I could see as I went into the case where I would end up—on the slag heap." And he was right.

Lord knew he would get into trouble because he interpreted "justice" in a manner quite different from the definition common today in most U.S. courtrooms. Justice, legally defined, is the administration of law and it is that definition that controls the courts, turning them into contests of skill where counsel for both sides seek to score points by outmaneuvering their opponents and dazzling juries with feats of legal legerdemain, while the judge sits as referee. Strategy and showmanship often outweigh truth as the deciding factor.

In Lord's courtroom, however, justice is defined the old-fashioned, moralist, even biblical way, as the administration of right. He prefers that the cases before him be limited to facts; he already knows the law. Thus, if someone tries to suppress those facts or in some way confuse the picture, he will say so, bluntly. If a witness obfuscates, he will "persuade" the person to be more open; if an attorney's questions stray from the point, he will ask a few of his own, just to get things back on track.

He will even try to even things out a bit if he feels an attorney is being "outgunned." In 1980, for example, six defendants were accused of shipping huge quantities of marijuana from Florida to Minnesota for sale. The young and clearly inexperienced assistant U.S. attorney trying the case was being opposed by seven attorneys experienced in criminal-trial matters. In a phrase, the novice prosecutor was in way over his head. On a number of occasions, the judge wondered aloud why the U.S. attorney's office did not send in some more experienced help (although he did so in such a way as not to embarrass the young man or prejudice the case), but it was to no avail.

Finally, the judge decided to even things out a bit, although again within what he considered the bounds of judicial propriety. At one point, after publicly instructing the prosecutor on how to proceed with the case, Lord turned to the jury and said, "Now, I hope that you don't object to my helping the government try its case." They didn't and five of the six defendants were convicted. The defendants, however, did object and used it as the basis of an appeal to the Eighth Circuit. By a vote of 6–3, the higher court ordered a new trial.

The Reserve case was one of those that have made Judge Lord so controversial. Given the power the company possessed in the state —it was not too long before that the mining interests almost completely controlled the state—it would take more than just being right for Lord to have come out of it unscathed. Knowing this, Lord could have taken the easy way out by going easy on the company; his concept of justice, however, would not allow him to do so.

Lord's precarious position was compounded even before the trial began: deadly asbestos fibers were found lurking both in the taconite tailings themselves and in the smoke being emitted from Reserve's massive smokestacks. Now, not only was the pollution of

Lake Superior even more ominous (it supplied drinking water for the entire region), but the ambient air for miles around posed a threat to anyone who breathed. Understandably, a state of near-panic swept the threatened areas. Lord helped to control that panic somewhat by ordering the U.S. Army Corps of Engineers to bring in fresh water to the area.

Judge Lord did his best to work out a settlement that would allow Reserve to continue operating while ending the pollution problem. His concern was for the people whom Reserve employed and the people Reserve's pollution endangered. Experts had proposed an on-land disposal plan and the judge attempted to get Reserve to agree to it. Reserve, however, rejected the plan. First it continued to argue that no health hazard existed. Second, it said that, even if such a threat did exist, the disposal plan was not economically viable.

The company then suggested an alternative: a deep-pipe disposal plan that it said was the only workable solution (provided, of course, that a solution was necessary). The plan called for a network of deep pipes that would carry the tailings to the very bottom of Lake Superior. There, because of their weight, they would no longer pose any threat.

Lord was not keen on the deep-pipe disposal plan because he felt it was an engineering impossibility. Still, it was something and he brought the parties together to discuss it. Then Lord learned that the plan had actually been rejected by one of the parent companies two years earlier. The plan being pushed by Reserve was thus nothing more than a smoke screen, designed to delay. The judge was not pleased. "Do you realize," Lord told Reserve's counsel, "that this court spent three days considering a plan which your company put forward as something feasible and possible, and that they wanted to do, that you had rejected in 1972?" His displeasure grew even greater when he discovered through subpoenaed documents that Armco had gone behind his back to Washington to discuss a possible out-of-court settlement with federal officials.

On August 1, 1973, therefore, the trial began. Shortly thereafter, Lord added Reserve's owners, Armco and Republic, as codefendants. He did so for several reasons. First, he anticipated that some residents in the area would eventually contract mesothelioma, a virulent and as yet incurable form of lung cancer caused almost exclusively by asbestos and that takes between twenty and thirty years to show itself. Reserve, however, was really little more than a paper company. He doubted that it would exist twenty to thirty years down the road and he wanted to protect the right of those people who developed mesothelioma to collect damages. That could only be possible if Armco and Republic were tied directly to the asbestos pollution, and that meant joining them to the suit. Second, Judge Lord assumed that a more direct involvement in the trial (and, thus, a more direct stake in its outcome) would provide the two companies with a more meaningful incentive to promote a settlement.

Reserve's parents, however, immediately appealed Lord's action and won a reversal in the Eighth Circuit U.S. Court of Appeals. Lord then found a way to rejoin them and this time he got his way: officials of both companies were subpoenaed and appeared as witnesses, and thousands of pages of documents from the two companies were entered into evidence.

Throughout the trial, the defendants employed the tactics of delay that so frustrate Judge Lord when life-and-death issues are at stake. The judge had repeatedly requested copies of existing on-land disposal-site plans, for example; officials from Armco countered by repeatedly denying under oath that such plans even existed. When it was eventually discovered from subpoenaed Armco documents that the company had investigated a number of such plans at length, Lord's frustration led him to take a more activist role in the discovery process and in his attempts at promoting a settlement that would end the pollution problem once and for all.

He had become convinced by then that Reserve's continued operation constituted a "substantial public health menace." He continued to demand that certain documents necessary to the government's case be turned over. He even threatened to fine Reserve sixty thousand dollars a day, an amount equal to the company's estimated daily profits, if it withheld those documents from the court. Reserve, however, continued to argue—much as Robins would ten years later—that the requested documents contained company trade secrets; as such, they were protected from discovery.

As Lord explained it, he was left with no options other than his brand of judicial activism, a role that at the time was inconsistent with the commonly held premise that judges had to maintain their passivity, no matter how provoked, in order to preserve their impartiality. (Even today, the concept of the "activist" judge is, at the very least, a controversial one.) "People's lives were at stake," Lord said, and yet Reserve and its parents were playing games with him. "They advertised themselves to be good corporate citizens," Lord explained recently, "but they misrepresented; they hid documents that I begged them to produce; they lied and cheated."

By April 1974, the trial had consumed 134 days. The trial record had grown to eighteen thousand pages and over sixteen hundred exhibits had been introduced. Still, the dispute was nowhere near resolution. The only course open to Lord now was to enjoin Reserve from further dumping of the taconite tailings into Lake Superior. He knew that the only way the company could comply with such an order would be to shut down operations. From personal experience, he also knew the kind of hardship such an act would impose on the company's thousands of workers who would be thrown out of work. He knew it because he had come from among those people and that area of the state. He was one of them and they were a part of him.

And so, on that April day, Miles W. Lord faced the most difficult decision in his career on the federal bench. Justice, however, his justice, dictated what that decision had to be. "In essence, defendants are using the workforce at Reserve's plants as hostages," Judge Lord wrote in his subsequent injunction. "In order to free the workforce of Reserve, the Court must permit the continued exposure of known human carcinogens to the citizens of Duluth and other North Shore communities. The Court will have no part in this form of economic blackmail. The defendants are daily endangering the lives of thousands of people. . . . This Court cannot honor profit over human life and therefore has no other choice but to abate the discharge."

The following day, Reserve shut down its operations; 3,100 people were out of work because of a stroke of Miles Lord's judicial pen. "[M]y heart goes out to them," a saddened Lord said in an interview. "As a result of the order I gave, my brother's brother-in-law was laid off . . . , my wife's cousin, dozens of young men—not so young now—that I grew up with."

Lord was born in Pine Knoll, Minnesota, in 1919. He was raised in the heart of Minnesota's Iron Range, where growing up made life in New York City's Hell's Kitchen look like a cakewalk. As Lord describes it, a boy would have to fight his way home from school each day—and young Miles Lord got home every day.

His "New England Yankee" family was typical of the families in the Iron Range, none of whom ever had it easy, and neither did he. His father was a lumberjack; most of his relatives were iron miners. As was common throughout the region, there was never enough work, and so there was never much money. The economic hardship of the time was so great that even the area merchants suffered mightily. Bills would often go unpaid for long periods; repairs would be put off indefinitely; homes rarely, if ever, saw fresh paint; good food was whatever was on the table; advanced schooling was a luxury. It was the kind of life-style you always yearn to leave but that never leaves you. You can try to forget it, or you can remember it and use what it taught you to help free others from having to live that way. Lord chose to remember.

"We didn't have supplementary unemployment compensation [then]," he has since recalled. "Nine of us [he and his brothers and sisters] lived on twenty-five dollars a month when the mines were closed each winter. I'm no stranger to unemployment personally. We always waited until the spring when the mines reopened."

There were good times, too. "The most popular guy in town was Peppy Vranish (the father of a friend of Lord's), an iron miner and a terrific dancer who also made the best white mule there was," Lord recalled during a 1978 reunion in his hometown. "They called it Peppy's Cognac. You either danced at Croatian Hall or the Finn Club. Peppy's house was about equidistant, which gave him a tremendous advantage. If you didn't have a girl, you'd run out between sets to Peppy's. If you had a girl, you'd run out to the car. In either case, you were in good hands."

Lord graduated from high school in 1937, but he did not do as well there as he could have done because he was too much the social butterfly in those days. He took a greater pleasure out of extracurricular activities than schoolwork. His favorite pastime was acting and he managed to snare the lead in virtually every school production from eighth grade through high school. Once he got to Crosby-Ironton Community College, however, he buckled down. After leaving college, Lord married and settled down. He tried to run a restaurant but failed at that and decided instead to get a law degree, which he did at the University of Minnesota Law School. In order to get through law school and support his family (the Lords had the first of their four children by then), he had to hold down three jobs: from 1 P.M. to 5 P.M. he was a janitor, from 6 P.M. to 10 P.M. a postal clerk, and from 11 P.M. until 7 A.M. a night watchman. Mornings were left for class. As for sleep, "he regarded . . . [it] as a Republican conspiracy, to be viewed skeptically," a writer once noted. He held other jobs, too, such as cat skinner, packinghouse worker, ditchdigger, fry cook, logger, electrical appliance salesman, bellhop, and tractor driver.

From there it was on to his first postschool job as an insurance adjuster, a job for which he (and his employers) soon realized he was not cut out. Lord suffered from a fatal disease for insurance adjusters: he had compassion. As he would later show on the bench, his concern was not so much with fulfilling the letter of the law as it was with fulfilling its spirit. After a short while on the job, therefore, he was forced to quit. "They criticized me for paying an old lady four hundred dollars for a broken knee when she would have taken fifty," he recalls. Lord, however, had reasoned that the woman needed the money more than the insurance company did. And, anyway, she really was entitled to the four hundred dollars. It was then that Lord decided to practice law in Minneapolis.

In law school, he had met the politically active Orville Freeman (later to become governor of Minnesota and secretary of agriculture in the Kennedy administration). Through Freeman, he met many of the other young leaders of Minnesota's Democratic Farm Labor Party (DFL), including one destined to put his unique and compassionate mark on the face of American politics and two who would seek to do the same: Hubert Humphrey, Walter Mondale, and Eugene McCarthy. He soon became active in politics, but his first attempt at running for public office was a disaster. In 1950, he had been in law practice for a year and had earned nine hundred dollars. He thought he was thus established enough now to try for public office. He ran for the state legislature and lost badly. With the help of his friend and fishing buddy Hubert Humphrey, then in his first term as a U.S. senator, Lord was appointed assistant U.S. attorney and gained a reputation for successfully trying tax cases.

In 1954, Lord's political fortunes changed. He received the DFL endorsement for state attorney general and was elected to the first of three successive terms in that post by defeating Republican Keith Kennedy in a bruising campaign. Years later, a fellow DFLer would reminisce with *Minnesota Star* reporter Jim Klobuchar about that race:

"The guy was an unquenchable campaigner. A political battle to him was like a war, all right, but he liked to fight with rubber torpedoes and flour bombs.

"He was campaigning in the farm country against Kennedy in this unmarked sound truck. It was a sunny day. Miles was filled with love for the good black earth. He found a kinship for the contented heifers he saw on this one farm. So as he was driving by, he picked up the little bullhorn and said 'moooo' to the cows. He did it again and the farmer thought it was some wise-ass city slicker making fun, so he shook his fist at the truck.

"Miles looked somewhat sad for a moment, then picked up the little bullhorn again and said, 'Be sure to cast your vote in the next election for Keith Kennedy, the man who loves cows.' "

Lord is quick to point out that he racked up "quite a record" as the chief law-enforcement officer of Minnesota. "In my years as attorney general," he would say, "I remember losing only one criminal case," adding that he "had a hell of a reputation as a trial lawyer. I've beaten the best of them." On Lord's staff for a time was Fritz Mondale, who would eventually succeed Lord as attorney general in 1961 when Lord moved over to the post of U.S. attorney.

The judge is quite proud of his record in that post, too. He has even been given some of the credit for putting Teamster president Jimmy Hoffa in jail. "Bobby Kennedy told me that I was the one who put it together," Lord recalls. Kennedy at the time was attorney general of the United States and thus Lord's boss. Lord's role was to plant an informer in jail with Ben Dranow, whom the judge described as "a bag man for Hoffa." The informer apparently managed to get Dranow to talk "and we knew everything."

To hear people (mostly critics) tell it, Lord is an example of an old political axiom: in politics, it's not what you do so much as who you know. Lord's steady climb up the ladder, they argue, was helped by his friendship with Hubert Humphrey. As the latter's career climbed the heights, Lord's career also benefitted. It was Senator Humphrey, for example, who got Lord named U.S. attorney for Minnesota by President Kennedy. And in 1966, at the urging of Vice-President Humphrey, Lord was named a U.S. district judge by Lyndon Johnson. ("He'll be a people's judge," Humphrey said at the time.)

There is truth to this, of course. However, former senator Eugene McCarthy has been known to call up Lord whenever such statements are printed in the press because he would like some of the credit, too. Most of the credit, however, must go to Miles Lord himself. He was a hard worker and a straight talker—and the people liked him for it. Perhaps "liked" is not the proper word; his popularity at times was enormous. In 1958, for example, a statewide poll sought to determine whom Minnesotans wanted as the DFL candidate for U.S. senator. On the list were such popular figures as Lieutenant Governor Karl Rolvaag, Representatives John Blatnick and Eugene McCarthy, and former U.S. ambassador to Denmark Eugenie Anderson. Among that crowd, Lord was the favored choice of an astonishing 49 percent of the people polled; no one even came close. (Lord decided not to run and McCarthy went on to win the nomination and the election.)

How close Lord was to Humphrey can be seen in the practical jokes the future judge played on his fishing buddy during an early Humphrey Senate campaign. One of Lord's jobs during the campaign was to keep the crowds interested at major rallies, as a sort of warm-up man for the big act to follow. At one such rally, Lord urged the crowd:

"Now, Hubert is going to be out here in a minute and we don't want him to get a bigger head than he already has. So, when he's introduced, I want dead silence. Or maybe just one or two people clapping. And then, when I'm introduced, let's bring the house down, okay?"

Okay, said the crowd, and when Humphrey came out the audience sat on its hands. Then Lord was introduced and it went wild. Humphrey could not understand what was happening.

He should have understood because Lord had pulled a similar prank just a few days earlier. The Humphrey caravan had encountered a bus full of senior citizens. Lord entered the bus first to warm up the crowd. When Humphrey entered a few minutes later, his best campaigning efforts were met with silence.

"What's going on?" he asked one of the seniors. "You have a

hell of a lot of nerve," came the reply. "That young fellow who was just in here said that there'd be a guy come on the bus impersonating Hubert Humphrey. He said give him the cold shoulder. Said his name was Miles Lord. Real nice young fellow."

"How much do I owe Hubert Humphrey?" Lord recalled years later. "Let's put it this way, something like how much do you owe your brother? Every time he has ever needed me or depended on me, or whenever I have in any little way a chance to help him, I've done it. Not because I owe him a dime but because I have thought he was good for the country."

Lord, jokingly, likes to take the "credit" for Humphrey's good works. "Walter Mondale goes around saying that Hubert Humphrey was his political mentor," Lord has said; "I'm the only guy who goes around saying that I was Hubert Humphrey's mentor." (Lord, incidentally, also takes some of the credit for putting Mondale in the Senate, saying that in 1964, after deciding to stay on the bench, he convinced then Governor Karl Rolvaag to appoint the state attorney general to the seat being vacated by Vice-President-elect Humphrey. An unframed photograph of Lord, Rolvaag, and Mondale, with the latter holding a newspaper headlining his appointment, is part of Lord's collection. On it, Mondale inscribed: "To Miles Lord, My choice for chief justice.")

Humphrey had been right in his prediction that Lord would be a "people's judge," as his agonizing over the fate of the Reserve workers showed after his injunction forced them out of work. The shut-down, however, was short-lived.

The defendants quickly went to the Eighth Circuit U.S. Court of Appeals in St. Louis for redress. The appellate court saw the action as extreme and immediately ordered a temporary stay of Lord's injunction, thus allowing Reserve to reopen. That began a year-long battle between Lord and the Eighth Circuit Court of Appeals over the case. The appeals court first extended the stay for seventy days, then put it on an indefinite basis on the argument that Reserve had acted in "good faith" in trying to come up with an acceptable environmental plan. Twice the case went to the U.S. Supreme Court (which kept sending it back down the line) and by late winter of 1975 had become stalemated; Lord and the government had nowhere left to go and Reserve continued to do business as usual.

Local writer Jim Klobuchar (whom Lord reportedly sees as something less than an ally) described a typical scene in Judge Lord's courtroom at that time. "The case is a peculiar mixture of tedium, sudden doomsday warnings, industrial power politics, judicial politics, scientific jabberwocky, old animosities and the new fears of Northern Minnesota—and the special flavoring of a personal justice imparted by Miles Lord," Klobuchar wrote. "It is a political and economic brawl and the warrior judge is in a dilemma: Where does he cease being a jurist and become an advocate? It is not only a legal battle, but a public relations battle and the judge is no foreigner to either arena."

Completely exasperated by this time over his failure to get Reserve or either of its parent companies to come forward with any kind of an acceptable plan, or even to bargain in what he felt was good faith, Lord virtually branded Reserve and its executives corporate outlaws by insisting that they had shown "bad faith" and had conducted themselves "beneath the standards" of American business.

The defendants once again rushed to the Eighth Circuit U.S. Court of Appeals. This time, however, Lord rushed right up with them. In an extraordinary move, Lord himself made a personal appearance before the Appeals Court to make an impassioned plea to be allowed to proceed with the case in his own manner.

"Looking beyond the rhetoric, it is of little importance whether or not Miles W. Lord personally presides over this case," Lord told the appeals court judges. "It is of great importance, however, that a federal district judge be vested with full powers and authority . . . to ensure the health of future generations. Neither this judge, nor any judge, can act effectively to protect the public health absent a clear mandate of support of this Court of Appeals. . . .

"While these proceedings drag on in the various forums, carcinogenic fibers continue to be dispersed, exposing thousands to a potential health risk. If the risk becomes a reality, hundreds may die."

Lord's plea, however, had planted a seed that would cost him dearly. He had said that it was unimportant whether "Miles W. Lord personally presides over this case" and now Reserve, reportedly at the suggestion of the appellate court itself, demanded that Lord be removed from the case. The plaintiffs, led by the states of Minnesota and Wisconsin, objected, saying that "the facts, the law and the public's health all demand" that Lord retain control of the case. Noting that the judge had "consciously jeopardized his judicial career" to warn citizens of the potential health hazards they faced from the taconite tailings, the plaintiffs said it would be "the ultimate irony in a case full of ironies" if Lord was removed. Even the Ford-era Justice Department agreed, saying that to remove Lord "would leave an enormously complex case in the hands of a new judge."

All of the pro-Lord arguments fell on deaf ears. The Eighth Circuit removed Lord from the case, saying that he "seems to have shed the robe of a judge and to have assumed the mantle of an advocate [for the environmentalists]."

On learning of the decision, the judge said, "I have done my best to provide for the maximum protection of the public health consistent with due process to all concerned. As of today, I can do no more."

Later, upon reflection, he would add: "Is it more important that you look impartial and let them get away with something? Or that maybe you'll get out of character a bit and just say, 'Hey, that's enough of this. Stop it. People's lives are at stake. You can't do this for profit anymore.' "

He even greeted the decision with some humor. Shortly after the ruling, Lord married a couple in chambers. Then he let the word out that the couple was in trouble because the marriage would be reversed by the Eighth Circuit.

Clearly, Lord was at least morally right in the Reserve case. Nevertheless, he feels that being right and doing right cost him. He was reversed "about 1.5 times in every ten cases before Reserve," he says. After Reserve, the record of reversals rose dramatically to approximately 50 percent "because people are human and the Reserve case was an embarrassment to the Court of Appeals," Lord says, adding: "I knew I was right and I expected the kind of treatment I got from the Court of Appeals because I am certain that you cannot pick on anyone who has as many friends as Reserve has in the way that I did without being severely criticized."

Being severely criticized, however, can be a two-way street and Lord felt no reason to not let the appellate court know how he felt about its actions. "I would have preferred the Court of Appeals to have stood beside me instead of standing on top of me," he publicly stated at one point. "I don't have any problem justifying my behavior," he said at another; "I think it would be their problem to justify their behavior." Lord, in fact, made so many statements regarding what the appellate court had done that Reserve sought to use the judge's words to draw more blood from him. Six months after Lord was removed from the case, a Reserve attorney sent to the Eighth Circuit Court of Appeals a fifty-five-page collection of speeches and articles by and about Lord in which the judge was critical of the court. Lord, however, shrugged it all off. "I am absolutely free to speak out about the Reserve case," he said. "I no longer have the case, but I have the First Amendment which protects my right to freedom of expression."

The people were still on the side of the people's judge. In a statewide poll taken after his removal from the case, 55 percent of the respondents said they had a favorable opinion of Lord while only 11 percent said they did not like him. In the same poll, only 21 percent approved of Lord's removal from the Reserve case.

One charge heard often against Judge Lord during his years on the bench is that he is too political, that he came from a political background, and that he remains a politician at heart. Several times over the years he sat on the bench, there were rumors that he would resign from the bench to run for the U.S. Senate; he even admitted a desire to do so more than once (when Humphrey stepped down to become vice-president in 1964 and when Mondale stepped down for the same reason in 1976).

Possibly the biggest overnight flap he caused while sitting on the bench was the day in 1977 when he put on his old DFL hat and publicly said he hoped that someone in the party, either U.S. Representative Don Fraser or state attorney general Warren Spannaus, would challenge Senator Wendell Anderson's renomination. Anderson had resigned as governor in order to have himself appointed to fill out Mondale's Senate term. While in the state house, he and Lord had clashed frequently during the course of the Reserve trial, with the judge saying that he thought Anderson had a "cozy relationship" with the mining company. Lord's opposition to Anderson's renomination, however, was less personal and more pragmatic. "If Anderson is the DFL nominee, I think a Republican will win," he explained. Further, Lord said that if no one else in the party came forward to challenge Anderson, he might be inclined to resign from the bench and do so himself.

The reaction was immediate. A judge talking practical politics publicly was unheard of in Minnesota or elsewhere. The reaction was so great that one would have believed that judges, who have to be in politics to have gotten their jobs in the first place, immediately lose all their loyalties and inclinations upon taking the oath. Editorials called for his resignation. The Minneapolis *Star* said, "Judge Lord should pipe down about partisan politics. . . . We wish he would shut up for his own good." The editorial even quoted from the Code of Judicial Ethics, which said in part, "A judge should refrain from political activity." Lord, however, felt (and rightly so, at least from the standpoint of honesty) that he was only doing in public what other judges did in private. He therefore ignored the outcry. Anderson subsequently was renominated and was soundly defeated in the election by Republican Rudy Boschwitz.

Those same newspapers would have had a real field day in 1968 had they caught Judge Lord shuttling between Hubert Humphrey's presidential campaign plane and Eugene McCarthy's. They would have accused him not only of playing politics while on the bench but of being unable to decide between two old friends and thus playing both sides of the street. "And they would have been wrong," said one who recalled the story. "[Judge Lord] didn't like the idea that these two friends were getting so bitter about each other, so [he'd] get off Humphrey's plane and jump right into McCarthy's trying to get them to make peace." The newspapers, however, would never have understood.

The idea that Lord was too political to sit on the bench was probably set to rest once and for all (at least as a serious charge) in a 1980 decision that made him very unpopular with Minnesota state officials and citizens' groups alike, including fishermen and recreational boaters, two powerful lobbying groups.

In 1978, Congress gave the federal government jurisdiction over a million-acre wilderness area in northern Minnesota, the Boundary Area Canoe Wilderness. Using the new law, the U.S. Department of the Interior limited the use of motorboats in many of the lakes and streams of the area. This upset the boaters, the fishermen, and the state government. Three suits were brought challenging the law. Plaintiffs included the state, a host of local communities, homeowners associations, civic and recreational groups, and business organizations. Nevertheless, Lord upheld the federal government's right to limit power boating. Brian O'Neill, who represented the Sierra Club in the suit, called the decision "a sweeping victory for the environmental community in Minnesota." Lord, however, did give the state a measure of victory by allowing it to continue to control logging and mining in the area.

If ever there was a case before him where he would bow to local political pressure, this should have been it; but anyone who believed that Miles Lord could or would be anything less than a judge while sitting on the bench knows little about him. What does it take to be a judge? After almost twenty years on the bench, Lord has a very simple way at looking at the role and responsibility of his office. "If you just don't read the lawbooks," he has said, "you can get lots done. Judges tend to use precedents instead of figuring things out for themselves. You can find a precedent for anything."

"I look out at the litigants," he has said, "and I ask, 'Are they rich and powerful, or are they poor and oppressed?' " It is not that he will prefer the latter to the former. He believes that, in most courtrooms, "there is one set of laws for the rich and powerful and another set of laws for the poor and oppressed." "Why is it," he often asks rhetorically, "when you plot in the barroom it's a crime, but if you plot in the boardroom it is not?" In his courtroom, he wants only one set of laws in which everyone is treated fairly and equally, with no regard given to station or influence. When his efforts to practice his egalitarian concept of law in a given case are thwarted, he becomes frustrated; when he is frustrated, he usually pushes himself harder and, in the end, gets what he wants, or at least some part of it. He usually also gets into trouble for it.

"I see myself as being both predictable and unpredictable," he explains. "When I've got giant corporations battling each other, I'm unpredictable. I find the learning process in these cases fascinating. But I think you can pretty much predict that when people are being abused by the monolith, by the great blind forces of society, I'll come to their rescue. I'll come down on the side of the person being oppressed. . . ."

Perhaps Lord's most controversial act in his battle against "the great blind forces of society" occurred on November 9, 1984. Two antiwar protesters, John M. LaForge and Barbara Ann Katt, had been found guilty of damaging $34,000 worth of military computer equipment at the Sperry Corporation plant in suburban St. Paul.

Lord, saying that he wanted "to take the sting out of the bomb and remove the halo over any device that can kill," gave them six months' probation, a sentence that immediately brought on a chorus of criticism. The judge also characterized the actions of LaForge and Katt as a "desperate plea to the American government to stop [this] military madness before it destroys humanity." People in "high places" believe Armageddon is inevitable, he added, and "much of our national effort appears to be helping in that process."

As for the so-called judicial temperament that some say he lacks, he says, "I think that can be overdone. To be effective as a judge and to win acceptance, I don't think you have to sit there like an undertaker. I think the real core of judicial temperament is fairness. Have you as a judge tried to grant a fair hearing? Have you brought all your resources to bear on a question? I think on social and economic issues, as an example, if the public is satisfied you have taken a good hard look, assembled all the facts, it will accept your decision—and public acceptance is what's behind the law, isn't it?"

In his time as a prosecutor and on the bench, Lord has become known for doing the unconventional in his pursuit of justice. Stories about him abound. One courthouse favorite concerns a witness who wasn't coming clean before a grand jury. She was a young prostitute with information on drug trafficking that the federal grand jury wanted, only she wasn't talking. Try as they would, the assistant U.S. attorneys could not get her to reveal what she knew. It was utterly frustrating.

Suddenly, the doors to the grand jury room opened and in walked Lord, then the U.S. attorney. He strode solemnly toward the front of the room and confronted the witness. "Young lady," he said sternly, "if you don't tell us something, I'm going to tell your mother what you've been doing." Then he turned and left the room. The witness knew that Lord meant what he said. She began to tell the grand jury everything it wanted to know.

Judges usually do not attend depositions. Lord, however, will do so if his presence can move the process along. Foreshadowing some of his actions in the Dalkon Shield case, Lord in an antitrust case sat in on the deposition of a drug company official who was apparently being less than cooperative. At one point, the judge interrupted the deposition to warn the witness, "That's not an answer to the question and you're going to have to straighten out and fly right or the court is going to have to impose a little fine on you." A short time later, Lord remarked of the witness, "He's done a lot better since we had our little chat."

Another famous Lord story concerns his son Mick's leg, broken in a 1963 football game. Seventeen years later, one Howard Lambert was before Judge Lord accused of conspiring to distribute lysergic acid diethylamide (LSD). The defendant pleaded guilty but refused to say what his source was for the hallucinogen. That position, however, is not the kind to take before Lord, especially in a drug case, because he is notoriously hard on drug dealers. Facing a ten-year sentence, therefore, Lambert risked a great deal by keeping quiet; Lord told him as much.

Then came the surprise. Lambert's attorney asked Lord to excuse himself because it was Lambert who had broken Mick Lord's leg in that long-ago football game. Lord said he remembered the game vividly, "I see my kid crushed from behind and I race out of the bleachers, bail over that fence, and run out to him. His leg is broken and I help carry him off the field." Lord added that he was certain a late hit had broken Mick's leg. "I've always wondered what kind of a person would do that," he said. "I really wondered about the S.O.B. all these years."

The story made local headlines for weeks as Lord decided what to do. Finally, he assigned the case to another judge for sentencing. The stories about the incident, however, had brought forward a lot of the men who had played in the game on both teams. By the time Lord withdrew, it was known that Lambert had not been the one who had broken Mick's leg. Both he and Mick Lord played on their respective defensive teams, so they could not have both been on the field at the same time. One of Lambert's former coaches came forward to say that it was doubtful that Lambert even played in the game in question. Lambert finally admitted he had lied out of fear of the sentence Lord would impose. Still, Lord withdrew, saying, "It is important to avoid even the appearance of a conflict of interest."

It was the avoidance of impropriety that got Lord in trouble at home on another occasion. He was hearing a case involving the Northern States Power Company when he suddenly realized that his wife held stock in the utility. Without even consulting her, he ordered his secretary to call his broker and sell the stock at whatever the current price was, saying, "I hope my wife will forgive me."

Another famous Lord story concerns international intrigue. It was 1969 and Lord was asked by friends to go to Rome and deliver a letter to the exiled King Constantine urging him to return to Greece, rally his people, and assume the throne. Lord took on the assignment with relish and, before long, he was at the gate of the exiled King's residence, demanding entry. It was refused and, after a fuss of the kind only Lord could create, the judge returned to his hotel to plot his next move. Within an hour, however, he received a call inviting him to dinner with Constantine. "I met a twenty-eight-year-old boy, looking like he was fresh out of Harvard, the King of Greece," Lord recalled some years ago. "And I sat there and had a few drinks with him and gave him the letters. And he asked me if I would be his political adviser."

"How about that?" Lord laughed, slapping his knee with glee. "I almost caused the overthrow of the dictatorship in Greece."

Local reporters remember the day Lord issued his long-awaited Boundary Waters Canoe Area decision. They had gathered in the courthouse corridors expecting to pick up copies of the anticipated decision. Lord saw them lounging around and made a shocking announcement, at least for a judge: "Come on in and bring your cameras; we'll break a little ground here." A sitting judge was holding a full-blown press conference.

Lord enjoyed himself that day. As a reporter attending the highly unusual session wrote, "U.S. District Judge Miles Lord, declaring that history was being made, held a press conference Thursday. That was unusual even for him. At the conference he criticized mining companies, the Minnesota Department of Natural Resources, and the Minneapolis *Tribune.* That was not unusual for him."

Near the end of the session, a photographer for the *Tribune* rushed in and asked Lord to pose for another photo.

"You're too late," Lord replied; "all the photos have been taken."

"Please, just one more?" asked the photographer.

"Nope," replied Lord, "so go back and tell [*Tribune* editor]

Chuck Bailey tough." Then, with a laugh, Lord relented; the photo made page one the next morning.

The measure of the man can perhaps best be taken in the two decisions he believes were the best he has rendered since being on the bench. "In one I decreed that women high school athletes should have the same options to participate as men," he recalls. "And in another case I held that children in a poor school district should have educational opportunities equal to those who come from wealthy school districts. The first has been reversed by the federal administration; the second by the state."

He is also proud of a settlement he worked out in a two-year-long class action lawsuit on behalf of the mentally ill in Minnesota. The suit attacked the way the state declared people incompetent and committed them to institutions and the lack of alternatives to hospitalization in Minnesota. The settlement Lord forced established a meticulous series of due process hearings, screenings, record reviews, clinical evaluations, and examinations before a person said to be mentally incompetent could be committed. Of the decree one commentator said, "A class action lawsuit that does something for a lot of people rather than making a lot of money for a few . . . stirs Lord's populist reformer's soul and inspires his best legal technique."

This quality made Lord both loved and hated by the lawyers who practiced before him. There seems no middle ground. In 1980, the editors of *The American Lawyer,* a legal trade publication, named Lord the worst judge in the circuit and one of the eleven worst judges in the United States.

The article cited a number of cases to support the designation but focused primarily on a 1969 case that was one of the more famous Lord had tried until then. It was an antitrust case involving a number of drug manufacturers who were accused of conspiring to fix prices in selling wide-spectrum antibiotics that were used in animal feeds between 1953 and 1966. The case was transferred to New York, where it was combined with numerous others concerning price-fixing in human antibiotics.

In 1971, a curious Lord called the administrative office of the courts in Washington to find out what had happened to the case. He was told that it was still hanging around and that he could have it back if he wanted to try it. However, he would have to take back all the consolidated cases. So, where he had sent to New York a single case, he got back fifty-five cases involving 22 million plaintiffs, including the U.S. Government; every manufacturer and distributor of farm feeds; and almost every insurance company in the United States. The case was just an unintelligible mess. Pretrial discovery and hearings lasted through mid-1974, and it was during this period that Lord supervised settlements amounting to about $200 million which removed all the plaintiffs save the federal government.

Trial began in November 1974 and lasted for sixteen months, with the federal government seeking $204 million in overcharges for drugs purchased for Veterans Administration hospitals and by other federal agencies and the Pentagon. Lord concluded that the case was too complex for a single jury, so he had a second jury box built in the courtroom and impaneled a second jury, each with a different set of issues to decide. "The courtroom resembles the floor of the New York Stock Exchange in its congestion of attorneys and a Wagnerian opera in its epic subplots," one newspaper report noted.

In May 1976, as the trial was in its sixteenth month, Lord suddenly declared a mistrial, stating that the "jurors are tired and confused" and the cumulative effect "of more than fifty [newspaper] stories about the trial, settlements and appeals in a year and a half is sufficient to cause doubts about the objectivity in the mind of any juror." He also accused the attorneys, with obvious cause, of dragging out the case. "They had this one witness on for three months," Lord was heard to explain sometime later; "I wouldn't have had him on for three hours."

The attorneys, naturally, were displeased with the decision. Several were quoted in *The American Lawyer* article to the effect that Lord's action was a gross violation of judicial discretion. An appeal was made to the Eighth Circuit U.S. Court of Appeals, which this time refused to characterize his action as an abuse of discretion; nevertheless, it required Lord to retain control of the case and either continue the trial or start a new one. Lord, in typical style, transferred the case to another judge and it was eventually settled.

Lord has defended his action in that case as having been judicially correct. He also said he was proud of several innovations he had brought to the case, including two separate juries to hear different facets of the complex suit and working out formulas to reimburse consumers who had been overcharged by the defendant drug companies. And he is proud of some of the decisions he made that have since been upheld by the U.S. Supreme Court, including the granting to foreign governments the right to sue U.S. corporations in U.S. courts. Nevertheless, it was his decision in this case that apparently got Lord chosen by *The American Lawyer* as the Eighth Circuit's worst judge.

Those close to Lord tell a different tale. They say that the dubious title was given to him because of comments he made regarding the civil rights of an escaped convict. The convict was a murderer who had threatened Lord's life and the life of his family. After his escape, he telephoned the judge's home to let Lord know that he intended to make good on his threat. Lord called on the public to assist in finding the man and putting him back behind bars. The editor of *The American Lawyer* then reportedly asked Lord how he expected to protect the man's civil rights with such comments. The judge couldn't believe it; his and his family's lives were endangered and he was supposed to be more concerned with protecting the man's civil rights. "First we'll clap him in irons," Lord snapped back, "and *then* we'll protect his civil rights."

Less than a year after he was named worst judge, using many of the same cases as examples, the Association of Trial Lawyers of America named Lord the outstanding federal judge of 1981. The forty-two-thousand-member group, made up primarily of plaintiffs' attorneys in civil matters, cited Lord "for being a staunch protector of the rights of the consumer, the environment, the worker, the citizen and minorities; and for being in the forefront of judicial innovation to insure that substantive rights are protected and not forfeited or lost in a procedural morass."

Lord learned of the award several weeks before it was to be given at the organization's annual meeting, but he kept it secret, telling only his wife and his four children. The reason for the secret? "I didn't want anyone to enjoin them," he quipped.

When he was selected worst judge by the editors of *The American Lawyer,* ostensibly on the basis of a survey, Lord had said, "When someone takes a poll critical of a judge, you deplore polls." When he won the trial lawyers' award, he said, "To be consistent, you should deplore a poll even when it is favorable. But I love it. . . .

I'm flattered and complimented." Asked to compare the awards, Lord refused, sort of: "It's hard to make a comparison between a little hole-in-the-wall publisher and some forty thousand trial lawyers."

The award also marked a time of some reflection for the judge. He told a local newspaper, "Being a judge is not a popularity contest. It's like shouting in the wilderness sometimes. But to know someone hears you gives you some sense of fulfillment." Still, he admitted there was a downside to such attention. "If you get too big for your britches, people tend to cut you down. I have cases in the Eighth Circuit every day. I'm getting along fine with them and I want to keep it that way."

This reflective mood, however, was not due only to the award. The judge now had greater responsibilities on his shoulders. Shortly after being named worst judge by *The American Lawyer* and not long before being named best judge by the trial lawyers, Lord in 1981 became chief U.S. district judge for the district of Minnesota, a post he was to hold until his retirement in 1985.

Lord's tendency to be outspoken is evident even in his humor. Asked by an interviewer, for example, what his favorite television shows were, Lord responded: "'Captain Kangaroo,' 'Twilight Zone,' 'Fantasy Island'—and Ronald Reagan's news conferences."

President Reagan is not one of Lord's favorite people. The President, he says, "frightens the hell out of me." Lord is not so frightened, though, that he won't take on the Reagan administration.

Early in 1984, for example, Lord enjoined Secretary of Health and Human Services Margaret M. Heckler from setting new, overly restrictive standards for Social Security disability benefits and ordered that approximately eight thousand people in seven states who had been removed from the disability rolls be reinstated immediately. Government attorneys then asked Lord to stay his order for ten days, but he would brook no delay. Some of those people, the judge explained, were now being forced to exist on the paltry $2,400 a year they got from welfare instead of the higher disability payments they were due. "That the poor must suffer while the affluent prosper is a political decision," Lord declared. "We've made a deliberate decision to let people go hungry.

"I can't see delaying relief to people who may very well be starving to death," Lord said in refusing to delay the order. Rather he would remove from its coverage any of the eight thousand people the administration could show him were not legally entitled to the disability payments.

"Hundreds of poor devils must go without benefits because the secretary ignores her own decrees" regarding who should or should not get benefits, Lord told the government attorneys. "In another place and another time, that would be shocking. But I guess we can't call it shocking when the government does it with a straight face."

The attorneys, however, would not give up. The order, they said, would cost about $8 million a year. That in itself, they argued, warranted a delay in the decree until the whole matter could be reevaluated. "If they slow down kicking people off the rolls," Lord shot back, "they'll have some time to reevaluate what they've already done." As for the logjam that would be created, the judge said, "The secretary will have to live in her own mess."

In a related action some time later, Lord mandated a whole set of "proper standards" for the evaluation of future disability applications, standards that were quickly stayed by the Eighth Circuit U.S. Court of Appeals pending a hearing on the government's appeal. Early in 1985, the Eighth Circuit upheld Lord's decision.

Perhaps Lord's biggest head-on clash with the Reagan administration, however, began in late 1983, in a case involving the Sperry Corporation. Sperry had been accused in three felony counts of using false labor statements to overcharge the U.S. Defense Department $325,000 on an MX missile contract. According to the charges against Sperry, which in fiscal year 1984 ranked twentieth among Defense Department suppliers, the company had agreed to charge the government for only a fixed amount of its research on an MX missile targeting computer system. However, when Sperry began to encounter cost overruns it preferred not to swallow, it falsified time cards on another contract, this one involving an airborne launch-control system for the Minuteman, to make up the difference.

On December 9, 1983, federal prosecutors direct from Washington walked into Judge Lord's courtroom to announce that they had reached a plea-bargained settlement with Sperry. It wasn't that they had sought out Lord, or that he had been involved with the case. They needed a judge to hear the plea bargain and accept it, and

Lord was available. He soon made them wish that they had drawn someone else.

Under the plea bargain, Sperry admitted its guilt and was to pay $650,000 in damages, $167,000 in interest, a $30,000 fine (the maximum allowable), and a $300,000 reduction in the amount of legal fees it could recover from the government. In a memorandum supporting the settlement, the Justice Department hailed it as a signal to other defense contractors "that mischarging [the government] will be treated as a criminal matter. With the prosecution of Sperry, we anticipate a change in attitude in the industry."

Lord's role that day was to be the rubber stamp. All he was supposed to do—in fact, all most judges would have done—was listen to the guilty plea and accept the terms of the settlement. Not Lord. "Do you know what I would do with the people who did this?" he demanded of the federal prosecutors. "I would take them over and sit them in a snowbank in front of [the] Sperry Rand [plant in St. Paul], and then I'd have two or three big harness bulls [police officers] come and lug them off to jail just like they did those antiwar protestors from over there last week."

Something was missing, Lord insisted, and he was incensed. A giant corporation was being allowed to walk away from a crime virtually unpunished. He began tearing into the prosecutors. They were good at prosecuting welfare cheats who are "going to jail for forty-dollar chisels or two hundred dollars. Here goes several hundred thousand dollars and no individual is responsible for it. It disappears into the deep, dark recesses of corporate power."

All but $30,000 of the $850,000 penalty (not counting the $300,000 reduction in recoverable legal fees), Lord pointed out, was tax-deductible and represented less than 1/1000 of Sperry's $1.4 billion in income from the Pentagon alone. This the government had branded as a major victory. It was a travesty, Lord insisted, and he would do something about it.

He was not prepared to accept the plea bargain at this time, he said. Instead, he ordered the Federal Probation Office to begin a presentencing investigation to determine whether individual liability could be assessed. He then adjourned the proceeding until the probation report was completed.

Moments later, probation officer Dale Carlton met with counsel for the government and Sperry outside Lord's courtroom in order to determine when he could have access to the evidence in the case. He would need it, he explained, in order to begin his investigation. That would not be possible, the government attorneys from Washington informed Carlton, because all subpoenaed documents in the case were being returned to Sperry that afternoon.

Carlton quickly returned to the courtroom and informed Lord of what the government attorneys had said. The judge, visibly disturbed, called both sides back into court, warning that he would hold federal attorneys in contempt if he had to in order to gain access to the evidence for Carlton. The government quickly relented but then stalled for several weeks before opening up its case files to the probation officer. Sperry, for its part, "didn't provide much of anything except the plea agreement, which I had already," Carlton recalled. In the end, Carlton reported back that it was impossible, given the documents the government had made available, to determine who personally was to blame for the felonies.

However, Carlton was able to supply Lord with something else that he had found during his investigation: a report by the Defense Contract Audit Agency that showed that Sperry was guilty of overcharging the U.S. Government $3.5 million—or more than ten times the amount the government prosecutors had claimed in the three felony counts. At a hearing called after receiving Carlton's probation report, Lord released the report and then angrily demanded to know why the government was not planning to bring action against Sperry for the entire amount.

Richard Sauber, who at the time headed the Justice Department's defense procurement fraud unit, told Lord that the difference in the amounts represented nothing more than accounting issues and as such were not subject to prosecution. "There are a number of issues that are unresolved," Sauber told Lord. "The vast majority of them are still open. They are ongoing issues. There may be . . . hundreds of thousands or millions of dollars in disputed costs."

Nevertheless, said Lord, it only pointed up once again the need for someone to pay for the crime, and yet "nothing [has] happened to anybody. It hasn't been called to my attention that any individual has been punished," he told the prosecutors. "I just have a view that this will never stop until the officers of a corporation are held accountable for the conduct of their subordinates."

There was little that Lord could do, however, to rectify the situation. The Justice Department had said that it doubted that a criminal conviction could be obtained if the case went to trial, and Carlton's review of the evidence seemed to support that claim. All that the judge could do was reluctantly accept the settlement. He had known that going into the hearing, of course, but he had called it nonetheless because he felt the public had a right to the information. More important, he later chuckled, "I just wanted [Sperry] shareholders to know."

Actually, Judge Lord had known since December 9 that there was little room in which to maneuver in the Sperry case. The case had been handled almost completely by the Justice Department itself; the local U.S. attorney was never involved, nor any of the local U.S. district judges. It was never even before him except for the one "hearing" at which he was expected to agree to the settlement. Delaying his decision until a presentencing investigation could be completed was a long shot that had little chance of succeeding.

In other words, there was little doubt in Lord's mind on that day —December 9, 1983—that he had lost that battle for justice even before it had begun. The fact that he had to threaten federal attorneys with contempt if they refused to cooperate with a federal probation officer was proof enough to him that justice would not be served in the Sperry case.

(Justice would be served in another case, a year and a half later, but it would only point up how right Lord's instincts had been about the Sperry settlement: that an industry giant was being let off the hook with only a very light tap on the wrist that would not deter anyone else in the defense industry from following in its footsteps.

In May 1985 the General Electric Company admitted to having submitted 104 false claims on a $47 million Air Force contract to install new re-entry vehicles on Minuteman missiles. As with Sperry, GE had falsified employee time cards to create the overcharges. Unlike Sperry, however, which plea-bargained its way down to a $30,000 fine, GE had to shell out $1.04 million because the prosecutor in its case, Assistant U.S. Attorney Ed Zittlau of Philadelphia, was not willing to let this industry giant off the hook. "I wanted GE to have to pay at least a million dollars," he explained in words Judge Lord would have loved to have heard from the prosecutors who had appeared before him, "so I went out and found more than one hundred falsified time cards and got indictments on each and every one. So the fine was based on 104 counts, and they had to pay ten thousand dollars on each count.")

As Lord walked back from his courtroom through the "tunnel" and out to the corridor leading to his chambers after the hearing, he once again despaired about the two systems of justice—one for the rich and one for the poor—and became more determined than ever to find a way to someday make his kind of justice work in his courtroom.

Once inside his chambers, Lord went through his regular routine: He loosened his robes, kicked off his shoes, and settled into his big black leather chair by his desk. He gave a perfunctory look at the small yellow pile of telephone messages; then he checked his calendar. He opened a drawer and removed a big cigar, bit off the end, moved the small garbage can to the right of his desk closer to use as an ashtray, and lit up.

Having finally made himself comfortable and relaxed with his cigar, the judge reached for some papers concerning the next major case before him. He leaned back in his chair, put his feet up on his desk, and began skimming over the documents. It was a civil matter, a product-liability case, and in a few moments attorneys for both sides would come before him to discuss procedures for the upcoming trial. In fact, he mused as he took a pleasurable puff from his big cigar, he thought he had seen several of the attorneys in court while he was dealing with the Sperry case, which probably meant that he was running late.

As Lord continued to look over the papers before him, three words attracted his attention: the Dalkon Shield.

7

BREAKING THE LOGJAM

The twenty-one Dalkon Shield cases on Judge Lord's calendar were not new, by any means; some had been filed as long ago as 1980 and, along with hundreds of others involving the same product, had threatened to bog down both the federal and the state courts in Minnesota for many years to come, as similar cases were doing elsewhere.

As chief judge of the district, Lord was responsible for the efficient administration of the courts in his jurisdiction. As such, he had long ago assigned direction of the federal Dalkon Shield suits filed in Minnesota to U.S. district judge Donald Alsop. At the time that he did so, the number of cases was manageable. As that number grew, however, Judge Alsop began to question whether he alone could clear the cases off the court docket. He knew for a certainty that he could not do so when, earlier in 1983, he had tried his first Dalkon Shield case, *Strempke* v. *A. H. Robins Company.* He had not allowed any new discovery in that case because the MDL supposedly had made all the discovery that was possible. Nevertheless, that trial had consumed nearly four months of court time. All six of the U.S. district judges in the state would have to be involved, Alsop reasoned, if the courts were to be able to get out from under. After a number of discussions among his fellow judges, the Dalkon Shield lawsuits were divided up, and Judge Lord found himself with twenty-one cases to try.

This in itself was unusual, and it points up just how seriously Lord and his colleagues viewed the logjam. Lord had a self-imposed conflict-of-interest problem that should have disqualified him. (It was a self-imposed problem because he was not required to disqualify himself.) In mid-1983, Robins hired the St. Paul law firm of Oppenheimer, Foster, Wolff, Shepard, & Donnelly. On the staff of the Oppenheimer firm was the judge's son-in-law; hence the potential conflict of interest. Lord agreed to accept Dalkon Shield cases only after "the Oppenheimer firm . . . made a prior agreement that the cases I took [it] would not handle."

The timing of the hiring of the Oppenheimer firm is, at the very least, curious. It took place just as Judge Alsop began to discuss dividing up the Dalkon Shield cases among the remaining district court judges in Minnesota. Given Judge Lord's handling of the Reserve Mining case, among others, his stated beliefs about corporate responsibility, and especially his penchant for not only allowing discovery but doing everything in his power to move the fact-finding process along, it would be understandable that Robins would not want Judge Lord sitting on a case involving the Dalkon Shield. Hiring the Oppenheimer firm thus would have been an ideal way to get rid of Judge Lord without much difficulty.

Both Robins and the Oppenheimer firm, of course, have denied that any such thing was considered. However, plaintiffs' attorney Dale Larson is convinced that the hiring of the Oppenheimer firm was a deliberate attempt to keep Lord out of the Dalkon Shield litigation. "When Judge Alsop had his first big litigation status conference following *Strempke* [at which time discussions were under way to divide up the cases], that was the first time that Oppenheimer showed up in court," Larson says. "And there's no doubt about it in my mind that Oppenheimer was hired to keep Lord out. For me, the confirming fact is that when we reached the point of ultimate negotiations with Robins and Lord's involvement was basically over, all of a sudden Oppenheimer was gone."

Whatever the reason Oppenheimer was hired, there was no question that Lord would have to sit on Dalkon Shield cases. There were just too many on the federal calendar and he was needed to help break the logjam.

Before Judge Lord got to his cases in December 1983, however, three other Dalkon Shield suits had already been tried in Minnesota federal courts and two more were nearing completion. The experience of those trials had Lord very concerned. Many of the issues in each trial were the same; many of the witnesses were the same; many of the documents entered into evidence were the same; many of the exhibits were the same. Yet each case was tried as though it were the only one that had ever come before a court. The result in *Strempke,* which Judge Alsop had tried, was a trial that lasted nearly four months, producing a transcript of nearly nine thousand pages. Thirty-seven witnesses had been called and over 570 documents had been introduced into evidence. Another trial, *Hahn* v. *Robins,* plowing exactly the same ground, had already lasted nearly two months and, as it neared completion, had produced a trial record of approximately 5,500 pages.

Judge Lord, who claims to like to "approach a case with as much ignorance as possible so that I can sit here in the same posture as the jury and get some wonderful surprises," had gone over the record of those trials only cursorily at this time, yet it was enough to make him realize that a different procedure was needed if the Minnesota federal courts (and all other courts, for that matter) were to get out from under and if the litigants were to have their rightful days in court. "If this goes on over and over across this country," the judge reasoned, "do you realize what will happen . . . ? [T]he ladies will be dead and gone before their cases get litigated."

The procedure that seemed to make the most sense to Lord was a consolidation of the twenty-one cases before him. He would greatly expand the jury (he was thinking then of "about twenty-five" people) and, at one time, hear the common issue of whether the Dalkon Shield could reasonably have caused any of the injuries set forth in the complaints of the plaintiff-victims. If the expanded jury found that the Dalkon Shield could have caused such injuries, then the jury would break up into several groups and each of the plaintiff-victims would get separate hearings on the question of whether the specific injuries they alleged were brought on by the IUD. Finally, if the "minijuries" in Phase Two found that any of the plaintiff-victims had sustained injuries because of the Dalkon Shield, a second trial before the full jury would be held to determine the common question of whether the A. H. Robins Company was aware of the dangers of the Dalkon Shield and, if so, what it did or did not do to warn physicians and women about those dangers. This would be the punitive-damages phase.

On December 5, 1983, therefore, Lord had sent a letter to all parties asking their "advice" on whether a consolidated trial was feasible. (In reality, what Lord wanted was their concurrence; he preferred not having to delay the trial while a possible appeal on an arbitrary consolidation order wended its way through the system.) He asked that counsel for both sides be present in his court on December 9 to discuss the proposal, as well as the procedures to be followed in the event of consolidation.

"I felt total relief when I read that letter," Dale Larson recalls. "At last, maybe this litigation will start to move, I felt, that the light would start to shine on it.

"The biggest problem with Dalkon Shield litigation overall, and I'm trying to summarize in oversimplistic form, was that the old rules, the rules most lawyers are guided by, were no longer the rules here. It had become evident to us [after *Strempke* and as *Hahn* wound down] that we could win all of the cases and totally lose the war. It was literally impossible to try all these cases, given their complexity and their length.

"Ultimately, too, there was a limitation on the resources of anybody to be able to handle that volume of cases. Unless we were able to achieve some means to bring cases together and to potentially resolve issues forever [legally known as collateral estoppel], we knew that it was very likely that the rights of the many women who'd been hurt by the Dalkon Shield would be jeopardized.

"Lord's consolidated approach was the first light to shine on these cases. It was inconceivable that we could lose these [consolidated] cases. And winning them meant that we would have the legal basis to even persuade the courts, that [the common issues in the Dalkon Shield cases have] really been fully litigated and these issues are resolved. And even if we did not get collateral estoppel, we would at least be bringing a group of cases to conclusion in a fashion where it would be very evident to Robins and its lawyers that the clock was finally running down; this game wasn't going to drag on for many more years. So we were perfectly happy to take a group of cases at a time and start trying them. To even achieve a consolidation, even without collateral estoppel, was a major, major step forward."

After receiving Lord's letter, the various plaintiffs' attorneys gathered at the cavernous offices of Robins, Zelle, Larson & Kaplan on South Fifth Street in downtown Minneapolis. They quickly agreed with Larson that consolidation was the way to go. In his letter, Judge Lord had also suggested that the various attorneys for the plaintiffs in the twenty cases (one had just settled) get together and choose someone from among their number to act as lead counsel. If consolidation was the way he would go, he wanted to have "one voice" speak for the plaintiffs in order to not waste undue time.

This, too, made sense to the lawyers grouped around the Robins, Zelle conference table and it was suggested that Dale Larson and his associate Mike Ciresi serve in that capacity. After all, they had tried *Strempke* and won; they were close to winning Martha Hahn's case and, although it is often hard to predict how juries would go, the plaintiff's case was just too strong; they had by far the most Dalkon Shield cases in the state (approximately three hundred, 80 percent of which they had gotten from Bob Appert and Jerry Pyle, the two attorneys Robins had sought to disbar); and the Robins, Zelle firm had the greatest resources, including 120 litigation specialists and a support force of paralegal assistants. Larson and Ciresi, therefore, were the logical choice.

However, not everyone attending the meeting was completely satisfied with the arrangement. The big stumbling block was how to guarantee that all of the plaintiffs would be equally protected, even if they were not Robins, Zelle clients. This led to a proposal that a minority plaintiffs' committee be formed. Larson, though, would not go along with it. As lead counsel, he said, he would protect the rights of all the plaintiffs, regardless of who actually represented them. He had no intention, however, of trying a case by committee and having every action he and Ciresi took argued over and second-guessed. If that's what everyone else wanted, he would go along—but not as lead counsel. The committee idea was soon dropped.

On the morning of December 9, Larson and Ciresi rode the elevator of the U.S. District Courthouse to the sixth floor and walked into Lord's courtroom. The judge was in the process of admonishing the Justice Department attorneys over their handling of the Sperry plea bargain.

Lord's courtroom is very much like so many other federal courtrooms throughout the nation: a sixty-by-forty room with a high ceiling and dark mahogany walls; double doors with glass panels at the back of the room serving as the access way for the public; five rows of benches separated by a center aisle; a mahogany bar with two hinged panels approximately twenty feet from the back of the room; a bench on either side of the aisle in front of the bar on which the U.S. marshal and other interested parties sat; two rectangular counsel tables with wooden armchairs on wheels; a fourteen-seat jury box (for twelve jurors and two alternates) to the right and a table for the judge's clerks beyond that, in the right-hand corner by the far wall, next to the door leading to the "tunnel" by which the judge enters and exits; and a wide screen rolled up in a blue metal case suspended from the ceiling. Front and center was a lectern with a microphone; before it was the well in which the calendar clerk sat to the left and the court reporter to the right. Above and behind the well was the bench, with two high-backed leather chairs, only one of which is usually occupied unless a magistrate or a second district judge is in attendance. On the far wall above the bench hung the Great Seal of the United States. To the left stood the flag.

It was a familiar sight to Larson and Ciresi. The two attorneys acknowledged the greetings of several of their colleagues in the case from both sides and then quietly sat down in one of the spectator rows to put the finishing touches on their plan for their first day before Lord. As such, they only caught little bits and pieces of the heated action at the front of the room.

After the Sperry case, Lord left the bench for a brief respite. When he returned, he raised the question of whether the matter of lead counsel had been addressed by the plaintiffs. "Have you had any success in doing that?" he asked.

Larson and Ciresi, now seated at the counsel table to Lord's left, rose and approached the lectern. "Your honor, I'm Dale Larson, of Robins, Zelle, Larson & Kaplan," the senior of the two explained, adjusting the microphone slightly. "We were able to get all of the plaintiffs' lawyers together this week and, subject to finalizing some of the arrangements, we will act as lead counsel."

"You and who?" Lord asked, looking at the second man.

"My firm," Larson responded, then, pointing to the man next to him added, "Mike Ciresi, specifically."

"Good morning, your honor," Ciresi said. "Good morning," Lord responded and then had enough of amenities. There was work to be done. "Well, come up here," he said, "and defense counsel, come up here, too."

Larson and Ciresi approached the bench, as did Jack Fribley and Mary Trippler, two local attorneys from the firm of Faegre and Benson, which was representing the A. H. Robins Company. "Did you get a copy of that letter, Mary?" he asked.

"Yes, we did, your honor," she responded.

"Well, I put forward some ideas there . . . ," he said, "[but] I don't want to make any plans until I know what you think about it."

The local Robins attorneys, whatever their private opinions, could not publicly think much of the consolidation plan because it went against the national defense strategy that had been established so long ago by the McGuire, Woods & Battle law firm. At the same time, they could not tell Judge Lord that this was the reason for their objection.

"Your honor," Fribley said, adopting the standard Robins line, "it is our position, in view of the twenty cases on the court's list that have been assigned to you and their state of unpreparedness . . . that consolidation at this time is not an efficient solution to the court's backlog. We share this court's desire to reduce that backlog. We believe that a mechanism is presently in place to do that." Fribley added that, in any case, each of the twenty lawsuits was substantially different in nature, which would preclude consolidation.

One of the main parts of the "mechanism" Fribley spoke of to Lord was a motion to move approximately thirty cases on the federal calendar to other jurisdictions "because the women [in those cases] have no connection whatsoever with Minnesota other than the fact that their attorney is located here." This was part of Robin's strategy of delay; the longer a plaintiff's case languished in the courts without being heard, the greater the likelihood either that the case would be dropped or that the plaintiff would be willing to accept a small settlement and be done with it.

"They'd like to get these cases transferred back to all kinds of states and maybe we wouldn't stay in the case," Ciresi thought as

Fribley argued his motion. The idea brought a smile to his face. "They want to get rid of us because we beat 'em in *Strempke* and we're beating 'em in *Hahn* and we got three hundred more cases to go. And they want to stick these cases on the bottom of other calendars so these women won't see their cases called for trial for another two or three years."

Robins also wanted to move as many cases as possible away from Judge Lord. The judge, ignorant though he was as to the reasons for the transfer motion at the time, nevertheless was as keenly aware as Ciresi of what a transfer would mean to the plaintiff-victims. "You mean they'll be sent someplace else and start again at the foot of the [court] calendar in another jurisdiction?" Lord cut in as Fribley explained the transfer motions.

"I'm not sure they would start at the foot of the calendar, your honor," Fribley countered. "They are cases we believe to be subject . . . to transfer to other districts because the women are there, the [medical] records are there, the doctors are there, and the only connection—"

Again Lord interrupted Fribley. "Did Judge Alsop give me any of those cases?" If not, he did not want to waste time hearing irrelevant arguments. Fribley told Lord that he had seven such cases. In order to move things along, Lord set a hearing on the transfer motions for the following Tuesday. As the hearing progressed, however, the idea that years-old cases would end up getting even older before they were resolved gnawed away at Lord; justice, he felt, was not well served in such an instance.

"I'll tell you," he eventually said to Fribley and Mary Trippler, "as far as transferring those cases out of here, I don't think you have to make that motion. . . . The ladies are here and they're ready for trial, and that's what we'll do. I can't see any interest in justice in putting those people at the end of the calendar again in another jurisdiction."

Larson began to say something, but Lord decided to cut him off with a compliment. "And then we have this wonderful local counsel who can handle it here," he said, pointing to Larson and Ciresi. "Who knows? [The plaintiff-victims] might not find such good lawyers in other places."

Everyone laughed. Fribley, however, appeared concerned. He had just lost an important delaying tactic and he obviously wanted to report back to Robins's national counsel with something positive. He therefore pressed anew his argument that Robins was not ready to go to trial on the twenty cases. "The problem I have . . . , your honor, is, of course, as you know . . . , we object to the consolidation procedure," Fribley said as Lord nodded and said "Surely," indicating that he recognized that the objection stood, "and especially under the timing that has been proposed."

Lord had set a trial date of January 3, 1984, less than a month away, with Christmas and New Year's intervening. Having just declined to transfer cases because of the long time they had already sat on the calendar, he was also not willing to buy the readiness argument.

"Here's what we'll do now," he told Fribley. "We'll set the January 3rd date as a firm date. And if we come to the day before New Year's and you can point out a good reason for continuing it, we'll have to think about that. Everything has to be done in a reasonable manner. Any unforeseen circumstances, we'll give consideration to. But it is inappropriate for you to stand here now, three and a half or four weeks before the date of trial, and say that you can't get ready on these cases."

The judge then went on to explain why he thought Robins's counsel had plenty of time to get ready. The biggest stumbling block, according to Fribley, was the taking of the depositions of all twenty plaintiffs. "If you put three people, each taking three depositions a day [from the plaintiffs]," Lord asked rhetorically, "how many days would be necessary to take the depositions—five, six days?"

"That might cover the plaintiffs' depositions, your honor," Fribley argued. "There would be [their] physicians' depositions, as well."

"They won't get on for quite a while," Lord said, because the first phase of the trial would deal only with the common issue of whether the Dalkon Shield could cause such injuries; the depositions of the physicians could be taken during that phase. "Put another team on that," the judge suggested.

The discussion then sparked another suggestion by Lord. "By the way . . . , if you have women whose cases have been ambulance-chased from other states by other lawyers in these cases," Lord said to the plaintiffs' attorneys, choosing his words so as not to offend anyone present, "and those women's cases have been pending for a year or two here, they should come and have their depositions taken and make it at the same time as they come to start the trial."

"That would be a great arrangement, your honor," Larson noted.

"So that they don't have to make two trips and spoil Christmas and so forth. . . . They can come after Christmas, you know. . . ."

All of this, of course, should have indicated to anyone in the courtroom that Lord did indeed intend to consolidate the cases, unless anyone could show him good reason why that would not be practical. In case anyone missed the point, however, he stated it clearly to Fribley when the defense attorney yet again tried to pursue his objection. "I do not accept—if you please, without any rancor—I do not accept your statement that this is not an efficient way of proceeding at this time. With the resources available and person power available in the form of lawyers"—Lord smiled and looked over to Trippler—"is ["person power"] all right, Ms. Trippler?"

"That's fine, your honor," and the Robins counsel smiled back.

Lord nodded and continued. "—this can be done. So tentatively my January 3rd date holds. . . . I have thought this out and I have given you what I have been thinking." Lord then paused in his comments; he realized that he had not yet heard from the plaintiffs on the subject. "Perhaps it might be wise to hear from Mr. Larson," he said.

Larson said the plaintiffs were "without exception . . . prepared and desirous of proceeding with these cases on a consolidated basis. . . . Your honor's approach to this, frankly, is a means by which these plaintiffs who have claims are going to have an opportunity, without threat of incredible expenditures of time and money, to have their claims resolved."

As Larson spoke, an anecdote popped into Lord's head. It would serve to lighten things up while at the same time get the consolidation question over with and begin the discussion of the mechanics of a consolidated trial. "Incidentally," Lord began with a twinkle, "I had this problem in [the antibiotics class action suit], where I had something like forty million plaintiffs, and the defendants demanded that each plaintiff come forward and testify about the damages which he or she suffered by way of overcharging when the individual plaintiff bought an antibiotic drug. And there I asked defense counsel, 'Have you computed how long that process would take?' They said, 'Yes.' I said, 'How long?' They said, 'Eight thousand years.' "

Lord got the desired effect: there was laughter in the courtroom. Then he got to the point:

"That was on the record; that was what they said. So, effectively" —Lord turned serious again—"they said that the cases could not be tried. And if you are at all aware of what interest rates are, and if it could be assumed that as of the date of the injury the lady [referring now to the Dalkon Shield plaintiffs] had the money due, then to delay five years at twenty percent interest means it costs [the defendant Robins] nothing to settle the case. So let us move forward on the cases I have. . . ."

Lord then began to lay out the procedures. The case would be complicated enough, he said, without endless time wasted over the admission of evidence. Any evidence (i.e., documents, exhibits, testimony related to generic issues) presented in the four-month-long *Strempke* trial would be admitted in the consolidated case without objection. If Robins appealed the admission of any such evidence in *Strempke* and that appeal were upheld, Lord would exclude that particular piece of evidence.

The judge also did not want to waste time qualifying expert witnesses. Résumés of each witness were to be passed among opposing counsel and stipulations reached to accept those witnesses who truly were expert. Attorneys, he noted, can waste a lot of time in questions establishing an expert witness's expertise.

He also wanted, if possible, to limit the evidence to the Dalkon Shield and what is wrong with it, without any unnecessary side trips into lengthy lectures on female anatomy. "It seems to me that a person would not have to learn all about the cellular and molecular structure of a woman's reproductive processes in order to resolve these cases. If they tell you that there is a string hanging down there [on the Dalkon Shield] and [it] sucked up germs, and that once the germs get there [in the uterus] they cause an infection, then is it important that you know all about everything else? Maybe it's not that simple, though; I don't know." It was that simple, Lord was told; there would be no lengthy lectures on female anatomy in general, or the female reproductive system in particular.

Time was also a factor, Lord said. Defense counsel for Robins apparently was able to put on its case in about a week's time, whereas counsel for plaintiff-victims had a tendency to go on for as many as five weeks. He wanted the plaintiffs to do everything possible to get in its phase one case in a week's time, too.

"Well, as I understand the initial proceeding," Fribley interjected at this point, "it would be a question—which is to me almost in the abstract, given the facts of these cases—'Is the device defective under [the definition of law]'?"

"Do they have any statistics on that, anybody?" Lord asked. The judge looked around the courtroom.

"I'm not sure what you mean," Fribley said. "The cases all involve statistics about rates of infection with this device versus other devices."

"As to those statistics," Lord tried to explain, "wouldn't the same evidence go into each case?"

"Yes, that's right, your honor."

"So it would be a common issue, at least?"

"That's right."

"Okay. Next?"

"Let's say we resolved that in two weeks or three weeks or whatever," Fribley began, but Lord cut in: "In a week, or about four days."

"Okay, I would assume, as I understand it, by all plaintiffs embracing this [consolidated] method of proceeding that there are obvious other liability issues. There's warning, there's express warranty, there's negligence."

"I think that [plaintiffs] are going to have to give up some of them, to get to trial," Lord said, slouching down a bit in his chair and resting his chin and right cheek in his hand.

Fribley seemed comforted. He would at least walk away with one positive point to report to Richmond. "That's what I was getting at," he told Lord. "I would assume, if we should prevail on the first trial [involving whether the Dalkon Shield could have caused the injuries], that liability would be foreclosed to all of the plaintiffs who participate . . . ?"

"I think they have to take some chances," Lord answered affirmatively. "I haven't talked to any plaintiffs about this, but . . . we just don't want to take that much time for trial. . . . So you've got to streamline these cases. And I cannot put all of the blame on the defendant for lengthening the cases"—Lord looked at Larson and Ciresi—"if you plaintiffs are tossing in all kinds of side issues about liability."

Larson indicated that streamlining was possible. "I haven't spoken with the other plaintiffs' lawyers about that, your honor," he said, moving closer to the microphone; "but certainly, if we're going to streamline this thing, we better sit down and try to resolve some of the other issues."

Nodding his head, Larson continued. "I think we can simplify this case and get rid of some of those issues and get on with it. . . . We're all here, and we can meet and talk about it." Larson did ask, however, for permission to require certain Robins executives to appear at the trial live, rather than through deposition testimony. He felt it would help shorten the questioning of these witnesses, including E. Claiborne Robins, Sr., the company chairman. Lord tentatively agreed to require the attendance of those witnesses.

Another streamlining device, Lord said, involved the length of time it would take for Robins's attorneys to depose the plaintiffs. He had a way of shortening that time significantly. "[T]he depositions aren't going to go into all of the things that they've gone into [in other cases], from what I've read in the [court] papers, about the ladies' past sex life fifteen years ago or whether—that kind of thing we're not going to talk about in this case," Lord ordered. "We're going to talk about things that are important and relevant."

The judge was repulsed by the questions, but that was not the reason he was ruling them out of order. The law of product liability, he felt, made them irrelevant. "[I]f an article is manufactured and put on the market and if, when it is used in a manner in which it reasonably could be anticipated that it could be used, it presents an unreasonable danger to the user," Lord would later explain the law, "then the manufacturer is responsible even though he used all due care in the manufacture of it." The Dalkon Shield was manufactured for a specific purpose—to allow women sexual freedom without fear of pregnancy. To what degree and in what manner a woman exercised her sexual freedom, therefore, does not matter.

He would consider allowing the "dirty questions," but only if

Robins could demonstrate a direct relationship between a woman's sexual habits and the cause of her injuries, and if this was explained to her before she had the Dalkon Shield inserted. This goes "especially," he said, for the plaintiff-victims' sex lives "prior to the time that they started to use the device."

"So," Judge Lord continued, now referring to previous plaintiffs who gave up their suits because they were subjected to such embarrassing questions for no reason (and showing a much greater degree of knowledge about the case than he admitted to at this point), "instead of having this a game of attrition, the company that sold the device that was put into the most intimate part of a woman's body should not now go into the most intimate of her personal affairs. . . . We're just not going to do that here. So [these] depositions will be a lot shorter and more to the point. . . .

"[R]emember now . . . , unless you could prove, unless there's evidence of a specific germ like syphilis or gonorrhea or herpes that somebody contracted as a result of sexual activities, at least prior to the time of insertion, there'll be no questions about [their sex lives]. As far as abortions are concerned during the relevant time, well, they couldn't have had one while they had that device in; otherwise, they'd be claiming for that—"

"Exactly, your honor," Larson agreed.

"—so abortions are out, not to be referred to, not to be inquired into. What else?" Lord asked Larson. "What is the other stuff that embarrasses these women into not filing [or proceeding with] their claims?"

"Oh," Larson answered, a bit embarrassed himself, "they ask them, you know, which way they wiped, how many sexual partners they have ever had, when they've had sex—"

Lord did not want to hear the litany recited. "None of their business," he cut in, "absent a showing that they've got a specific intercourse-related disease like syphilis, gonorrhea, or herpes. . . ."

After some further discussions, Lord had covered as much ground as was possible that day. "I don't know what else there is to discuss at this time," the judge finally said. "I want you to know that any decision I have made here is made only on the information that I have today, and that if further information develops that is cogent and strong information as to the lack of wisdom of any ruling I make, I will be willing to give consideration to amending it at that time. So it is not appropriate for either of you to quote panic in the face of what I say here because I have only said proceed with alacrity to try to accomplish this and if something comes up that is insurmountable we will give consideration to changing that order."

Throughout the first day's hearing, Lord seemed to be leaning a bit to the Robins side. He had gotten the plaintiffs to simplify their case and to agree to limit their Phase One questioning to one week (as opposed to the five weeks, say, that was used in the Strempke case). True, he had banned the "dirty questions," but only until such time as Robins could show a definite relevancy to those questions; and he had agreed with plaintiffs that certain Robins executives would be required to testify, but again only if they could show the importance of such a requirement. He even urged a quick settlement and warned the plaintiffs not to be too greedy.

For their part, the Robins attorneys appeared to be laid back, as if not to tip off the judge that they meant to utilize as many of the traditional Robins obstructionist tactics as they could get away with. Now, as the pretrial hearing wound down, Fribley spoke up.

"One final matter, your honor, simply so my silence on the subject wouldn't be construed as agreement," Robins's local counsel said, following the instructions given him by the drug firm's national lead counsel. "In terms of live corporate witnesses, my understanding of the law is that without a subpoena served upon them they cannot be compelled to appear. I don't know who will be available then—"

Lord stopped Fribley cold. That was not the kind of thing he liked to hear in his courtroom. "You don't want to stand on that, do you?"

"As a legal position, yes sir," Fribley responded.

"You stand on it as a legal position," Lord countered, "and as a *practical* position you better have the people here."

This was not a threat on Lord's part, but a genuine concern for the defendant's case. Lord knew to what effect an attorney for the other side could play up the fact that certain witnesses failed to appear.

Indeed, as the discussion continued, Mike Ciresi was smiling to himself as he contemplated the use he would make of missing witnesses in his summation in the Martha Hahn case only six days later. "Dr. Freund didn't come up here," he would tell the *Hahn* jury. "Dr. Clark, E. C. Robins, Sr., E. C. Robins, Jr. . . . , where are they? They were the corporate management who made the decision [to market the Dalkon Shield]. Why didn't they come in . . . to subject themselves to the scrutiny of your observations . . . ? [Dr. Owen was here. He said,] 'I wasn't directly responsible for the Dalkon Shield; Dr. Kitty Preston was.' Where is Kitty Preston? I'd sure like to know where Kitty Preston is. I'd sure like to have her up on that witness stand and let you evaluate her testimony. . . . Full and open disclosure? Responsible and prudent manufacturer? I submit it's not. I submit it's willful indifference. I submit it's a cover-up."

That was what Judge Lord hoped to avoid in his courtroom, where he preferred cases to be tried on facts, not inferences; it may not be legally necessary to bring those witnesses here, he reasoned, but it made a great deal of sense from a practical standpoint. Fribley said he understood, but he nevertheless continued to argue against the judge's tentative ruling. At length, Lord put an end to the discussion:

"You have, in effect, an order to show cause why they should not be produced," he told Fribley. "I think they ought to come because I think what we are going to do is set some patterns for the rest of these [3,310 Dalkon Shield cases nationwide] and make it possible for Mr. Robins and all your clients to go back to producing drugs and saving lives, and we'll get it over with, and also the insurance company [Aetna] will be relieved to find a formula by which they can get rid of these claims and not spend all their money defending them."

With that, the hearing ended. The Robins obstructionism was about to begin. The main weapon in the Robins armory was to be the delaying motion. In all, Robins would file seven such motions: for reconsideration and modification of Lord's order for depositions; for a protective order on evidence produced during discovery, in hopes of keeping that evidence sealed by the court and unavailable in any other cases; for an order to prohibit the disclosure of a summary Lord's staff had prepared on all documents for which privilege was claimed; objections to the discovery proceedings; for a stay in the proceedings until Robins could move for Judge Lord to disqualify himself from the case; for the disqualification of Judge Lord; a combined motion to quash deposition subpoena and, once again, for a protective order.

It had been the judge's intention to streamline the cases and, as he had indicated to Fribley and the others, to set up a mechanism by which all other Dalkon Shield cases could be resolved with a minimum of time wasted. Instead, because of Robins's obstructionist tactics, the consolidated Dalkon Shield cases would be anything but streamlined. Aside from the motions (or, more likely, because of them and other Robins tactics), between that December 9 and February 29, 1984, when Lord's direct involvement in the consolidated cases would end, there would be more than sixty-five separate pleadings, creating a paper "mountain" almost a foot high; there would be ten written orders, most involving discovery and the taking of depositions; numerous oral orders issued during the course of the seventeen pretrial hearings, which in themselves created a paper mountain of over 1,260 pages; an even greater amount of paper would be generated in the depositions themselves, which would be spread out over 5,721 pages, added to the 3,386 pages of depositions that had been taken during the various multidistrict litigation proceedings.

Merely the preliminary Robins tactics of seeking to remove cases to other jurisdictions, trying to force a separate trial on each case and, above all else, threatening not to produce requested witnesses rang a bell in Lord's head—the same bell that always rang when someone in his courtroom was trying to use legal legerdemain to thwart the interests of justice. It caused him to begin to review more closely the data already supplied to him regarding past Dalkon Shield cases that already had been tried.

Lord noted that Robins executives had poor memories when they gave depositions or testimony. They never could remember certain things pertinent to the plaintiff's case, although they never had any trouble remembering anything pertinent to Robins's defense.

Lord was particularly annoyed at the deposition testimony given on September 19 by E. Claiborne Robins, Jr. The president and chief executive officer of the A. H. Robins Company had made a big point of his management style—the delegating of authority—but otherwise could remember nothing about the Dalkon Shield. Dale Larson had questioned the younger Robins in Richmond:

Q. Have you ever discussed the Dalkon Shield with your father?

A. In relation to what?

Q. To anything. Has the term "Dalkon Shield" ever come up in a conversation that you've had with your father?

A. It has.

Q. Many times?

A. No.

Q. Do you recall the first time?

A. I do not.

Q. Can you tell us approximately when it was?

A. No. I don't remember. . . .

Q. Approximately how many times have you discussed the Dalkon Shield with your father over the years?

A. I don't know.

Q. Would it be more than a dozen?

A. I don't know.

Q. Can you recall any of the occasions?

A. I cannot. . . .

Q. Apparently, none of those conversations were sufficiently significant so that you have any recollection of them, is that correct . . . ? I'll be happy to rephrase it. If you can recall any conversation, I just want to know about it, Mr. Robins. If you can't, you can't.

A. I cannot recall. . . .

Q. Do you have any recollection as to what year . . . you [first] came into contact with any discussion about the Dalkon Shield at a board meeting . . . ?

A. Since that was over ten years ago, I do not remember.

Q. Needless to say, you obviously don't remember the initial board conversation about the Dalkon Shield either, correct?

A. I do not. . . .

Q. Excluding conversations with your attorney, do you have any recollection of any discussion with any company member, employee, board member, or consultant about the Dalkon Shield . . . at any time . . . ?

A. I do.

Q. How many conversations of that type do you recall?

A. Only one.

Q. When was it?

A. September of 1980, I believe. . . .

Q. Was the subject of that meeting specifically the Dalkon Shield?

A. It was a letter relating to the Dalkon Shield. . . .

Q. Was that one of the "Dear Doctor" letters?

A. Correct. . . .

Q. Now, as I understand it, Mr. Robins, outside of this one conversation concerning the Dalkon Shield . . . , you don't have any recollection of any other conversations with anyone within the company at any time . . . , is that correct?

A. Correct. . . .

Q. [A]s you sit here today, is it your understanding that the Dalkon Shield is a safe and effective device if used properly?

A. I would say that's probably correct.

On the morning of December 20, Lord opened his newspaper to find that yet another Minnesota jury had ruled against the A. H. Robins Company. The day before, the jury in the Martha Hahn case had awarded her $750,000 for the agony she had gone through both before and after her Christmas Eve operation that saved her life but ended her ability to ever have children. Despite all that he was learning about how previous Dalkon Shield cases were handled, however, he went out of his way to be fair at the pretrial hearing that he held that day. At that hearing, Alexander Slaughter of McGuire, Woods & Battle made his first formal appearance, apparently to see how far Judge Lord could be pushed.

Once again, the two central issues were consolidation and time. On consolidation, Lord made it clear that he intended to proceed with the plan. In fact, he said, Robins would be better off if he did.

"[I]n this instance, I won't pretend that I don't have any knowledge whatsoever until such time as it is submitted," Lord began. "I think that's kind of ridiculous, in the light of all the briefs that have been submitted to the various courts [which I've read]. . . . At least fifteen times, I think, the defendant's brief [in this case] mentioned that they would be deprived of due process, deprived of a fair trial and be prejudiced. . . . In fact, it might be favorable to the defendant in many respects. . . . On this question of punitive damages[, for example] . . . , the punitive damages given to some twenty plaintiffs might be a lot less per case than the punitive damages given on a case-by-case basis. The jury just gets a broader perspective of it."

Another argument against consolidation that Robins had set forth in its trial brief—which Lord made certain to compliment highly, considering what he was about to say—was that the issue of product liability was so different in each case that a generic trial on that issue would be impossible. This, Lord made clear, was not an argument he could accept, based on his research.

"The more I read, by both sides, the more I am convinced that, insofar as the product liability aspects of [the Dalkon Shield], its propensities for dangers and so forth, the history of its development, what was or wasn't known to the extent that that is relevant, are all common questions. Just no doubt about it. And anybody that argues to the contrary," he said pointedly, "I have some question about their sincerity."

As for the time question, the Robins people were still saying that a January 3 trial date was just too soon for them. They were looking for something closer to six months to prepare adequately for the consolidated trial (to which, they continued to remind Judge Lord, they still objected).

"How many weeks ago did I first send out the note saying that we were going to try to consolidate these things, do you know?" the judge asked attorney Fribley.

"Your honor," came the response, "I received this December 7th, which would be two weeks ago tomorrow."

"Now, during that two weeks, have you taken the depositions of—" Lord paused in midsentence. "First of all, how many local plaintiffs are there in these cases?"

"I think there are fourteen, your honor," said Fribley.

"Have you taken the depositions of any of those fourteen women?"

Only one, so far, the judge was told, and there were seventy-two more depositions they needed to take. Lord then suggested that the Robins attorneys put more lawyers onto the deposition-taking, even from the Oppenheimer firm, if necessary, adding that six people taking twelve depositions each could cover the list in twelve days' time.

He also admitted that he had been a bit "too ambitious" with the January 3 starting time, and purposely so. "My thought would be that we would probably delay the starting date until January 15th. In some ways, you know, you just set a date to get people's attention; in this one, I thought we could start, but I am convinced it would be more fair to wait. Six months is a pipe dream. You don't need six months to do this."

Fribley then proceeded to ask some questions of Judge Lord regarding what would or would not be proper in the Phase One trial. "[A]s I understand Phase One," he said at one point, "to the extent it involves warning, that is intertwined in the issues that are going to be in Phase One."

"Let me talk to you about that a little bit," Lord interrupted. Fribley's mention of the word "warning" gave him the perfect cue to ask a question that had been bothering him ever since he had begun to delve deeper into the Dalkon Shield story. "I read in the plaintiff's brief that A. H. Robins had never even up to now ever got hold of the women and told them to take those things out. Is that true?"

Fribley nodded. "If the plaintiffs are referring to an effort by the company to contact the women directly, that would be true, that is right."

"And it's the women who are hurt, isn't it?"

Yes, Fribley said, but plaintiffs' counsel "would want us to contact every customer who ever had a Shield inserted, I'm sure."

"Do you have a computer?"

"I'm sure [Robins has] computers."

"I don't want to be rough with you," Lord then said, "but I've time and again [said] that we should bring the law up to the age of the computer. And within three days with the technology we now have available, we could notify every woman in the country. Or the detail man could stop at the doctor's office and help [him] to go through his records and see who he gave one of these to, and within two weeks the ladies would know enough [to] take them out."

Lord now suggested that he might not allow Robins to try to lay the blame for a woman's injury on her physician—another standard Robins tactic—unless the company could show that the physician knew all that Robins knew about the Dalkon Shield.

Fribley ignored the implications of this statement for the moment; instead, he saw an opportunity to return to his favorite cause:

winning a long delay. He advised the judge that, at the very least, it might be possible to show that the women had been warned by their physicians to remove the device, but that they did not heed the warnings. The problem, he argued, was that this would have to be explored during the taking of depositions and he, Fribley, did not believe there was enough manpower to depose everyone in time even with the twelve extra days Lord had provided.

In responding, Judge Lord once again indicated that he was by now well versed in the history of Dalkon Shield litigation. McGuire, Woods & Battle have lawyers working for it "in every state in this Union," Lord said. "All they have to do is call Oregon and talk to somebody they knew on a first-name basis and say, 'Hey, we've got one coming up out here. Get that old doctor's deposition.' They call Arkansas, and the same. You see, a nationwide problem, a nationwide company—and one of the mightiest insurance companies in America. They could move heaven and earth, if they want to. And anybody that takes a realistic look at it knows—"

Lord paused and looked directly at Alexander Slaughter, who was seated at the defense counsel table. Then he looked back at the lectern where Fribley was standing. "I am advised that the folks in Richmond run all these cases," he said to Fribley in a bit firmer, more deliberate tone than he had used previously, "that there are local people that appear, but the cases are basically run from Richmond. And, as a consequence, let Richmond take over the deposition problem. It is their money. . . . They have got skilled lawyers, the issues are not that much different [from other cases]; they can just pick up those depositions. So I have suffered all I am going to about the hardship they have, when they have literally thousands of lawyers at their disposal. So I won't hear that any further."

Fribley tried to reassure the frustrated Lord. "Well, your honor, there will be a concerted effort made among all the defense lawyers available to this corporation to take these depositions."

"They could have them all done by Christmas if it was their desire to do so. . . . You agree with that, do you sir?"

Lord had directed his question to Slaughter, not Fribley. It took the McGuire, Woods attorney by surprise. "I'm sorry, your honor?" Slaughter answered from his chair at the defense table. "I say, you nodded your head—" Lord began, but by then Slaughter was back on track. "Yes, your honor, we have lawyers available in other states."

"Okay, so that isn't an issue anymore."

Having cleared up the depositions matter for now, Lord returned to a discussion of procedural matters. Regarding the admitting of exhibits without having to wrangle with repeated objections and extensive laying of foundation, Larson told the judge, an effort would be made to agree on the dozen or so exhibits unique to the consolidated cases before they were introduced during later stages of the trial. "[W]ith respect to Phase One exhibits, frankly, I don't see any problem. They've used the same exhibits in the two cases we've tried, and we've used the same exhibits, so—"

"The one thing I don't want you people to do is to pretend that this is the first case on this subject," Lord said to all counsel. "That's just ridiculous. We're in the middle of a mess and we've been through the many facets of it many times. . . . If you have any unusual [exhibits] which you haven't put in before," he was speaking now to Larson, "point them out. But then, the defendants are entitled to know how much you're going to streamline your case, and I pressed you for that." Larson nodded in agreement. "So at least you should point out to them what the parameters of your case are. . . . What are you going to leave out? You've got to leave out something."

"We're leaving out a lot, your honor," Larson said. "We've got it streamlined pretty good by now, I think, after going through this a couple of times."

"Get hold of Mr. Fribley," Lord interrupted, having taken enough time on the matter. "It isn't necessary to issue an order on everything with two practitioners like you, who know each other well and are going to be living here long after A. H. Robins goes home. You work it out." Turning to Fribley, Lord added: "And . . . you find out what plaintiffs have, and then tell us what you are going to do."

Eventually, the hearing got around to the question of Lord's order that certain Robins executives appear to testify before the jury. Fribley had told Judge Lord during the December 9 hearing that, without subpoenas, the requested witnesses might not appear. Now Slaughter was taking the issue one step further. Some of the people involved were no longer under Robins's control and, so, the company could compel their attendance. And that included, Slaughter said, E. Claiborne Robins, Sr., who was both chairman of Robins and a company consultant, but not actually an employee. "Our client," Slaughter then told Lord, "has not decided, given its legal position, whether the ones will appear that they do control."

Quietly, Lord answered the Richmond attorney, "Yes," he said, meaning that he understood the legal position involved. However, he also wanted Slaughter to understand his position. "There have been some cases where, when responsible officials of the company do not come, the plaintiffs are then allowed to argue the absent witness and, you know, make quite a point of it," he said. His tone implied a great deal more than his words spoke. "You might almost be better off to get them out here and get it over with."

"Yes, your honor, I understand your position," Slaughter said, unmoved by the implied threat. "The only thing I wanted was to make sure we did not mislead the court at all on that point. And we will give the court notice, before the scheduled trial date, of what that decision would be. . . ."

That decision, as of January 5, was a tentative no. It was left to Fribley to inform Lord of the decision that day, "So the court knows where we stand, it is the company's position today . . . [that it] would not bring these . . . people here for the plaintiff's case. . . . [T]hey are not necessary for the plaintiffs' case and they have no right to bring them here."

"Don't these people want to tell their story?" Judge Lord asked, in words reminiscent of Ciresi's summation in the Hahn case. "Wouldn't they be interested now . . . in coming here and telling us their side of the story . . . , which should be fairly important? Why would they, at this juncture—and this is just a little bit of human relations, I don't see it as legal strategy; you know, I've read all the briefs and seen the things they said [E. Claiborne Robins, Sr., for one] did or didn't do, without reciting them—why wouldn't the man want to come here and tell the jury his version of the story in the context of these cases?"

Again, as in the previous hearing, Fribley tried to assuage the judge without giving an inch. "Your honor, we're talking about a couple [of] things here, and one is a tactical matter, I would submit, and that's the issue of whether we will be calling company witnesses. We do not know what the plaintiffs' case will be yet, so we do not know what the company witnesses will be."

Also as before, Lord wasn't buying any of it. "In all due respect, I have read a good deal about this, and there can only be so many differences in these cases. If you don't know what their case will be, ask them; they'll tell you exactly what it is. And," he said pointedly, "you might do that before we make a final decision on whether or not these witnesses will attend."

Fribley then raised an ancillary issue. Larson and Ciresi had the previous week served formal notice that they wanted to depose the four present and former employees of the A. H. Robins Company whose presence at the trial was still in doubt—Allen Polon (who had replaced Ken Moore as project manager of the Dalkon Shield in late 1973 and "rode it right to the end," as Ciresi puts it), and Drs. Ellen J. Preston, Jack Freund and Fred Clark. They also indicated that they intended to ask for permission to depose E. Claiborne Robins, Sr., if it became more certain that he would not attend the trial.

"Your honor, we view these four depositions, which are all noticed for next week in Richmond, as being totally inconsistent with this court's plan for commencement of the trial on January 16," Fribley argued. "Plaintiffs indicated [on December 9] they were ready to go on the 3rd [of January]. . . . They indicated that again in the hearing on December 20th. There was no mention by the plaintiffs at either hearing of the need to take further discovery depositions of defense witnesses."

Lord, however, had quickly grasped the reason for the depositions. "Well," he told Fribley, "they probably wouldn't have to if they had those . . . doctors here. Couldn't we shortcut it that way? Just have the doctors here and let them depose them on the witness stand?" Larson nodded in agreement as Lord continued. "Otherwise, it sounds like you want to have your cake and eat it, too. They say, 'We want the witnesses; we'll be ready.' You say, 'You can't have the witnesses.' Now they say, 'We will depose them.' "

These people had been deposed before, Fribley countered, during the MDL proceedings. There was no further need to question them now.

Not good enough, Lord countered. "If they have been deposed

before, they should be able to read the transcript and repeat the answers, so you folks probably don't have to be there for the depositions—unless there's something new coming up that you anticipate," Lord said. "And if you anticipate new material, why shouldn't plaintiffs be able to discover into that area?"

"Your honor, I don't know what they intend to inquire into," said Fribley. "And perhaps there should be some delineation of that before we take it much further."

Larson was then asked why he wanted to take the depositions. He would prefer to have the witnesses live, he said, but Robins was saying that those witnesses might not attend even if ordered to by Judge Lord. If the only way he could get them was through deposition testimony, then that was what he felt he had to do. And he wanted the testimony recorded on videotape, Larson added. "We feel these witnesses are critical to be viewed and to be heard by the ladies and gentlemen of the jury that we'll have. And it is just back to the same old thing, your honor: They are not going to bring them live; they are going to try not to. And, at a minimum, we ought to have them by videotape deposition. . . ."

More discussion followed, including whether Dr. Clark and E. Claiborne Robins, Sr., could attend the trial in Minneapolis even if the judge ordered that they had to appear; their health, Lord was told, was poor and they might not be able to make the trip. Judge Lord ordered Alexander Slaughter, who was present at the hearing, to bring in the medical records of the two men so that they could be evaluated by a court-appointed physician. Slaughter reluctantly agreed to at least discuss the matter with his clients as far as E. Claiborne Robins, Sr., was concerned, but said he could not do so about Clark, who was not his client. However, he told Judge Lord, he would take up the matter with Clark's attorney, adding that "we will be back to the court on our position on these things."

Finally, to move things along, Lord said he would take the matter of the depositions under advisement. Four days later, on January 9, he issued an order approving the request and, to provide time for all concerned to be at the taking of those depositions, delayed the trial by another week. The new date was January 23.

In the end, this tactic proved to be a major error on the part of Robins and its attorneys. "They had brought in a ton of lawyers," Larson explained. "They had Faegre and Benson, they had Slaughter, they were about to bring in [Chuck] Socha from Denver, they had the Oppenheimer firm, Aetna had its own lawyers, and I can't remember how many there were, but I remember on one occasion I counted seventeen up-front lawyers representing various A. H. Robins interests, not counting those back in, say, the Faegre office. They were there because they were going to fight a war of attrition and they were going to espouse cooperation with Judge Lord and then do everything they could to drive everybody mad.

"But it was at this point that Lord saw exactly where they were going, when they refused to bring up any of their officers, their top people, for trial and in the same breath told Judge Lord that they don't think they're going to let those people be deposed. That was just like waving a red flag in front of any judge. Lord began to get deeper into it; he just wasn't going to have it. Their own conduct, to bog this thing down in interminable issues, led to him opening up discovery. Had they agreed to bring these people up to trial, we probably would have lost the opportunity to get any discovery."

Another matter taken up at the January 5 hearing was the issue of the "dirty questions." It was raised by plaintiff's attorney Kenneth Green and it involved the furnishing of his client's medical records to the Robins attorneys. "We have furnished all the medical records that we have," Green told Lord. "Some of them have not been available. We don't have the service number of her former husband. He was in the service around 1961, '62; they want that service number and I am assuming they want to get those records and that they want to take depositions of somebody. She has doctors. Her most recent doctors—"

Green was jumping around faster than Lord could keep pace. "Let's stick with one thing at a time," the judge suggested; he wanted to find out what the woman's former husband had to do with anything.

"Okay," Green said, and then picking up exactly where he had left off in midsentence, "are at Redwood Falls—"

"Well, wait a minute, you went ahead of me even then. How about—"

"Okay," Green jumped in. "The other records we're talking about are just as ancient—"

Lord was quickly becoming frustrated. "Excuse me," he told the attorney. "My turn?"

With that, Green was quieted and the judge asked why the records of the husband were being requested. "What could you defendants find out about the husband that would tell you about this lady's case? That ex-husband, was it?" he asked Green. "Correct," the attorney responded.

"Well," Fribley began, "clearly, your honor, exposure or treatment of the ex-husband for any kind of sexually transmissible disease during the time when he was living with his wife would be relevant to a source of potential infection."

Lord was annoyed. "Do you have a doctor who will testify that, if this guy gave her 'clap' in '58, that she would retain those germs in her body to have them rise up against her after she put the Dalkon Shield in?"

"I don't know the facts of this particular case," Fribley answered, "but I would certainly think that's a possibility."

"I'm not talking about possibilities," Lord said in measured tones. "I am talking about a doctor who will get on the witness stand and say to a reasonable medical certainty that the fact that she had gonorrhea in '58 was the inciting factor which caused her infection in '74, or whatever."

Fribley, however, would not give up. "I would think so," he said. "In particular cases, that testimony would be forthcoming."

"If you can bring me evidence that you have a doctor who will get on the witness stand and testify to that to a reasonable degree of medical certainty, I'd probably let you make the inquiry. But I want to hear the doctor myself; bring him in, subject him to examination and cross-examination. We can do that in a pretrial context at the time the thing comes up."

The argument went on for several minutes more, with Slaughter and Chuck Socha (pronounced so-ha), of the Denver, Colorado, firm of Tilley and Graves, both trying to add weight to Fribley's argument and Larson coming to Green's aid. (Socha, one of Robins's national lead trial counsel, had officially joined the consolidated defense team that day. According to Larson and Ciresi, he was to be the second half of Slaughter's "good guy, bad guy" routine before Judge Lord. In effect, his role, according to the plaintiffs' attorneys, was to bait the judge so that he would respond with some kind of impropriety that would establish a record of prejudice in the event Robins needed to appeal any orders or any eventual verdicts.)

Finally, Lord had enough of the debate. Prove absolutely that the testimony is relevant, he stated, and it will be allowed. Otherwise, "we're not going to do unnecessary discovery. And I . . . should think ten years would be enough to produce medical records; I don't know who would want to go back further than that for any useful purpose in deciding these cases. . . ."

On Thursday, January 12, the Dalkon Shield spotlight momentarily moved to St. Paul, where a federal jury in Judge Alsop's courtroom had just returned a $300,000 verdict against Robins in the case of *Mary Guenther* v. *A. H. Robins Company.* The verdict got a lot of play. The Minnesota score was now four to one against Robins. Robins apparently got the message; the next day, it settled twelve of the consolidated cases before Lord.

It was now ten days before the rescheduled trial was to begin. On the same day, Mike Ciresi filed a collateral estoppel motion prepared by the Robins, Zelle staff on the issue of negligence. That issue had now been decided beyond doubt, at least in Minnesota, he argued; there should no longer be a need to retry that issue.

In a way, it was fitting that Ciresi filed the motion that day, Friday the 13th, because had Lord, in his zeal to streamline the cases and move matters forward swiftly, decided then and there to grant collateral estoppel, it would have been the worst piece of luck Ciresi would ever have. The attorney, of course, was looking out for the best interests of his clients and Dalkon Shield victims in general. Indeed, a collateral estoppel motion in the Dalkon Shield litigation was and is long past due. Not having to retry the negligence question would greatly shorten the length of the many trials, thus limiting the money needed by plaintiffs in pressing their cases. Correct as that motion was (and still is), Ciresi had no way of knowing then that letting Judge Lord continue the negligence issue would end up being the single most important event in the history of Dalkon Shield litigation.

Fortunately for Ciresi, Lord has a thing about wanting to find out facts for himself, especially when he feels (as he now apparently did in this case) that one side preferred to keep those facts hidden. As the judge told Roger Brosnahan, an associate of Larson's and Ciresi's who argued the motion before him (or, more appropriately, who tried to) on January 25, the consolidated cases were too important to allow a hasty ruling on collateral estoppel. He would wait until the actual trial was under way before deciding on the motion.

The trial had been scheduled to begin on Monday, January 23. Larson and Ciresi, however, had gone to Richmond to depose the witnesses as per Lord's order. The depositions, however, were not going well at all and they could not complete them in time for the trial date. More accurately, perhaps, as they explained to the judge, they were being forced to overcome so many roadblocks that they were having difficulty even starting the depositions. Lord, therefore, granted another delay, to February 1. He also at this point began taking a more active hand in the depositions.

One major roadblock Larson and Ciresi were being forced to overcome was the endless series of objections being raised by counsel for Robins. It took over a half hour, for example, to get out from under a myriad of objections and elicit an answer from Dr. Jack Freund regarding who had the authority at Robins to issue product recalls. It took about the same time to get from E. Claiborne Robins, Sr., information regarding whether the company had ever discussed whether to issue a recall.

Especially where the elder Robins was concerned, this was an almost debilitating problem for plaintiffs' counsel because Judge Lord had ordered that his deposition testimony be given in hour-and-a-half spurts so as to not overtax the seventy-five-year-old board chairman's health. (Lord had based this decision on the testimony of Robins's physician and the concurrence of a court-appointed physician who reviewed Robins's medical records.) Effectively, then, the plaintiffs' attorneys could ask only a handful of questions per session. (MDL lead attorney Bradley Post, for one, remembers his experience deposing Robins, Sr. "His angina seems to act up every time you ask him a difficult question.")

Another major problem was memory; as in the past, the Robins witnesses just couldn't seem to remember anything of substance. In order to jar their memories, and particularly that of the elder Robins, Lord in a telephone conference call on the twenty-fourth ordered the company to turn over to Larson and Ciresi fourteen years' worth of minutes of its board of directors' meetings. Versions of those minutes—supposedly edited only to remove items that legally could be considered privileged—had been turned over years earlier to the multidistrict discovery under Judge Theis, but they showed no references to the board ever having discussed the Dalkon Shield. Considering all that happened regarding the Dalkon Shield—including the FDA request that the product be withdrawn, the mushrooming lawsuits against the company, etc.—this was absurd on its face (although, for some reason, no one had ever challenged this assertion before in the twelve years of Dalkon Shield litigation). Both Robins, Sr., and Robins, Jr., had testified under oath that they could not recall when such discussions took place or what was discussed. Lord felt that the time had come for the unexpurgated minutes to see the light of day.

Defense attorneys, after much wrangling over questions of privilege, agreed to turn over the minutes to Judge Lord the next day in Minneapolis, for him to review what was privileged and what was not. In that same telephone call, Lord warned Robins's counsel about the endless objections. He repeated that warning in court on January 25. "[I]f there are obstructionist tactics used—delay, quibbling, interruptions to 'educate' the witness and so forth—I will impose sanctions," he told Alexander Slaughter.

As for E. Claiborne Robins, Sr., if he won't be allowed to answer questions in Richmond, Lord told Slaughter (who had flown to the Twin Cities with the minute books), the chairman will be made to answer them in Minneapolis. "[I]t's up to the lawyers," he explained, "because I know that in the hands of a skillful cross-examiner, that man will give answers. Any person will, when they are under oath. So, if he is allowed to talk, the deposition will be completed in plenty of time. If he is not allowed to talk, then the lawyers will have to explain to him why he is required to come to Minnesota. So let's not get into that any more. I have given all the warnings I need to give.

"Did you want to say something, Mr. Slaughter?" Lord asked.

"No," the Robins attorney began, but he did have something to say and he decided to go ahead. ". . . I just wanted to make our record clear that we still do not concede the court's authority to make these people come to Minnesota, any of them. . . . I thought Mr. Robins, Sr., since [his doctor], as I understand it, said that he shouldn't come up here, that that may be moot. I assume the issue will come back up in respect to other of the persons who are named in—"

Lord was becoming increasingly impatient. "I don't want to articulate it over and over because sooner or later you say something that they say is prejudicial or will hurt somebody's feelings—but if the lawyers will allow him to have his deposition taken, he will probably not have to come. If the deposition is so delayed and so obfuscated, he may be required to come, and we'll have to get a special coach for him. I've had people come up, people who were supposed to be sick or worse sick, get on a train, hire a special train, a car on the train, and have a doctor, they have a nurse, they come, they can stay [at the hotel] right across the street, and if they couldn't leave the room then we can take the jury over there, all twenty-six of the jurors. We can do a lot of wonderful things if we work together. So let's leave that right where it is for now."

The debate continued nonetheless. Eventually, therefore, Lord made another suggestion. "If you are unable to proceed down there, what about having the judge go down and preside over the depositions?" he asked.

"I will consider that," said Slaughter. The Robins attorney, however, suggested that Lord let another day go by first, to see whether the depositions were moving along.

"Unless you almost finish the depositions today," said Lord, "it would probably save me time to jump on an airplane—even if I had to pay my own way down there; and I'm not soliciting funds from you guys"—Lord smiled and the attorneys laughed—"to go down there and preside over the depositions and have a nice, clean-cut presentation of it, get rid of all the 'straw' and just have plain 'wheat,' and we can go home again. . . . I will just get on an airplane tonight and hitchhike around. I've done that before."

He made no decision to fly to Richmond at that time, however. The decision came later in the day, after yet another conference call from the deposition site complaining about the endless stream of objections, the obfuscatory answers, and the delaying tactics.

"I was sitting upstairs in the legal offices, Dale was in the auditorium, and we were on a conference call with Lord, and he said maybe he'd come down there and give us a hand, what did we think?" Ciresi recalls the conversation. "I just wished that Dale would have been there because we would have just looked at each other and just sort of smiled. And we both gave the same answer. 'Well, your honor, I believe that'll be very helpful.' I remember we then went back to the depositions"—Ciresi laughs at the memory—"and there was a perceptible difference even that day. I was deposing [Dr. Fred] Clark and his attorney Robert Houghton's eyes got like a saucer when he heard that a federal judge was coming down here and was going to be sitting on a deposition."

As Lord and two law clerks flew to Richmond that night, the judge reflected on what he had learned from his review of the minute books brought to court that day by Alexander Slaughter.

"I [had earlier] read the deposition of young Mr. Robins . . . ," Lord would explain sometime later. "In that deposition, it appeared to me to my satisfaction that [he] had no knowledge whatsoever about the propensities of the Dalkon Shield to cause harm. He denied . . . knowledge of any litigation. He said these were matters which he delegated and many times repeated that his management style was such so to have made it appropriate to leave all this stuff at the lower echelons. He kept talking about his medical people. And one would think in a reading of that deposition . . . that the whole Dalkon Shield [problem] . . . escaped his notice. . . .

"[Then] I looked at the minutes of a meeting of the Board of Directors and, without saying what's in there, or any specific issues, the minutes . . . had page after page after page of detailed reports by Mr. Robins Jr., the president of the company, on the affairs of the company. . . . I concluded that . . . if he knew so much about all these affairs of the company that he could recite about acquisitions and sales and market ratios and profits and all these things—and new products, he reported in detail about new products—if he knew all those things, then a jury would be entitled to know whether or not he also knew that much about [the Dalkon Shield]."

For that reason, Lord decided to provide the plaintiffs with newly edited versions of the board of directors' minutes, the judge explained.

There was more, however, that he had found. "[Alex Slaughter had] furnished a section of the Board of Directors meeting which refers to the Dalkon Shield but excised any reference to a report [on the status of litigation] by Mr. [Roger] Tuttle[, Robins's in-house lead counsel through 1975]. Now, the context in which that went into the Board of Directors meeting led me to believe that the Board of Directors was familiar with what Mr. Tuttle was doing."

Lord had then asked to see the Tuttle reports. He knew that both Robins, Sr., and Robins, Jr., had essentially denied ever receiving detailed knowledge of Dalkon Shield litigation. Yet, when he saw "that here were periodic reports to those very individuals from a lawyer setting out the names of the cases and the claims made, it had been my thought that that was not privileged [either]. . . . I [knew] of nowhere else you could get that kind of impeaching material."

The judge knew how valuable that information could be to the plaintiffs. The past testimony of the two top officers of the A. H. Robins Company could be impeached. It could be shown that they did have detailed knowledge of matters they consistently denied knowing about. And that meant that it could be shown that the Dalkon Shield cover-up might be traceable all the way to the very top of the A. H. Robins Company, all the way to the chairman of the board and the president—all the way to E. Claiborne Robins, Sr., and E. Claiborne Robins, Jr.

He was determined that the jury, when it was empaneled, would have a fair chance to get at the truth.

8

THE JUDGE TAKES COMMAND

For a judge—even one not as busy or as hassled as the chief judge in charge of all the federal courts in his district—to sit in on the taking of a deposition is unusual. For him to leave his jurisdiction and fly to another state to do so is almost unheard of. And yet, on the evening of January 25, Chief Judge Miles W. Lord was doing just that because something was seriously wrong and only his presence had any chance of correcting it.

For Lord it was a nuisance. However, based on everything he had heard regarding the depositions then going on involving E. Claiborne Robins, Sr., and Dr. Fred Clark, the onetime medical director and then research and development chief of the A. H. Robins Company, the testimony being given and the objections being made had turned the process into a circus of evasion and delay. Only he, as the judge sitting on the case, had the power to close down that circus and put the depositions back on track.

That Lord's presence was needed in Richmond if the plaintiffs' cases were going to move forward there seems little doubt. To fully appreciate the circumstances that caused him to fly to the scene, it is necessary to examine the goings-on "up close and personal," as it were.

Robins had made available a boardroom for use during the depositions of E. Claiborne Robins, Sr., and Dr. Fred Clark. The front half of the two-tone-brown rectangular room was given over to the people directly involved: the witness being deposed sat at a table close to the far wall directly in front of a tan-and-brown leaf-patterned set of drapes that covered, of all things, a one-way mirror; to the witness's right at the table was his attorney. A second table was catacorner to the left and was reserved for plaintiffs' counsel. In the space created by the catacornering sat the court reporter. Catacorner on the right side of the witness table was a third table, reserved for other counsel who chose to sit in, as for example an attorney for Robins or for Aetna. Each of the tables were covered with a long blue tablecloth that reached to the floor. In front of the witness was set down a thick black loose-leaf volume containing the various plaintiffs' exhibits upon which many of the questions would be based. The volume was tabbed to separate each exhibit and to make locating any particular one easier.

The other half of the room was given over to the two camera crews (Robins had insisted on duplicating the videotaping of the depositions) and any observers who chose to be present. In the cases of both Robins and Clark, one of those observers was the witness's personal physician who was empowered by Judge Lord to ask for a recess at any time he felt his patient's stamina was wearing too thin.

The room was cramped and, with the hot lights of the television cameras, it was hot, too. Still, Ciresi found that there were some things to laugh about in spite of the conditions.

"Our 'taping crew,' for example, was one guy with a little camera. That was a cute thing," he laughs heartily at the memory. "Here's this one guy in the middle with his little camera, and they had these two great big cameras, one on either side, with a chair, you know, the whole nine yards. It looked so funny we had a picture taken of it."

Not so funny was the suspicion shared by both Larson and Ciresi that Robins was surreptitiously monitoring the depositions electronically. Although this made little sense—videotapes of each session were instantly available and there were daily transcripts of the proceedings—the two could not shake off the feeling that it was being done.

Ciresi points to one incident during the early days of the depositions. The Robins videotape crew at the time had a van on the outside of the building where the testimony was being taken. The van served as a mobile control booth. Larson and Ciresi were convinced, however, that it was also being used to monitor the depositions. At one point, therefore, Ciresi left the deposition site, went outside to the van, and began banging on the locked door, demanding entrance. He was told that only the taping crew was present and that no one could be admitted. Still he demanded to be let in. When the door was finally opened, he did indeed find others there. By the time of the Robins and Clark depositions, the control room had been moved indoors.

A similar incident involved Judge Lord himself. "During a recess in the E. C. Robins deposition," Ciresi recalls, "Lord was walking through the hallway, past the control room, and he heard Dale and me talking over a loudspeaker of some kind, so he went in there and found that the mike was still on. He blew his stack." (Lord remembers it a bit differently, apparently; he has reportedly said that he overheard the two attorneys *whispering* over the loudspeaker.)

As a result of such incidents and their own suspicions, Larson and Ciresi made it a practice to discuss important matters only in their hotel rooms. Perhaps they were "being paranoid," but they felt that there was good cause.

The deposition of the frail-looking Robins was always the first to be taken each day, out of concern for the board chairman's health. On the left lapel of his gray-checked suit jacket was clipped a small microphone. Beside him to the right was Charles E. Osthimer III, the young A. H. Robins attorney who had recently lost the Hahn case. On the table before Robins was the plaintiffs' exhibit book to which he would frequently be asked to refer.

Dale Larson handled the questioning of the elder Robins. He spoke in a slow, methodical manner, often drawing out his words for emphasis. Frequently during his examination of Robins, he would look to the front of the room at the camera crews to be certain not to miss the cue that the videotape was running out and a brief recess was required to put in a fresh cassette.

After one such recess on the morning of January 25, Larson, wearing a snappy three-piece gray suit, continued the line of testimony he had started before the last tape had run out. "Mr. Robins," he began, "as I understand your testimony, there has never been a time period from 1970 right up to the present when the

A. H. Robins Company hasn't had ample resources, financially, to recall the Dalkon Shield from consumers by advertising or other means if it chose to do so, is that correct?"

"Object to form," the bearded, heavyset Osthimer interjected. With no judge present to rule, the objection was meant for resolution at a later date, when the question and the answer would be excised if the objection was sustained. Robins understood this by now and so, despite the objection, he answered:

"Well, we have had adequate resources to do anything reasonable, but we have never had advice of the best qualified people that such a step was necessary." He spoke in the quiet, calm, and lightly accented tones of the Southern aristocrat he had become.

"I move to strike the latter portion as unresponsive," Larson said for the benefit of the absent judge. Then, looking down at his legal pad a little to the right on the table in front of him, he continued. "It is also true that you and Mr. Robins Jr. have at all times during that same time frame had adequate personal resources to recall the Dalkon Shield from women consumers by advertising and other mass media means if you chose to do so, correct?"

"Object to the form of the question," Osthimer said.

"I don't know the answer to that question," Robins answered.

"You just don't know whether you had adequate resources?" Larson asked.

"No, I don't," Robins said, shaking his head a bit to and fro. "I haven't any idea what kind of resources you are talking about."

Larson gave an audible sigh, something he did frequently during the deposition when he became frustrated by Robins's "I can't recall, I don't know what you mean" answers. Sometimes the sigh was genuine, resulting both from his frustration and exhaustion. At other times, however, it was meant to impress upon the future jurors how unresponsive Robins was being from the plaintiffs' attorney's point of view. "All right," he said, "you don't know what kind of resources would be required to advertise and/or announce through a media campaign the intensive recall of the Dalkon Shield from consumers, is that correct?"

"I would have no idea what would be involved." As Robins spoke, his hands were cupped before him on the table.

"And you don't recall ever considering the amounts that might be involved in such an effort, is that correct?"

"Object to the form of the question," Osthimer said yet again.

Robins began to answer, but Larson stopped him. Turning a bit to face Osthimer and moving slightly forward in his chair, the plaintiffs' attorney said in a decidedly harsher voice than he used for his questioning, "We are going to stop right now if you start objecting, counsel. I told you that at the outset; now . . . , I suggest that you call Mr. Slaughter before we get on the phone and talk to Judge Lord, because I'll tell you right now, based on the conversations he stated on the record, he is ready to sanction counsel and sanction this party [Mr. Robins], and I suggest before you get on the phone [with the judge] that you check with Mr. Slaughter, if you haven't checked with him specifically. Judge Lord has ordered clearly, unequivocally, that you are not to enter those types of objections on this record and he has done so twice, two days in a row."

"Well, that is not my understanding," Osthimer countered.

"Well," said Larson, sighing once again, "we're going to stop and we're going to call him." Then, turning to the witness, he said, "I'm sorry, Mr. Robins, but your counsel is violating a direct court order here and I have no, no alternative but to get the judge on the phone. And I know what his attitude is going to be about it, counsel."

Larson indeed did know what Lord's attitude would be: anger that his orders were being disregarded. Once again, the judge ordered that the objections be limited to matters of privilege only; he also once again allowed Larson to probe into Robins's financial status. That is what Larson did as the deposition resumed.

"As we sit here today, Mr. Robins, what is your net worth?"

"I don't know," Robins replied. "I really don't know. . . ."

"What is your best estimate?" Larson then asked.

"Well," Robins paused to frame his response carefully, "this can vary from day to day . . . because of the amount of stock that I own in Robins. . . . For example, a month ago it might have been as much as $18 million more than it is today. . . . [W]e're talking about paper, which . . . moves up and down, and what it is today might be considerably less tomorrow. So it is very impossible to, since that is the major part of my net worth . . .—"

Larson ended the rambling Robins monologue in midsentence by asking his question another way. "And in terms of an estimate again, as we sit here today, what would you estimate that net worth to be, and give a range if that is more comfortable for you?"

"I would say seventy to seventy-five million dollars, somewhere in that range. . . ."

"Now, Mr. Robins," Larson asked, "you are aware that women in Minnesota were sold and inserted with your Dalkon Shield device, is that correct?"

"I am not aware of it except that I assumed that some were inserted in Minnesota."

"Okay," Larson sighed. "And you, well, you knew they were being sold in Minnesota, did you not?"

"Well, I couldn't tell you whether there were any sold in Minnesota, or not, but I assume there were," Robins said.

"All right. If there were, those devices all had this multifilament [Larson pronounced the word mul-tie-filament] tailstring on them, correct?"

"I'm not qualified as a physician or as a scientist enough to discuss anything connected with such a matter," Robins came back. "I don't know. . . ."

"So nobody has ever told you that the tailstring on the Dalkon Shield that your company sold was a multifilament tailstring, is that correct?"

"I don't recall it being discussed."

"And nobody has ever told you that that tailstring . . . had from two to four hundred filaments inside a plastic sheath, is that correct?"

"I would know nothing about that."

"And nobody in your company ever told you that the tailstring that your company sold on the Dalkon Shield was open at either end, is that correct?"

"I would know nothing about that. . . . It would not be up to a layman like me to know that," said the man who is considered a medical marketing genius and who, a half century earlier, had searched through the medical literature looking for the drug product which physicians needed and which could be marketed directly to them, to build an empire.

"But my question again, Mr. Robins, is nobody told you these things, is that correct?"

"I don't recall it."

"And that would be true right up to today, is that correct?"

"That's correct."

Larson soon left that line of questioning and went on to other points regarding the tailstring. At one point, he asked Robins: "You were aware during that period, 1972 right through 1975, were you not Mr. Robins, that your company was looking for a non-wicking tailstring to replace the tailstring being sold on the Dalkon Shield . . . ?"

"I don't recall this at all . . . ," Robins answered. "I have no knowledge, as far as I know, that—" Robins paused very briefly and then rephrased his response, "I don't recall such knowledge. . . ."

"Mr. Robins"—Larson again changed course—"let me turn you to . . . exhibit 599, which is dated . . . November 9, [1972,] another memo by Mr. [Ken] Moore, the project manager [for the Dalkon Shield]. Would you review that, please?"

Helped by attorney Osthimer, Robins soon found the appropriate document in the binder before him and began to read it. It was Ken Moore's very lengthy summary of the interdepartmental meeting on the Dalkon Shield problems at which time he had discussed the possibility of replacing the tailstring with the Teflon string manufactured by Gore-Tex. After a minute or two of reading, Robins said, in a muffled, offhand way, "I'm sorry to take so long, but these are such long memos." He adjusted his black reading glasses and continued studying the document.

Finally, after Robins put down the book and removed his glasses, Larson asked, "Mr. Robins, is it your testimony that you have never previously seen or reviewed [that document]?"

"I don't recall it," said Robins looking up at the attorney.

"So you might have, but you can't tell us as you sit here today, is that right?"

"I don't think I have seen it. I would think I would recall it."

Again, Larson sighed audibly. He was getting nowhere and he was frustrated. "I just want to know for sure on this record for the ladies and gentlemen of the jury whether you mean to say you definitely haven't or you just don't know for sure?" Just as there was no judge, there was no jury, although a jury would eventually view the deposition.

"Well," Robins said, "I say I don't recall it, so I can't say whether

I have or haven't, but I . . . think it's very likely that I have not seen it."

A short while later, Larson was questioning Robins about his company's relationship with Aetna. "I was reading from the interim defense agreement that Robins had entered into and signed with Aetna," Larson recalls. "It was evident from the inferences arising from that document [and the specific language used] that Aetna had knowledge of the Dalkon Shield's problems and the company's method of response to it because sometime in 1977 they had negotiated away Aetna's ability to deny coverage based upon fraudulent promotion and concealment, etc."

"Are you aware," he asked, the interim defense agreement in his hand, "that the A. H. Robins Company and . . . Aetna entered into agreements concerning how [Dalkon Shield] claims would be handled?"

"I'm not aware of the details, no," Robins answered, in the same calm, even-toned voice he had used throughout the question-and-answer session. "Our legal department would know that."

"Are you aware Mr. Robins that at least by 1977 according to this particular agreement, Aetna"—Larson paused briefly to clear his throat—"waived certain apparent defenses that it had to deny coverage, based upon apparent evidence that it had of injuries being 'expected' or 'intended.' Ah, are you aware of that at all?"

"I'm not sure I understand the question."

"Are you aware that the Aetna insurance company had certain defenses, ah, pertaining to injuries resulting from the Dalkon Shield that might be 'expected' or 'intended' by the A. H. Robins Company?"

"I still don't understand the question. I'm sorry; I must be dense."

"I'll try again, Mr. Robins."

"Would you re-word it, perhaps in another way, a clearer fashion?"

"Are you aware that there were limitations in your insurance policy for injuries that were 'expected' or 'intended' by the A. H. Robins Company?"

"I'm not sure that there were any things intended or expected, if that—is that the word, intended or expected?"

"Yes."

"I don't, I don't think any such, I'm not aware of any such thing existing. . . ."

"Alright, Mr. Robins, so ah, you're not aware that the Aetna insurance company"—Larson cleared his throat again—"advised A. H. Robins at any time that it had no coverage for Dalkon Shield claims because the injuries resulting from the Shield were both 'expected' and 'intended' by the company, is that correct?"

"I don't think that's a correct statement. I don't think they made any such statement. Uh, I was, I'm, the only thing I'm aware of is that we had no insurance coverage, I believe, after 1978, was the date."

Throughout the session, Robins had continued to speak in his calm, even, quiet tones. Only once did he show any emotion—and when he did the emotions were defiance, anger, and resentment that the good name of his company was being besmirched.

Larson sighed audibly yet again; the exhaustion was beginning to show and his patience was wearing thin because of it. Quoting again from the agreement, he asked: "Are you aware that the Aetna insurance company claimed that it did not have any coverage for Dalkon Shield claims because of A. H. Robins's 'failure to disclose important and relevant information,' as well as 'supplying false and misleading information' concerning—"

"Now wait a minute—"

"—Dalkon Shield—"

"Now wait a minute, wait a minute—" Robins's voice rose higher.

"—cases?"

"You're implying something that isn't so," the elder Robins said with obvious annoyance in his voice. His face tensed up and his whole body became animated. There was no longer any sign of the frail man who had been testifying. This was the man who had built a billion-dollar company from nothing.

"I'd just like to say right at this point, I will stake the reputation of our company, for integrity, with any company in the United States, and if you would ask any ten thousand people, or thousand people who are knowledgeable in this city . . . , I'll be perfectly willing . . . to rely on their answer. It would be favorable." This last word was uttered emphatically, as if every syllable were a shell being cannonaded. "We are known as a company who not only, uh, does the right thing"—pause—"but we're known as a company who are compassionate and are more concerned with getting good products than we are concerned with profits. I'd stake that reputation against any company in the United States. And, uh, all you would have to do if you'd really wanted to would be to go out on the streets and ask the question of people who, uh, had some knowledge of the company, what the reputation of the company was. Now that question that you just asked me—excuse this long answer—implies that we do not have integrity."

With that Robins sat straight back in his chair, hands on the arm rests, his lips pursed tightly, looking firmly and challengingly at Larson and visibly angry.

In Dr. Clark's case, it was not how little the witness said in answering the questions put to him, but how much he said while saying so little. Dr. Clark had raised this to something approaching an art form. Typical was an exchange that day between Mike Ciresi and Dr. Clark.

The scene was very much like what it had been earlier in the day during the deposition of E. C. Robins, Sr. Dr. Clark, a distinguished-looking man with dark gray hair and wire-rimmed aviator glasses, was seated in the chair Robins had occupied, the lapel mike now clipped to his suit jacket. On the table before him was the plaintiffs' exhibit book. His attorney, James E. Farnham, was seated to his right; Ciresi was sitting at the catercorner table to his left. Between the two tables sat the court reporter. Opposite Ciresi at the table Judge Lord eventually would occupy sat Robert Houghton, who was representing the A. H. Robins Company at the session.

The questioning at this point related to the former Robins research chief's June 8, 1970, meeting with the coinventor of the Dalkon Shield, Dr. Hugh Davis, and his subsequent June 9 memorandum in which he reported, among other things, that Dr. Davis's published pregnancy rate of 1.1 percent for the Dalkon Shield was no longer valid and that the study itself was no longer valid because changes had by then been made in the IUD's composition. In the past, both Dr. Davis and Dr. Clark had argued that the memorandum was faulty in a number of respects; that the memorandum was not based on notes Dr. Clark had taken during the course of the meeting; that they had no recollection of where the information regarding the higher pregnancy rate had come from; and that they had very little recollection of what was discussed at the meeting.

"Did Dr. Davis provide you with information concerning his experience with the Dalkon Shield?" Ciresi asked, sitting sideways from the table and leaning comfortably back in his chair, a note pad on his raised lap.

"He discussed various experiences of his with the Dalkon Shield, yes," Dr. Clark responded a few seconds later, after gathering his thoughts.

"And as he discussed that information, you were taking notes, correct?" Ciresi followed up.

"Not entirely correct," Dr. Clark explained in a slow, apparently thoughtful manner. At times, as he spoke, the physician would move his hands across the table directly in front of him, as if cleaning off invisible crumbs or smoothing out the wrinkles in the blue tablecloth. "During the process of the two, two-and-a-half-hour meeting I had with him, I jotted down one word here and one word there. If that constitutes your definition of taking notes, then maybe yes, but it would not be quite mine." The witness shook his head slightly to and fro. "So the answer to . . . your question is no, in the way I interpret your words."

"Fine, doctor," the plaintiffs' attorney said. Once again, he thought, he would have to play it Dr. Clark's way, breaking his question down into its component parts and arriving at the desired answer one step at a time. "During the . . . meeting that you had with Dr. Davis, you were discussing the Dalkon Shield, correct?"

"Correct."

"And during the course of that discussion on an intermittent basis you would take down information on to your notes?"

"Well," Dr. Clark paused yet again to think through his answer, "as I said before, I would write a note, a word, down here and there, as is my custom when I am sitting in meetings. I'm a doodler and I doodle."

"So you were doodling and writing a word down here and there—"

"I'm not going—"

"—during the course of your meeting with Dr. Davis?"

"I am neither going to quibble with you nor elaborate on what I have already tried to respond to."

"Well, doctor . . . , what *were* you doing at that time . . . ? [Y]ou have mentioned that you are a doodler and you would take a word down here and there."

"Yes."

"My only question to you, is that what you were doing during your meeting with Dr. Davis?"

At that point, Robert Houghton interrupted. "I would object to counsel's statement since it is improper as to form," the lanky and balding blond Robins attorney said. "It is argumentative and it also mischaracterizes the testimony of Dr. Clark."

"We'll let Judge Lord decide that, counsel," Ciresi countered, turning back to the table and moving forward as he spoke, "and we can at any time break this deposition and call Judge Lord directly as he ordered us to do if we are having problems getting responses or any problems at all with the questions, or whatever. So I am prepared to go out and call Judge Lord if you think that I am harassing Dr. Clark, or I am being argumentative. I simply asked him a question with respect to what he was doing during the meeting. . . ."

"And I believe that question has been answered," Houghton replied.

"Twice," Dr. Clark interjected, nodding his head for further emphasis.

With that, Ciresi turned back to the witness. "Doctor, during the course of this conversation with Dr. Davis, were you doodling?"

"I do not recall," Dr. Clark responded after a brief pause. "I am a doodler and my habit pattern in sitting at meetings is usually to do what I call doodle. I am not even sure I could describe to you what I mean by 'doodle.' I make lines, I draw pictures, I scratch a word 'yes.' I scratch through that. I use that as a, a what?"—Dr. Clark groped for the right words—"a way to, to use nervous energy. That is 'doodle' in my words, and I do not remember precisely what I doodle, but I would almost bet that I did doodle during that conversation because I did write, did have a piece of paper and had written an occasional word on it which I then used later on my trip [back] to Richmond, and wrote out in longhand the words that eventually became typed and is the document that you have in front of you now [the June 9 memorandum]. . . . Beyond that, I have no recollection."

"Did you take down information during the course of that meeting that Dr. Davis was orally giving to you concerning the Dalkon Shield?"

"As opposed to taking down other information that somebody else might have said?" Dr. Clark was fencing with Ciresi. "No, I, all I can do is use my own common sense and recollection to the best of my ability, and the words that I jotted down would have been from Dr. Davis, they wouldn't have been from anybody else. That was the meeting I was in."

"I think that was my question, doctor," Ciresi interjected.

"Well," Dr. Clark said smugly, "I thought the answer was so self-evident, I didn't even have to answer it."

Ciresi smiled. Leaning back again in his chair, he continued. "And did you take down that information which you considered to be information you wanted to include in any memorandum that you would prepare for the A. H. Robins personnel regarding the possible acquisition of the Dalkon Shield?"

"Would you repeat all the words in that question again?"

"Sure. Would you read the question back, please, Mr. Reporter?"

Dr. Clark leaned a bit sideways to the left as court reporter John Brennan read back the question.

"In the way you word your question, no," the doctor responded as Brennan concluded.

Once again, Ciresi had to try to break down his question into smaller parts. "Did you take down information concerning the Dalkon Shield for the purposes of writing a memorandum or having a memorandum prepared concerning the possible acquisition of the Dalkon Corporation?"

"In the way you word your question, no." Dr. Clark was not giving an inch.

"Did you take down information concerning the Dalkon Shield?" the plaintiffs' attorney tried again.

"Yes."

"Did you take down pregnancy rates?"

"I do not recall."

"Did you take down insertion numbers?"

"I do not recall."

"Did you take down experiences that Dr. Davis had with respect to adverse effects with the Dalkon Shield?"

"I do not recall."

And so it went. Neither Robins nor Clark could recall essential details. Clark in particular and even Robins at times were argumentative and unresponsive. However, as the two attorneys explain it, there was more to it than that.

"There were so many sideshows going on," Ciresi says of the scene in Richmond. "They'd have to break every twenty minutes with Robins, Sr., on the hour with Clark. They'd go off with Robins, Sr., and check his blood pressure, and Clark had a doctor there and he would check him out. Clark's wife was there—you know, sitting like Maureen Dean—and she'd sit in the back. She looked like if she had a shotgun I'd be dead right now.

"And they'd keep bringing in different attorneys, you know. So we'd have Robins on the stand in the morning, and then in the afternoon we'd ask Clark, 'Well, Dr. Clark, when did you first advise Mr. Robins of blah, blah, blah?' and he'd say, 'Oh, I never advised him of that,' and I'd say, 'Would it surprise you to know, Dr. Clark, that Mr. Robins sat in that same chair no more than an hour and a half ago and testified under oath that you did tell him that?' and he'd say, 'Well, Mr. Ciresi,' and these lawyers didn't know what was going on because they weren't keeping track of what went on before."

One early example, of this, Ciresi recalls, involved the question of whether Dr. Clark had been notified about the request that he be deposed. "Socha said on the record, 'You have to talk to [Robins attorney Frank] Tatum, he's responsible for that, he's been in contact with Clark'; then Tatum said on the record that 'Socha was responsible, you have to talk to him.' So I said to Socha, 'Would it surprise you, Mr. Socha, that Mr. Tatum said, etc.,' and finally he said, 'I'm not going to be cross-examined by you.' "

As time wore on, both Ciresi and Larson knew they could not continue taking the depositions of either man without some form of help from Judge Lord. "Their intrusions in the examinations plus that example of them jerking us around was what led Lord to say that this is enough; we're going to proceed with my agenda," Larson explains.

Thus it was that Judge Miles W. Lord of the District of Minnesota found himself in Richmond, Virginia, at 11:20 A.M. on January 26, the day after the deposition testimony already cited here had been given, opening the next session in the continuing deposition of E. Claiborne Robins, Sr.

Lord was seated at the long blue-cloth-covered table catercorner to the right of the witness table, a long thin microphone pointing toward him. Instead of his judicial robes, he was dressed in a two-piece gray suit, with a gray striped tie and white shirt. His jacket was open and the thumb of his right hand was hooked to the inside of his belt. His chair was perched upon its two back legs and the judge's head and shoulders rested against the brown wall behind him.

Even though he was a federal judge, Lord did not have the authority to sit on a case in Richmond unless specifically assigned there, or unless the parties to the action consented to his doing so. On the 25th, it had seemed as though both parties wanted the judge to come to Richmond. He had already come to the conclusion that every move he made in the case had to be on the record, and any agreements reached with the Robins counsel had to be there, too, in their own words. Otherwise, they could argue later that the judge misunderstood what they had said. He decided, therefore, to get Robins's lead counsel, Alexander Slaughter, on record as approving his being there.

Judge Lord turned his head sharply to the right, looking past the three still-dormant television cameras to the seats at the other end of the boardroom. "Before we start with the tape and the TV now, Alex Slaughter, I haven't been assigned here by any intercircuit assignment," the judge began as court reporter John Brennan recorded his words. "In my attempt to help you by presiding in this deposition, I would ordinarily have required that Mr. Robins, in these particular circumstances, come to Minneapolis, and I asked at the hearing [yesterday] whether anybody had any objection or thoughts they wanted to express about my presence or about coming out here. Do you have any observations you want to make on that?"

Slaughter rose and came forward as Lord spoke. "I had assumed I would like to look at it just to make sure that it is technically appropriate. . . . [P]robably, in one of your own cases, you have the authority to move where you like[, but] I would like to have somebody look at that just to make sure that we are technically accurate."

"Well, if I didn't have that authority, would you want me to leave?" Lord asked.

"Not at this time," responded Slaughter. "I would like to reserve that."

That was exactly what the judge had been afraid would happen; he was right in getting it all on the record now. "No," Lord said calmly, moving all four legs of his chair back onto the floor and leaning forward now, "I don't want to reserve it, I want to know now before I utter the first word and make the first ruling."

The always confident Slaughter apparently was not quite certain what to say next. "May I consult for one minute with Mr. Forrest [Robins's vice-president and general counsel, who was also present at the preliminaries]?"

A moment later, Slaughter turned back to Lord and said, "No, we have no objection to you supervising Mr. Robins's deposition."

The judge nodded his head. He was pleased. "And I would take it that that would mean that I would have the same power here as though we were taking the depositions in Minnesota?"

"Yes," said Slaughter.

"Very well," Lord said.

After another moment or two, the cameras were turned on and focused directly on the judge. For the videotaped record, he stated, "I am Judge Lord from Minnesota, here with the consent of both parties who agree that for the purpose of this deposition, I should preside with the same powers as though the deposition were taken in Minnesota." Looking at Dale Larson, the judge added, with a bit of a smile, "Now, let us proceed." He pushed his chair back up on its back legs and the deposition of E. Claiborne Robins, Sr., was again under way.

At one point during the session, Larson referred Robins to a 1973 document regarding the wicking of the tailstring and asked him if he had seen it. "I don't recall receiving this document," Robins said.

"In 1973, were you ever advised that physicians were reporting that the string was acting as a wick along which pathogenic organisms would travel from the vagina into the uterine cavity?" As was his custom during these depositions, Larson asked his questions in a slow, deliberate manner, drawing out many of the words for emphasis.

Osthimer objected to the question. "Overruled," Lord said matter-of-factly almost as the objection was out of Osthimer's mouth.

"I think we have had a number of questions along this line," Robins said, adding his objection to that of his attorney.

"Answer this one, sir," the judge said calmly but firmly.

"Well," Robins said, turning to his left now to look at Larson, "as I stated earlier, this is a theory, wicking is a theory, and to my knowledge has never been a proven fact in humans."

Larson sighed another time. Robins, he thought, was still playing the game of answering questions no one asked while not answering the questions he was asked. "Could you read [the question] back please?" Larson instructed the court reporter. Judge Lord, however, cut Brennan off. Turning to Robins, Lord said, "I direct you to make a more responsive answer, sir. We can't wait all day."

"Well," Robins began, as if to argue the point. Lord wouldn't allow it, however.

"He asked you if you had ever been informed that wicking was alleged to be a problem," Lord said in a firm voice.

"I have never heard that it was a problem," Robins answered. "I have heard that it has been postulated that wicking could occur."

Good enough, the judge thought. To Larson, he said, "All right."

"Is it fair to say, Mr. Robins, that you knew that in 1973?" the attorney asked.

"I don't recall whether I knew that in '73 or not. I doubt it."

"Did you know it during the period that you were selling the Dalkon Shield?"

"I don't know—"

Osthimer cut in. "Object to the form of the question," he said.

Judge Lord found that hard to believe. "How could you object to the form of the question on a straight question like that?" he asked incredulously.

"It was argumentative, your honor," the lawyer explained.

Shaking his head almost sadly, the judge said, "Overruled."

". . . Were you advised in 1973 that there were serious causes of pelvic inflammatory disease being reported in Dalkon Shield wearers?" Larson asked.

After more objections, Robins was instructed to answer the question. "No, I was not."

"Were you aware in 1973 that there was a hazard of infection to women who became pregnant with the device in [place]?"

"I am not aware that there was a hazard . . . ," said the chairman.

"[Is it] your testimony before the ladies and gentlemen of the jury that you have never reviewed documents of the A. H. Robins Company which report that bacteria can enter the tailstring?"

"Objection to the form of the question; assumes facts not in evidence," Osthimer interrupted.

"Overruled," Lord said. He wanted to put an end to this, however, so he added, "You may have a standing objection along that line. You won't have to make it anymore."

"I don't recall . . . ," Robins answered.

Larson then asked Robins to review product literature for the Dalkon Shield. "Mr. Robins," the attorney then asked, "was the literature that you were giving both physicians and users describing and representing the device as, quote, medically safe, unquote?"

"Isn't this what we just had?" Robins countered.

"I'm referring to specific terms, Mr. Robins," Larson said with his seemingly ever-present sigh.

"I'm not sure I understand what you mean by specific terms," Robins came back.

"I'm referring to representations to physicians and users that the device was, quote, medically safe, unquote."

At this point, Osthimer objected and Lord overruled the objection. The judge, however, had become suspicious of the answers Robins was giving to simple questions. Leaning back in his chair, he began looking more closely at the witness and his attorney.

"I think I answered that question," Robins said, appealing to the judge.

"Answer it again, then, please," Lord said firmly. "Let's move on."

Robins then began another of the argumentative answers that were so frustrating Larson. Lord decided to ask the question his own way, simply, directly and to the point. "Did you advertise that it was medically safe is the question," the judge asked of Robins.

"I don't really know the answer to that question," Robins responded.

Lord, however, was not interested in the answer as much as he was in what he had just seen. He had suspected that Osthimer was using some sort of signal to prompt Robins into those unresponsive answers. As he had finished his brief question, he saw Osthimer's elbow move very close to his client; anyone watching at that moment would have said that Osthimer's elbow did in fact touch Robins. That was what Judge Lord saw and he didn't like it.

"If you're bumping him," the judge said, "I'm going to ask that you move down there." The judge pointed to the far end of the witness table.

Even before Lord finished his sentence, Osthimer was defending himself. "I didn't touch him, your honor," the lawyer said.

"Now, please," Lord began; he knew what he had seen.

Anticipating Lord's comment, Osthimer said, "No, I did not touch him."

Robins came to Osthimer's defense. "No," he said to Lord, shaking his head back and forth. "Oh, no, he didn't touch me."

"Your elbow was pushing [him] . . . and you moved his arm," Lord said annoyedly.

"On the contrary, your honor," Osthimer argued.

"I'll move further away," Robins suggested and he moved his chair about an inch or two to his left.

Lord was satisfied, but only for a second; Osthimer had changed his position in his chair, bringing his feet closer to his client. "Move your feet," the judge ordered Osthimer.

The attorney again defended himself. "I moved back, so the witness—"

Lord cut him off. "Move your feet away, too. I don't like what's going on."

With that, the deposition continued. Larson tried to get the witness to admit that the company's board of directors had known of the problems the Dalkon Shield was creating. "Now, it is a fact, is it not, Mr. Robins, that your company has never told either physicians or wearers of the Dalkon Shield that they have an increased risk of pelvic inflammatory disease as distinguished from all other IUD users, is that correct, sir?"

"I am not sure about that," Robins said. "I don't know that I could answer that intelligently, because I really don't know. . . . All I know is that we did send out a letter suggesting it be removed.

. . . [Y]es, we sent out a letter in 1980 in which we warned physicians."

Larson was obviously frustrated with the answer. So, apparently, was Lord. The judge decided, therefore, to pose the question himself.

"Let's take it this way," he began, "in that letter, did you tell them that there is a greater risk of PID in your device than in any other device on the market. . . . Did you tell them that?"

"To my knowledge, I don't recall the exact wording of the letter, but I don't think we did," Robins responded to Lord's query.

"Well," Lord said, "you can read the 'Dear Doctor' letter if you have to. Let's move on."

Larson continued to press ahead with his questioning. Judge Lord, meanwhile, was keeping a watchful eye on the witness table, to see whether Osthimer had found another way to prompt Robins. At one point, or so it seemed to him, he caught on to Osthimer's new tactic.

"Mr. Robins—" Larson began at one point.

"Yes."

"—addressing yourself to the ladies and gentlemen of this jury, you've been aware as the chief executive officer and now the chairman of the board of the company that if there is information in your medical department files that the string is multifilamented, has a wicking tendency, that physicians out in the marketplace are not going to know that unless your company gives them the information, isn't that correct?"

"I'm not sure that that's correct. I'm not, I really don't—" Robins was now looking down at the table, slightly to his right. Just then, Osthimer's left hand rose and made a waving motion. "I can't answer any more. I'm sorry, but I—"

Judge Lord had caught the scene. "The hand signals, please dispense with them," he broke in, addressing attorney Osthimer. "You understand what I said?"

"No I didn't." Robins thought Lord had been talking to him. "What did I—"

"Your lawyer is telling you when to stop and when to start—"

"Your honor—" Osthimer sought to interrupt.

"—and that's not appropriate," Lord finished his sentence.

"I didn't see them, I'm sorry," said Robins. "I was—"

"Your honor—" Osthimer again tried to say something.

"You stopped immediately when he waved," Lord said firmly to Robins. "Now let's go on."

"Your honor," Osthimer finally said, "that was twice that you have implied that Mr. Robins and I have some sort of signal going and I want the record to reflect—"

"I just saw you hold up your hand when he stopped and if the camera was on you it would show that. Let's proceed."

"I'm sure it did, your honor," Osthimer admitted, "but I submit to your honor that I have in no way attempted to signal Mr. Robins or to control Mr. Robins's testimony."

"I just suggested that you not make those gestures."

"I really do not feel that the court's implication is warranted," the attorney continued. "I think that Mr.—"

"I didn't say anything bad about you," Lord began calmly, "I just said that you're making those gestures." The judge's voice suddenly took on a sharper tone. "Now stop it or I'll excuse you from this deposition."

"Well, your honor," Osthimer began slowly, "I have a right—"

"Now let's proceed," Lord cut in harshly.

"—to be here—"

"I've heard enough," the judge said with finality, his mouth chewing furiously on a wad of tobacco, a not-so-secret pastime of his. "Proceed," he added, waving his arm upward to Larson.

A chastened Osthimer sat back in his chair as Larson picked up where he had left off.

Throughout that deposition session and those that followed, Lord showed great concern for Robins's health, frequently interjecting himself into questions to ask if the chairman was in need of a few moments' rest.

"Are you aware," Dale Larson asked a little later, "that [distinguished] physicians who head up [ob-gyn departments at] such [institutions] as the University of California . . . [and] Harvard . . . [have] stated publicly their opinions that that tailstring is a hazard to women and dangerous and defective for many years?"

"I am not aware of that," Robins responded.

"Nobody has ever communicated that to the board, or you at any of the board meetings, is that correct?" Larson asked in the slow deliberate manner he had carried throughout.

"I don't recall it ever being discussed," said Robins.

". . . Have you ever, or has your company to your knowledge, ever made any effort to directly contact and learn about the opinions of physicians who believe that the [Dalkon Shield] tailstring is defective and causes disease?"

"You would have to ask our medical department. I don't know."

With that answer, Lord jumped into the questioning. "You have never sent them to ask those questions, that's what you're saying?"

"Right, right."

Lord was about to continue when Osthimer stepped in. "Your honor," he said in an agreeable tone, "I am going to object to that, because that assumes facts not in evidence. I object to your question."

The judge did not understand the objection and said as much. "[M]y question was, have you ever sent any people out to do that personally?"

"No."

". . . And you don't know whether or not anybody has ever gone out to do that?" Lord continued.

"That's correct."

"You don't have any information or documents that would show that?"

"That's correct. I don't know of them."

At this point, Lord asked a question that concerned him greatly; it was the same one he had asked attorney Fribley on December 20. "Why don't you recall those things on the basis of what you know now?"

Robins at this point demonstrated that he had taken Lord's suggestion (which had been made at an earlier session) and had read the September 25, 1980, letter known as "Dear Doctor II." After Osthimer objected to Lord's "participating in adversarial proceedings and assisting plaintiff's counsel," Robins responded to the judge's question by saying, "Your honor, you understand, we did send out a letter in 1980 suggesting that physicians remove the Dalkon Shield and any IUD that had been in service for more than two years, I believe it was."

To this, Lord said, "Well, see, I wasn't even aware of that, that's how new I am to this case. But I thought there was some argument between you and counsel about not recalling?"

Clearly, the judge, who had suggested that Robins read "Dear Doctor II" in the first place, had thought that Robins was referring to a *recall* letter. In July, in his bid to have Judge Lord disciplined, Griffin Bell would refer only to the judge's comment regarding "Dear Doctor II" that "I wasn't even aware of that" as proof of how ignorant Lord was of the facts in the Dalkon Shield case. ("Judge" Bell, as the former Carter-era attorney general likes to be called, refused to explain to us why he had so distorted Lord's remark. He said he'd let the record speak for itself; it does.)

Picking up on the recall theme, Larson a few moments later asked Robins, "You have never instructed anybody to have any member of the company or any outside consultant contact physicians who believe and have claimed that the device has caused disease in their patients, is that correct?"

"I don't think we have sent anybody out, no. . . ."

"And you have never gone outside the company to an outside [medical] consultant and asked . . . that medical consultant whether or not you should recall the device from women, correct?"

"That may have been asked of our consultants, but I do not know."

"And you don't know what the basis is, apparently, for this recommendation from your medical people not to recall the device?"

"No."

"You just don't know?"

"No."

On the afternoon of the twenty-sixth, Judge Lord gained even further insight into the obfuscatory tactics that had necessitated his coming to Richmond to supervise the taking of the Robins and Clark depositions.

Clearly, his presence was making a difference, at least as far as moving the testimony along was concerned. This often was true of Dr. Clark's long, sometimes argumentative, sometimes obfuscatory answers.

In one instance, Mike Ciresi was trying to get Dr. Clark to reveal how many cases of pelvic inflammatory disease would have needed to come to Robins's attention before a warning was included on the Dalkon Shield labeling. As soon as Ciresi finished the question, Dr. Clark shook his head in a stunned what-did-he-say manner. Immediately, Robins attorney Houghton jumped in with an objection. The question as phrased, he argued, called for an assumption—that PID could be caused by the Dalkon Shield. Finally, Lord, his chair pushed up onto its back legs and his head and shoulder resting against the wall, took over:

"Let me take a little run at this, if you don't mind," the judge said to Houghton, who was sitting to his right. Then, moving his chair forward and turning to Dr. Clark, he asked, "Is . . . pelvic inflammatory disease serious?"

"It can be," Dr. Clark answered.

"It can be. Does it subside by itself?" Lord continued.

"It can," came the response.

"So what percentage is serious?"

Dr. Clark paused for a moment and began moving around in his chair as if suddenly uncomfortable. "That's a very difficult question . . . ," he answered finally. "I don't know whether anybody can answer that for everybody's piece of mind. . . ."

Lord tried another route. "At least a substantial percentage of it is serious?"

"By substantial—" Dr. Clark began, his left hand now picking invisible lint off the tablecloth, but the judge wasn't going to let him digress into one of his lengthy nonresponsive responses.

"We needn't quibble about that," Lord said. "I'll stop and ask you another question. Would you recommend treatment if people have it?"

"Yes."

"Would you recommend prompt treatment?"

"In the sense of not delaying for a week or two for treatment, yes, I would, yes."

Judge Lord pushed his chair back up and rested his head against the wall. He chewed vigorously on a wad of tobacco for a moment, then got to the crux of his questions: "And why?"

There was only one way Dr. Clark could answer that question. "In an effort to eliminate it as quickly as possible so as to prevent it from becoming chronic and more severe."

"All right," Judge Lord said, having established that PID was serious enough to be treated immediately. "If you knew something was going to cause it, would you try to stop it?"

Again, Dr. Clark had only one answer that he could give. "Yes," he said, folding his arms together. "If one were convinced that an isolatable cause was present, yes, one would try to eliminate that cause."

"And you think it was important to do that?"

"Yes, but if I may—"

Dr. Clark apparently was attempting to qualify his answer as far as the Dalkon Shield was concerned, but the judge was ahead of him. "I don't want to argue that this did or didn't cause it," Lord cut off Dr. Clark, "I'm just asking you these hypothetical questions."

"But on—" Dr. Clark began. Then he stopped to think for a moment and began again. "I think with a couple of sentences, I can illustrate the difficulty of answering that," he said.

Lord, however, anticipated what Dr. Clark would say. "You don't know what causes it for sure," the judge asked, "but if you did know, would it be important to stop that?"

"Yes," Dr. Clark responded, "I would say it's important to stop it if in fact one knew, yes."

With that, Lord turned the questioning back over to Ciresi. The young plaintiffs' attorney then began to focus on the "dirty questions," trying to get Dr. Clark to call them irrelevant.

"Doctor," Ciresi began, "during the time that the Dalkon Shield was marketed by the A. H. Robins Company, the medical department was aware that the device would be used by women who would have more than one sex partner?"

It was a question for which a one-word answer would suffice. Dr. Clark, however, was back in form. "Well," he began, and then he paused again, a bit longer this time. Finally, he said, "People within the A. H. Robins Company including the medical department were aware of the changing social mores that were occurring at that time and in a speculative vein it probably did conclude that somewhere in the course of one million . . . or two million women, there would be women with multiple sex partners. I'm not sure that anybody in the medical department gave it any more thought than that, however."

"Is your answer yes?" Ciresi asked, trying to pin down the seemingly unpinnable Dr. Clark.

"Well, with, not as bald as you said it, but with the . . . considerations that I added, yes."

As Ciresi was attempting, with each successive query, to tear down the "dirty questions" tactic, Dr. Clark's answers seemed to come slower and slower, with long pauses before answering. This apparently made Judge Lord curious. He had already that day come up twice against what he had thought was the surreptitious prompting of E. Claiborne Robins, Sr. He had walked into the control room during a break in the Robins deposition and found that Larson and Ciresi's private and whispered conversations were being overheard. Now, he was obviously suspicious about Dr. Clark's "hearing aid," an earplug in Dr. Clark's left ear, with an off-white wire that ran down the outside of his dark blue suit jacket to somewhere under the table. It looked much like the devices television reporters who are listening to their directors use. Lord had been told that the plug was hooked up to the sound system and was needed by Dr. Clark to help him to better hear the questions. The judge had accepted that at first, but now, apparently, he was beginning to wonder whether Dr. Clark was listening to his own "director" from outside the room.

"Do you have a hearing aid beside the one you have on, doctor?" the judge asked of Dr. Clark as Ciresi was about to begin another question.

"No, I don't," Dr. Clark answered.

"Well, do you have one? Do you ever use one?" Lord asked.

"No," Dr. Clark said.

"Why are you using it today?" the judge continued.

"Because I have problems with my left ear."

"And you don't ordinarily wear a hearing aid?"

"I do not. My wife keeps telling me, and other people, that I should, but I am too vain, I suppose, to—"

The judge, however, had made his point. If Dr. Clark was receiving outside prompting through the device, he had no way of proving it; but at least he had made known his suspicions this time without having to make any accusations, as he had done with Osthimer's signaling.

Ciresi then moved on to the question of whether the A. H. Robins Company represented to physicians that the Dalkon Shield was safe when it began to market the device in January 1971. Again, Dr. Clark felt the need to provide expansive and slowly expressed answers that narrowly defined the question before responding to it in his own unique fashion.

The plaintiffs' attorney thought Dr. Clark's answer was unresponsive; so did Judge Lord, who allowed the question to be asked again. This time, however, Robert Houghton objected. After about a minute or two of quibbling and nitpicking, the judge decided to get the answers his way.

"Did the literature which you sent to the doctors state that it was a safe device?" he asked Dr. Clark.

"I do not recall that it did or did not," Dr. Clark answered, turning to his right to face the judge. "In any event, physicians would interpret the word 'safe' with respect to a medical device or a drug, and in this sense it doesn't really make a difference."

"And the physician then would—" Lord began.

"—would recognize that 'safe' is not a one hundred percent word in this . . . sense," Dr. Clark finished Lord's sentence, adding, "and that is where I am having trouble with the question."

"Maybe I could help you, sir," the judge then said between "chaws." "When a physician measures the [risk]-benefit analysis, decides whether something is safe or not, measures how much good it will do . . . , he compares it to the risk, right?"

"Right."

"If you tell him it's safe, he has got to know what the risk is, right?"

"Right."

"And he should be told that there are certain things, adverse things, that can happen here, shouldn't he?"

"Right. He has—" Whatever Dr. Clark was going to say, he apparently thought brevity was a wiser course at this point. "Yes."

Lord now tried to drive the point home. "If you don't give [the physician] that information, he has no basis to question the safety of it, does he?"

Dr. Clark, however, was ready this time. "That is not quite correct, sir . . . ," he told Judge Lord as gently as possible. "[The physician] is expected to utilize his own training and background and his professional literature and his professional organizations to provide him with a background to interpret and to utilize."

The judge, however, would not be dissuaded. "Who would have the most responsibility for knowing whether a product had side effects, the manufacturer or some researcher . . . ?"

"I don't mean to beg off your question," Dr. Clark argued, "but this would depend—"

"Why don't you answer it . . . ?" Lord shot back as Dr. Clark spoke.

The doctor, however, would not be cut off. "—to the nature of the specific product as to which way that answer would go, so to some products that I can think of, it would not be."

Dr. Clark then launched into a lengthy dissertation of a 1968 medical journal article on IUDs. The judge, however, was in no mood to hear anything more than a direct answer to his question. In typical style, he leaned back against the wall, smiled, and calmly cut Dr. Clark off after about a minute or two. "You know," Lord said, "you have two hours to talk and you can take it all up in a monologue . . . [but] I am trying to help move this [along and]," Lord turned to Robins's attorney Robert Houghton and continued in a confidential tone tinged with a laugh, ". . . some of the witnesses have a bad habit they've gotten over the years without any supervision. . . . I want to help educate the witness to where we want to focus in on."

Once again, the judge got the response he sought. Everyone laughed, the tension caused by the rambling answers was eased, yet the point had been made, for now at least: sooner or later, the plaintiffs' questions would be answered, and the sooner the better for all concerned. Lord then turned the questioning back to Ciresi.

(Lord has since added Dr. Clark to his repertoire of anecdotes. "Let me give you an example of the kind of answer you get from Dr. Clark," he would say. " 'Dr. Clark, was it your habit in driving to work to drive down the highway that leads from your house to the place you work?' 'Well,' Dr. Clark would answer, 'let's now redefine habit. I have no such habit. Habit means something that's imposed upon you that you cannot control. . . . I could have gone that way. I could have gone another way. But this was the shortest way, It wasn't my *habit,* it was just the shortest way. I went [that way] every day, however.' ")

As the day drew on, Lord felt much of the frustration that Larson and Ciresi had been experiencing. Nevertheless, as even Clark's attorney was to point out that day, his presence was doing what it was supposed to do. "[I] think your questions are useful . . . ," Farnham told Judge Lord. "[They] focus on specific facts which it is far easier for the witness to answer than it is to answer a question which is conclusary in its terms. . . . [S]o I would encourage your honor to ask the pointed specific questions."

Pleased though he was at these remarks, it did little to abate his frustration. He rocked more frequently in his chair and tried to find comfortable positions in which to sit or stretch. He seemed to long for the end of the day's session, so that he could regenerate himself and prepare for the next day's round of battling with the Robins tactics of delay and obfuscation. Things were moving along; but the strain was showing.

If it was rest he sought, however, he was not yet to get it. As the Clark deposition ended for the day at midafternoon, the judge was informed that the Robins attorneys were challenging one of his discovery orders. Lord immediately ordered his two clerks to gather everyone up and bring them back to the deposition room.

The judge from Minneapolis was going to hold a hearing in Richmond.

9

A MATTER OF DISCOVERY

"Yesterday, in Minneapolis, we were looking at corporate minute books," Lord explained as the hearing opened in the Robins boardroom. The only difference was that the videotape crews were gone and so were the witnesses. "In the minute books was found a reference to the periodic reports of the then chief counsel for the company concerning Dalkon Shield litigation. We asked for production of those periodic reports. They are in the hands of the court for *in camera* review. We have discussed ways in which the fact of their existence could be used by the plaintiff without invading the privilege. . . ."

"Could I make that clear," Slaughter interjected, "that the court ordered us orally . . . to produce all documents which might refresh Mr. Robins's memory—Mr. Robins Sr.—relating to the matters under interrogation . . . ? On certain of those documents, a claim of privilege was made. The claim extended to these so-called reports on litigation to management. I don't believe any of them came from the chief legal counsel, but came from another lawyer who was in charge."

"What was his name?"

"Tuttle."

"I thought he was chief legal counsel," Lord said. "I'm not familiar with who's on first base." This was not an unusual admission considering the number of attorneys who had been moving in and out of the case by this point, seemingly at random. Lord had the same trouble keeping track of the many U.S. marshals under his jurisdiction back in Minneapolis. His solution to that problem was to have passport-size colored photographs of each of them encased in plastic on the bench, with their names inscribed. That kind of solution, however, was not practical here.

"But given that context," Robins's lead counsel continued, "these are litigation reports to senior management and certain others about litigation pending against the company. They appear to have been made from a period beginning in '72 through late '74. . . . [We object to] any disclosure to the plaintiffs or the use in the litigation of the privileged material. . . . The information in the documents is available from other sources. This is purely a lawyer, albeit within the company, reporting to his superior on the status of litigation. . . ."

"How would you propose that these plaintiffs find out what reports were made to the Board of Directors by the lawyers about the case?" Lord inquired. "They have denied that they knew about the cases, effectively."

"There have been statements in depositions about who knew what at what particular time, and they vary. These, again, your honor, are not to the board."

"Oh, I think they are."

"No," Slaughter insisted.

"Let's look at them. Who are they to?" Lord picked up a stack of papers and began searching for the distribution list.

Slaughter sought rather frantically to divert him. "Your honor," the attorney said, "there's no point in getting off on that."

Having found the distribution list, however, Lord would not be diverted. Nor was he confused about who these people were. "Oh," he said playfully, "to individuals, to individuals like, for instance, [chairman] Robins, [then president William] Zimmer, [senior vice-president Ernest L.] Bender . . . [vice-president and general manager Charles E.] Morton, [executive vice-president George E.] Thomas, [public relations chief Richard A.] Velz, [vice-president—sales John L.] Burke, [vice-president and medical director Dr. Jack] Freund. And that's not—is that the board, or is that just a—"

"Zimmer and Robins were on the board, and the rest—I don't know when Thomas was on the board, but he's the only one."

Lord smiled briefly. "I was technically in error," but he had made his point. "What I intend to do, so that we can zero in on this," Lord continued, "is to give . . . to the plaintiffs' counsel enough of a description of [these twenty-odd reports] so that they can take a couple of them [and] say, 'Did you see a report like this; did you know that the report contained—,' and get some of the detail out of it without the legal strategy. The existence of a case and the allegations made in [that] plaintiffs' complaint are all that I intend to give, and . . . who got the report, what the date of the report was, who wrote it, and who got carbon copies. . . ."

"Your honor," Slaughter said with some feeling, "I object to the court's disclosing this to opposing counsel, because this is privileged material. . . . [O]ur position is that it's—and it's a correct legal position, I believe—is that all of this is privileged because of the, of what it is. It's a report by a lawyer responsible for litigation to management about the litigation."

"Well, I have to overrule you on that. There's nothing privileged in there, and the document will speak for itself. And, if there is anything privileged in there, you and your young associates will have a chance to go over [the summary] with my law clerks and strike it. . . . I know of no other way to get this information and to prove that the information [about the Dalkon Shield] was called to the attention of the Board of Directors. . . ."

"These weren't to the Board of Directors," Slaughter corrected.

The judge, however, was no longer in a mood to argue semantics. "Well, to the top management of the company, some of whom were on the Board of Directors."

"Could we make this [summary] sheet an exhibit to this transcript, so we will have a record . . . ?" Slaughter asked, letting Lord know that he had not heard the end of the issue.

"My ruling is made," Lord snapped. "You may make an exhibit out of that document, but don't let the fact that you make an exhibit out of that document slow down the fact that we want it typed up for use tomorrow morning. That's all for that, I think. . . ."

Slaughter, however, was not yet ready to let go. "[I]f we could respectfully disagree—"

Lord had had enough. "You can disagree, you can appeal, or take whatever action is appropriate," he said carefully and calmly. "But I've looked at it. I have been very solicitous to avoid any reference to attorney-client communications in a sense that is really harmful, and I've cured it. And so that will be the rule."

Dale Larson then approached Lord. The interim defense agreement between Aetna and Robins suggested, at least, that the insurance carrier at one point had resisted paying out for Dalkon Shield injuries because Robins had supplied it with fraudulent information. Larson wanted the relevant documents. "I think it's further evidence of the intentional nature, or the willful nature of the conduct of A. H. Robins Company," Larson explained.

Slaughter immediately objected. "It's really irrelevant here as to what the Aetna thought or didn't think at particular times about the claims or whether they had coverage on the claims," the Robins attorney argued. He then pointed out that, without the attorneys present who represent Robins in the Aetna matter, the discussion ought not to continue. "I don't think it's fair to get into the matter without them having a chance to be heard."

"Get them here . . . ," Lord demanded. "When are you going to have them here?"

"As soon as I can get them."

Larson and Ciresi clearly looked pleased as the session ended. They considered the minutes critical to their case and now, they felt, they would get their chance to see the relevant portions of them.

"Because of Judge Lord's intervention, we had learned through E. C. Robins, Sr.'s, deposition that there was a host of references to Dalkon Shield problems in the board of director's minutes," Larson explained later. "These should have been disclosed during the multidistrict proceedings, but weren't; they were neither legitimately privileged nor attorney's work product items. And they were important. According to the implications—we didn't actually see all of them before the cases were settled—but it was just evident that there was information in those minutes that showed knowledge on the part of the board of directors which their top officers, who were members of the board, namely E. C. Robins, Jr., and E. C. Robins, Sr., had denied any knowledge of under oath. Robins had edited out these references before turning them over to the multidistrict proceedings; they had edited them without any court's or lawyer's supervision.

"Obviously, our whole view of Robins's conduct was that it had knowledge back in the early 1970s, as well as clearly by 1974 and 1975, and yet we were faced with this lack of documentation on that knowledge. It's one thing to go into a courtroom and say, 'Of course, they had to know,' and it's another to have evidence that they did know. So the thrust of our effort was to in effect show that lie, if you will. They were coming off in the depositions as 'hear no evil, see no evil, etcetera,' and it was evident that they had knowledge, that they had reports that reasonable people would have acted on.

"So the board of directors minutes had clearly and deliberately been edited to eliminate any knowledge of problems or deficiencies with the Dalkon Shield. Now, why was that important? Because the knowledge existed all the way up to the top, to the highest man, and under the law that goes to the punitive side of the case. Also, although our cases were civil, that actual knowledge, coupled with the denials and lies on their part, reflects, to a jury at least, a criminal mentality.

"And then there was just something incredulous *[sic]* about a company of that size, a so-called Fortune 500 company, that its board would have such knowledge and would then not act; that it would instead say, 'Let's protect our assets.' "

About two hours later, the hearing resumed. William P. Kogar of the firm of Mays, Valentine, Davenport & Moore was there representing Robins's Aetna interests.

During the recess, however, Lord had been told that there were now objections to his being in Richmond. He wanted that matter cleared up before proceeding any further.

His chair was again pushed back to the wall and was balancing on its two back legs. "[Is there] any dispute about the fact that even though I'm sitting in Virginia—I'm not even sure I'm sitting; I'm sort of tottering—I would have at least as much power to order discovery while sitting here as I would have if I were sitting back in Minneapolis? Does that create a problem for anyone?" he asked.

"It does for us," said Slaughter, and that was all Judge Lord had to hear.

"Well, then, I won't have any further hearing on this," he said, looking at Slaughter. "We'll go back to Minneapolis and have it. So the hearing is over. . . . I know that you're wrong in trying to limit my power, but I don't care about that. I'll go back to Minneapolis and do my work." The judge made clear, however, that he still intended to stay in Richmond long enough to supervise more deposition-taking.

Kogar was the next to approach the bench. As a latecomer to the proceedings, he wanted to know what was going on. Specifically, he was interested in knowing why he had been summoned. The judge and Slaughter attempted to explain the situation to Kogar. "I don't fully understand what the problem is," the attorney said at length.

"Well, come to Minneapolis if you're interested in talking about it, then," Lord said. "Apparently, I shouldn't go forward anymore here."

"Am I to understand that you have directed me to come to Minneapolis?" Kogar asked.

"No," Lord responded, obviously annoyed by the whole proceeding. "I just say that I'll be talking to Robins about those files, and some of those files may or may not concern their litigation with Aetna Insurance Company. We'll be making certain resolutions on it. You are welcome to come or stay or do whatever you want. I'm going back to Minneapolis."

"Some of it may involve the Robins litigation with Aetna, is that what I understand?"

"That's what Mr. Slaughter indicated he thought that might be referring to. I don't know. I haven't looked at the documents; my law clerks have."

Once again, Slaughter thought it appropriate to correct Lord. "No, your honor, they haven't looked at those documents," he offered.

The nitpicking was getting to Lord. "They have looked at documents that said Aetna may not cover us because of fraudulent promotion, and such and such. Now," he said pointedly, "that kind of gets you into the question of what the conversations were about Aetna, and so forth, and what [Robins's senior management] knew at the time. So let's go back to Minneapolis and resolve that and"—looking at Kogar now—"nobody has to come if you don't want to. . . . I will feel a lot better, too, back in Minnesota making these judgments."

Getting back to Minnesota without holding any more hearings, however, proved to be a problem for Lord. The judge had become fed up with the accommodations the A. H. Robins Company had supplied for the deposition-taking of E. Claiborne Robins, Sr. The room was too small to hold all of the lawyers, paralegals, clerks, and stenographers and the two videotape crews. All those people stuffed into the room also made it too hot and uncomfortable. On top of everything else, however, there were constant interruptions from Robins staffers constantly walking in and out of the room. "With people running back and forth," Lord later would recall, "we must have had twenty-five people scurrying back and forth in and out of that room." It was almost as if the Robins people wanted it that way.

Most important, though, was Lord's belief that there was surreptitious prompting of the witnesses and possible eavesdropping on Larson and Ciresi. He wanted the depositions taken in an atmosphere he could control.

The problem bothered Lord all that night. Finally, at seven the next morning, Friday, January 27, he instructed his two law clerks, Roberta Walburn and Keith Halleland, to contact all of the attorneys and inform them that he was moving the deposition site to "a much more appropriate place," the U.S. District Courthouse in Richmond. Twenty-five minutes later, Alexander Slaughter received a call from Lord himself telling the attorney that he wanted E. Claiborne Robins, Sr., brought to what he would later describe as the "quiet, serene atmosphere of the federal district courtroom."

"That was so hectic I [thought] Mr. Robins would have a heart attack," Lord subsequently explained, "if nothing else than from the commotion around there."

Moving the deposition site, however, also meant holding a hearing on the matter, if for no other reason than he by now expected that the Robins attorneys would demand one eventually so why not get it over with—even if he had already forsworn holding further hearings anywhere but in Minnesota. After he opened the session, he looked directly at Slaughter and asked if anyone objected to moving the deposition-taking to the courthouse. As Lord expected, Slaughter objected. Robins's physician had advised that the seventy-five-year-old chairman "shouldn't be put in a courtroom atmosphere," and now the judge was proposing to do just that.

"Now," said Lord, "the courtroom atmosphere is something new. You've just injected that. It had nothing to do with the question I posed to the doctor, which was the travel to Minnesota in the cold weather. But go ahead."

"Well, I don't believe the cold weather had that much to do with it," Slaughter retorted.

"That was the basis that your own doctor used was the cold weather." Temperatures in Minneapolis often sink unhealthily below zero in winter.

"Well, I'll send for [the doctor's] affidavit, your honor, which we filed."

"It won't be necessary," Lord said matter-of-factly. "I remember what's in it. Go ahead."

Slaughter, however, would not be put off. "I would like to have it, your honor, to attach it to this record."

Once again, the judge was being forewarned of a possible appeal. He decided to put the shoe on Slaughter's foot for a change. "Have you produced the [summaries of the Tuttle reports] my law clerks [dictated to your people yesterday]? Are they over here?" Lord knew they were not there.

"No," came Slaughter's reply.

"How come?"

"I would like to take that up on the record," Slaughter responded.

"Do it later," said Lord, "but I had asked your young assistant, Mr. [Terrence] Bagley, to send for that stuff about forty-five minutes ago. How far is it from here to the Robins company?"

"It's right far from Robins Company," said Slaughter, "[but] those documents aren't at Robins Company; they're at our office."

"How far is that?"

"About three blocks."

"I asked him for those about forty-five minutes ago. I did not expect that you would resist that and, as you have the memo of the doctor brought over, also have those memoranda that my law clerks made, dictated to your people at A. H. Robins yesterday, which you promised."

"I don't believe so," said Slaughter, again trying to grab Lord at a technicality, as if building a record showing that the judge was too loose with facts. "Technically, your honor, they were dictated in a machine to be transcribed by our office at the court's request."

Slaughter's desire for exactitude no longer annoyed Lord. "Well, have it brought here, anyway," he instructed calmly.

Slaughter agreed and then opened a new issue: the "rough justice procedures" Lord had been using to order the production of documents. The judge was doing things so informally—and so swiftly—that Robins was not getting a chance to dig into its almost bottomless bag of legal tricks to prevent discovery. Naturally, he did not put it that way to Lord.

"As the court is aware, there are rules and procedures for producing documents," Slaughter told the judge, "having an opportunity to respond to motions to produce . . . , and having [written] orders from the court specifying documents to be ruled on. The court, since it has gotten very involved in this process, has begun making more or less spontaneous oral orders, sometimes pursuant to the plaintiff's request, sometimes not."

"Sometimes . . . when I find documents in [the minute books] which mention other apparently relevant evidence which is excised from the material that has already been produced, I [want] to look at them," Lord explained; if Slaughter was setting up a record for appeal, he wanted that record to reflect his thinking, as well as his actions. "And that is the oral orders that I gave. I wanted to see what was referred to in the minutes of Board of Directors meetings on, for instance, February 4 of 1975, where the Tuttle report was deleted with reference to . . . all kinds of information which is not necessarily privileged. But go ahead."

"As the court is aware," Slaughter continued, "we brought the minute books . . . to Minnesota and the court reviewed those *in camera.* But again, there is no written motion before the court. And what I am concerned with at this point is the court more or less rambling through the documents, ordering orally here and there that we produce things without the opportunity for us to adequately respond and prepare and argue the matters before the court. I did not mean to offend the court—"

"Sure."

"—but that is what it appears to me that we are up against."

Lord smiled, more to himself than anyone else, as if to say, "So Slaughter was setting up a record for an appeal." Well, he would set one up right beside Slaughter's. "[I]f it appears that way, you should have mentioned it at the time that you produced them because, at the time that you produce something to me without any argument and you agree as to how we should put it together, it's hard for me to say, 'Mr. Slaughter, we should have done this pursuant to notice, fourteen days for this notice, sixteen days for that; delay the trial another time.' It's rather difficult for me to answer statements you are making about me making random oral orders. I thought we were working together on this . . . ?"

Lord then felt that an example was called for that would make his point clearly.

"[Some of the] material which I directed to have reproduced," the judge noted, "was the material that showed that at every . . . meeting of the Board of Directors . . . , [E. C. Robins, Jr.,] recited to the Board of Directors in detail all about its finances, about its new acquisitions, about its sales, about its profits, about its losses, about examining new buildings. This man . . . , E. Claiborne Robins Jr. knows all about everything. And I thought, in light of the fact that [in] the only deposition that I read of him . . . he said that his management style was to delegate everything, and he knew nothing about anything . . . , [that] these Board of Directors meeting minutes showed that to be very questionable. . . ."

The argument was getting nowhere and Slaughter finally thought it best to move on to some of his other objections, particularly the taking of Dr. Fred Clark's deposition and moving the E. Claiborne Robins, Sr., deposition to the courthouse. On Clark, Slaughter pointed out that he had been deposed many times in the past and even on videotape, so there really was no need to continue to take his deposition now. Lord, however, saw matters differently as far as Dr. Clark was concerned.

"I watched Dr. Clark perform yesterday," the judge said, "and my guess would be that he is better at running a courtroom than almost any judge I know. . . . [I]f he carried on in his other depositions like he did for the first one-third of yesterday's deposition, nobody ever got anything out of him. . . ."

"Well, he has testified a number of times, your honor, and he has testified by deposition a number of times," Slaughter repeated.

"He is an expert witness," Lord said.

"No, he is not an expert witness," Slaughter countered.

"He is expert at being a witness," Lord insisted.

"No he's not."

"He seems to be."

As for the elder Robins, Slaughter produced his physician, who stated that he feared Robins would suffer a heart attack if forced to testify away from the familiar surroundings of the A. H. Robins Company. Lord, by now, was tired of arguing. He wanted to get on with the depositions and return to Minnesota. He conceded the point and ordered everyone back to the A. H. Robins Company for the depositions.

It was obvious to Lord, as he returned to Minnesota late on Friday the twenty-seventh that the trial could not actually begin on February 1, as he had hoped. There was little time, however, to notify the prospective jurors not to show up that day for empaneling; nor was he so inclined, believing then that an already empaneled jury might be just the thing to convince Robins that he would not put up with any more delays.

On Monday, he conferred with Robins's Minnesota counsel Jack Fribley and Roger Brosnahan, Larson's and Ciresi's partner. He suggested that the jury be selected on February 1, and the trial then continued for two weeks until all of the pretrial loose ends were eliminated. Both sides agreed, or so Lord thought as he entered the courtroom that Wednesday morning. Waiting for him, however, was Denver attorney Chuck Socha, Robins's lead trial counsel, and Socha was not pleased. "I don't believe that that was the agreement," Socha said. "At least, it is my understanding that was not the agreement. It is my understanding that the court in essence announced that that is the manner in which the jury was to be selected."

"The trouble with this case," Lord grumbled, "is that A. H. Robins speaks with too many mouths and that one lawyer agrees to something and the other one comes in and acts surprised about it . . . ," a complaint raised by many of the judges who have presided over the Dalkon Shield cases from Miami to Denver to Oregon and stops in between. The judge looked over to Alexander Slaughter, who was seated at the conference table, letting Socha play his "bad guy" role for all it was worth. "Mr. Slaughter, from now on, since you seem to be the management of all this litigation, I am going to tell you that the acts and utterances of any Robins attorney in any circumstances is binding on you and every other lawyer representing Robins. . . . And after this I don't want anybody to ever again call me on the telephone [regarding this case] unless there is a court reporter present. I have had enough of misunderstandings about what was said, what was agreed to and what was not said. There must be a court reporter on the phone when you call me." The judge then made it clear that the agreement stood; the jury would now be chosen.

The prospective jurors were brought forward from the spectator rows a few at a time and placed on the two benches before the bar. Lord always enjoyed the exchanges with would-be jurors and he began to lighten up again. "Good morning, ladies and gentlemen," he said, and the hundred-odd prospective jurors responded in unison as if he were Johnny Carson doing a monologue, "Good morning, Judge Lord." Everyone laughed. "I just wanted to tell you Mr. Socha . . . that I told the jurors I want a nice response when I said that, as I walked through the hall this morning. Some of them have been here before." Again, there was laughter. Lord was letting Socha know that this was his turf and that he and he alone was in control.

Lord now began to address the prospective jurors directly, trying to weed out those who did not want to serve but who were reluctant to say so. "For this case, I have to figure on having people here who will be serving off and on—not steady—between now and maybe the first of June. . . . [H]opefully, some day the ground will thaw and then those of you who live on farms will want to hitch up old Dobbin to the plow and go out—and start with the forty-thousand-dollar tractor." Again, there was laughter.

The judge continued. "The other thing is how lonesome it can get sticking around in Minneapolis with your family and your children and your grandchildren off at Fairmont, for example—which is . . ."—the judge paused—"is it 147 [miles], 180, how far is Fairmont?"

"One-twenty." The answer had come from a prospective juror in the back of the room.

"A hundred and twenty?" Lord said with mock astonishment. "They've moved it since I got here. I used to drive it in a 1932 Chevrolet."

Throughout the morning, Lord whittled down the pack. Finally, he instructed his clerks to "order up" more prospective jurors. Meanwhile, he set about hearing Robins's as yet unresolved "privilege" arguments over Lord's plan to turn over to the plaintiffs the Tuttle memoranda and even edited versions of the minute books themselves, at least those portions that related to Dalkon Shield litigation.

The arguments had not changed in any way; what was getting to Lord, however, was that other out-of-state attorneys for Robins were being brought in for the sole purpose of presenting those arguments, then riding off into the Minnesota sunset. The judge had no way of really knowing these people, or even if he could take their representations and arguments at face value. "They appear one day and give a very sincere argument, then leave, and [you] find out it was made of whole cloth. . . ." Finally, Lord wanted to put an end to what he called "the hit-and-run treatment."

"That's been their tactic all along," Mike Ciresi explains, "to say this individual knows a little bit, this one knows a little bit. I mean, you can see they'd stand up, one attorney would say one thing and you knew goddamned well that the other one sitting there knew differently. In *Hahn,* they tried the same thing. They brought in Osthimer, they brought in Houghton, they brought in all these different lawyers to try different cases. . . . They brought in a guy from Washington, D.C., to try a case before Judge McLaughlin; they brought in Tom Kemp to try the case opposite George Gubbins. They brought in all these lawyers—and all these people popped up again when we started taking depositions. And they'd make certain representations to the court that was different in one courtroom as opposed to another and the judges are just sitting there. For instance, Osthimer made some representations to Judge [Paul A.] Magnuson that I knew goddamned well were not true and Osthimer could say that because he wasn't involved in, say, *Strempke* or with what was going on in other places. And he could always say, 'Well, I don't know about that, your honor,' So I'd say, 'Why don't you check on it?' and he'd say 'Well, I'll check on it,' but they never do and you get caught up in other things.

"I think their intention, from the day that Lord got involved, was to prod him and bait him into making some type of error so they could make a record. They knew we were going to trial on this and they wanted some type of record of what the judge had 'done' to them and I thought it was remarkable the patience that he showed during those entire proceedings, faced with this type of, really, total disrespect for the court."

Judge Lord was no longer going to allow this sort of thing in his courtroom. "What I would like to do at some point here," he said, "would be to have each of the out-of-town lawyers take a little oath that they'll agree to abide by the rules and regulations of the court here in Minnesota, will voluntarily subject themselves to the jurisdiction of the State Board on Ethical Practices, and that they'll not contest the jurisdiction of any Minnesota tribunal to take . . . the same steps against them as they could against anyone who is admitted to practice in Minnesota."

Slaughter immediately jumped into the fray. Philosophically, he was for the idea, he told Judge Lord. As a practical matter, however, he would not agree to such an oath without first checking the Minnesota code and seeing how it compared with the codes to which he already subscribed.

The judge then insisted that he wanted the issue of the oath resolved before any further arguments were made on the defense motions. "Anybody that doesn't want to sign such an oath," he added, "they don't have to come here, you know. . . . [J]ust repeat the oath you've already given somewhere else. It's only a geographic change. I wouldn't want you to be any more responsible [for your actions] here than you would be in Virginia. . . ."

In fairness, however, he gave the Robins attorneys twenty-four hours to consider the proposal and, if they so desired, to present arguments against the plan.

Having settled that for now, Lord continued discussion of the discovery issue. Larson and Ciresi requested that discovery be opened up even further. The depositions that had already been taken, they argued, were filled with such things as "I don't recall" and "That was so long ago" that the only way to get the deposed witnesses to admit to anything would be to show them documents and ask them to refresh their memories.

"I believe, your honor, we have a right to find out what facts were communicated to those people," Ciresi argued, "because they want to say that the Dalkon Shield wasn't recalled or it was not defective because there was no clinical significance to the injuries that were occurring; it wasn't happening in enough women; wasn't killing enough women; wasn't injuring enough women. . . . We would like to find out—and I asked Dr. Clark, 'Did you ever discuss at any of these meetings with all your medical people or when you had meetings with company officials, "Gee, how many women out there are being injured with this device, how many might be injured . . . ?" ' "

"If you had that information," Lord asked, "what would you do with it?"

"Your honor, I think it could be used for two purposes," Ciresi advised. "Number one, it could be used to impeach some of these people directly on direct questions they were asked. Secondly, it could be used maybe to refresh their recollection[s] because they just don't recall these things."

Lord said he would accept written arguments on further document production and would take the matter under advisement. The voir dire continued until a panel was chosen. Court adjourned after 6 P.M. It had been a long and frustrating day.

When court reconvened on February 2, Lord was told that the Robins attorneys would not sign the oath. The judge then immediately announced that he was excusing Slaughter, Socha, and all of the other out-of-staters from any further appearances in the six consolidated cases (two more had been settled by this time). Fribley and the other Faegre and Benson attorneys, he said, were quite capable of handling the defense for Robins without any help.

Fribley, however, had been instructed by Slaughter that he could not proceed alone and he so informed the judge. More debate followed and, after a brief recess, it was agreed that, after all, an oath of some kind would be signed by any out-of-state attorneys appearing on Robins's behalf.

Lord, however, was not finished. He had been handed a motion the other day, he said, that was so disjointed that it was unintelligible. James Fitzmaurice of Faegre and Benson, who had been brought in to argue the oath problem with Lord, had stated that Slaughter wanted to assure the court that, "as a responsible party at his law firm, there is no question that you cannot address to him, and he'll give you an account, offering who did what, when, where and how."

The judge decided to take Slaughter up on his offer. "[W]ho wrote that brief I commented on . . . ?" Lord asked.

"I'm not real sure, your honor," came Slaughter's reply. "I think Robert E. Pane."

"You think who?" Lord asked next.

"I think the senior person was Robert E. Pane," Slaughter answered.

"Where does he . . . live?"

"Richmond."

"Now isn't that something," Lord said. "I'm reading a brief . . . which I think is an abomination and even the lead counsel for the company doesn't know who wrote that. What kind of a way is that to practice law or to have to try a case? I want everybody to sign every document that they have anything to do with from now on. I want their name on the bottom of it, the name of the person who actually conducted the work, did the procedure, made the search, drafted the document. And I want those people to sign, those very people, to sign this oath. . . . [T]hat is an order and I'll have no further argument about it. . . . We are going to pinpoint responsibility." (This is exactly the same order that would be given to Robins in June by an equally exasperated U.S. district judge C. Weston Houck in the South Carolina case of *Diana S. Pate* v. *A. H. Robins Company.)*

The situation, however, was far from settled. In fact, it was about to become even more frustrating. Rather than argue on the merits, Lord came to believe, the Robins attorneys were doing everything they could to obfuscate and delay any decision on his part. There was, for example, the unresolved question of whether the plaintiffs could view any documents in Robins's possession about whether Aetna felt the drug company had engaged in fraudulent practices in its promotion of the Dalkon Shield.

On Friday, February 3, Lord ordered that the papers be brought to Minnesota pending a hearing on Monday to decide the question. Over the weekend, however, Robins showed it still had some more unused tricks in its legal bag. Together with Aetna, it ran to a friendly judge in the federal court in Richmond and secured an ex parte order allowing the papers to be turned over to Aetna and removed to Connecticut, so they were no longer in Robins's possession. (An ex parte order is one in which one side in a litigation files a motion and secures a ruling without notice to the other side.) Lord was furious when he learned of this on Monday. "There will be no 'cat and mouse games' here," he vowed that day. Later on during that session, Lord introduced two attorneys, Peter N. Thompson and Thomas C. Bartsh, and announced that he had appointed them special masters of the court to oversee any discovery order he might eventually issue. He also provided counsel for both sides with a draft of the wording of the order he intended to issue.

Another example of the Robins tactics came at a hearing on the proposed order held the following day, February 7, when another new face representing Robins, attorney Duncan Getchell, argued that no new discovery was needed because discovery had been completed during the multidistrict proceedings under Judge Theis and any further documents that existed were privileged information not subject to discovery.

Lord knew this was not the case and said so. Getchell then amended his statement to say that there probably were unprivileged documents that had never been produced, but that they were irrelevant to the proceedings.

After court, Lord telephoned Judge Theis in Wichita to discuss the MDL proceedings. Theis told Lord that his discovery orders left open to each individual court hearing Dalkon Shield cases the matter of whether to continue discovery. That evening, the two special masters, Thompson and Bartsh, were dispatched to Richmond pending Lord's order.

The next day, Lord issued that order, a detailed 3,500-word document in which the judge declared that Robins and its attorneys had waged a "war of attrition" against plaintiffs and their counsel and complained that company lawyers had even nudged company officials to stop them from answering questions during deposition sessions, apparently preferring not to have their objections to certain questions entered into the record.

Lord detailed a number of "exceptional events" that had occurred since he consolidated the twenty-one cases, among them the fact that, while both E. Claiborne Robins, Sr., and E. Claiborne Robins, Jr., claimed "poor recollection of events and limited participation in the concerns of the company," the minute books the judge had examined showed that they had "a detailed knowledge of the corporation's affairs," presumably including the existence of thousands of documents that the company, in thirty-one trials to date, had not admitted existed and had not turned over to courts despite various discovery orders, although it had claimed to have fully complied with all such orders.

Lord then went over some of the Robins courtroom tactics he found so abhorrent, including Robins's "practice of obscuring the responsibility of its attorneys so that it is impossible to determine at any given moment who is accountable for representations made to the court. The defendant also has rotated its attorneys in and out so that the court must start up from ground level over and over in order to brief the new arrival."

He also described the Robins attorneys' conduct in the various discovery arguments that had been held. "The pattern is the same" each time, Lord stated; "the defendant either appears to accept the court's orders without objection and then fails to abide by them, or recoils at the slightest hint of a new directive and asks for additional time to prepare its response."

Finally, Lord got to the heart of his order—the most sweeping discovery ever in the twelve-year history of Dalkon Shield litigation: All documents were to be turned over to the court "as soon as possible," including all correspondence between the company and its insurer, Aetna; all documents relating to Aetna's denial of further coverage; all written material that was given to or prepared by Robins's vice-president and general counsel, William A. Forrest, Jr., from June 1, 1974, onward; memoranda from other company attorneys to company officials; and all documents relating to the safety of the Dalkon Shield and the company's knowledge of potential defects.

"What I am attempting to do here and give herald to," Lord said of his order, "is a system whereby some five thousand cases which threaten to tie up the federal courts . . . , can be resolved. . . . This additional discovery will aid the resolution of all these outstanding cases."

In opening court that day, February 8, Lord made it clear that he was no longer going to sit by and see justice denied. "I have heard the arguments of counsel regarding the proposed order," he began. "I have issued my order. There will be no further argument on it. Hand the order out," he said to his clerks.

As the attorneys began to read the document, Lord made clear that it was final as far as he was concerned. "Any stay is denied," he ruled in anticipation. "As a consequence, we will move on to some new business."

Slaughter immediately rose in protest. "Your honor," he said, "May I make a statement in respect to a stay . . . ?"

"I have said there will be no further argument on this," the judge said firmly, "The stay is denied in the order."

"The court is requesting me to sit down?"

"Yes, if you please."

In Richmond, the two masters were informed that Lord's order had been formally issued. They immediately went, first to the Robins headquarters and then to McGuire, Woods & Battle to begin the process of discovery. Instead of cooperation, they met with repeated objections. The attorneys asked for more time to study the order. "I responded that we, as masters, were not in a position to stay the court's order," Thompson subsequently recalled, "particularly after the court had denied [Robins's] request for a stay." Thompson added that, at the time, it appeared to him that Robins "had not determined whether it would comply" with Lord's order.

The next morning, February 9, Alexander Slaughter appealed the order to Chief Judge Donald Lay of the Eighth U.S. Circuit Court of Appeals. Slaughter asked Lay to stay the discovery order pending an appeal to the full Circuit Court. He also asked Lay to delay yet again the start of the trial, this time so that the issues of Lord's discovery order could be decided.

As Slaughter was presenting his appeal to Lay in St. Paul, Robins vice-president and general counsel William Forrest was to be deposed in Minneapolis; the two masters, meanwhile, were continuing their efforts to begin cataloging the thousands of documents Lord had ordered produced. Under the circumstances of the appeal, however, Lord voluntarily ordered a postponement of all the Richmond activity until Judge Lay could rule.

Within moments of learning what Slaughter had done, Larson and Ciresi hurriedly prepared briefs in defense of Lord's actions. Lord's consolidation of cases, they would tell Lay, was consistent with what two other judges in different jurisdictions had by then done. As for Lord's having become too involved in the case, they said, he was not the first judge "who has been frustrated by the attempts of Robins to thwart discovery through overwhelming objections in order to prolong and delay proceedings." On the question of the new depositions Lord had ordered, that was necessary, the attorneys argued, because Robins had changed its defense since the time the officials were first questioned.

By noon, all motions had been filed and the long wait began. Many that day thought back to the Reserve Mining Case and wondered whether the Eighth Circuit would yet again slap down Judge Lord.

At 5 P.M., Judge Lay ruled in favor of Lord. The order, he said, was "couched in protective terms so as to require review by the court on claims of attorney-client privilege." Lord's rulings in the case, Lay added, did not appear to be "an abuse of discretion," and they "were [not] outside the sphere of judicial power." The appeal on the discovery order would be heard by the full court in one week's time, Lay said. In the meantime, there would be no stay; discovery would continue under the guidelines Lord had set. In Richmond, the masters were told to proceed. Bartsh, however, had to return that evening to Minneapolis to clear up an unrelated matter.

The next morning, Lord appeared on the bench looking drawn and tired. Overnight, he had learned that Robins intended once again to dip into its bag of legal tricks and file with him a motion for recusal, asking him to step down from the case because of bias. He had intended to supervise the Forrest deposition, which was being videotaped beginning that morning in his courtroom. Instead, beside him in the second black leather chair on the bench was Magistrate Patrick J. McNulty, whom Lord had summoned from Duluth. Everyone in the room knew something dramatic was about to occur.

Lord ordered the cameras that were in place to record Forrest's deposition to roll. Black-robed and solemn, he picked up a document and began to read. He did his best not to show any emotion. His voice, however, betrayed him. There was a slight tremor in it and he had difficulty at times reading the words he had written. He also digressed from the written text on several occasions, further revealing the passions he fought so hard to conceal.

"I wish to read to you an order that was filed with the clerk at 7:30 this morning . . . ," Lord started haltingly, reciting the words one at a time and emphasizing each one. "This court, in an effort to have these consolidated Dalkon Shield proceedings processed in an orderly and expeditious manner, makes the following observations and enters the following orders:

"This court has deliberately attempted to administer these proceedings in such a manner as to reflect the fairness and impartiality that is expected of this tribunal. This effort to maintain not only impartiality but the appearance thereof has been made most difficult by the sensitive discovery issues facing the court involving attorney-client and work product privileges." Lord looked up from his text toward the counsel tables before him. "It was for that reason that I appointed masters to shield me from criticism resulting from that kind of order," Lord said, and then he returned to his written order. "Understandably, the closer this court—I ad-libbed that last line—the closer this court approaches the ultimate time for a ruling upon actual production of documents to the plaintiffs, the more apprehensive become the possessors of the documents and the more heightened becomes the rhetoric of the courtroom. As the arguments against production of the documents exhaust themselves, the tribunal itself becomes the target. This court has tasted of this cup before and has had its fill.

"There is pending before the Court of Appeals of the Eighth Circuit a petition for mandamus in which defendant seeks to foreclose plaintiffs from even 'glancing toward' what the defendant broadly alleges to be a work product, work product and privileged materials. During this interim period while these matters are before the Court of Appeals, all discovery must move forward. Yet this court would feel ill at ease if it were to preside over the scheduled depositions of company officers during this tense interval."

Again, Lord departed from his text. "I've already had some experience—I'm ad-libbing this—I've already had some experience with the kind of drama that takes place in the courtroom under these circumstances," Lord said, adding after a dramatic pause, "and in this case specifically." Now Lord resumed reading. "This court does not desire to partake in this discovery while looking over its shoulder at a recusal petition. Therefore, in an effort to give continuity to the process, yet still maintain the ongoing discovery in a calm and tranquil atmosphere, this court will temporarily cease its involvement in these depositions."

Magistrate McNulty, Lord then ordered, would be in charge of the depositions and would oversee the work of the masters in Richmond until the Eighth Circuit ruled. Jack Fribley, Lord continued, was to proceed "forthwith, I add forthwith, to Richmond, Virginia, to act as liaison between the masters and A. H. Robins personnel and attorneys . . . to avoid wrangling and unpleasantries which might otherwise occur." Lord looked up yet again. "I will hear no further argument—and this I'm ad-libbing—on the need to have him present for this deposition; they have literally hundreds of lawyers who could preside over the depositions for the defendant."

After completing the reading of his order, Lord rose and walked to his left off the bench and out of the courtroom, instructing his clerks to distribute the written order as he went. He had opened the door and was set to leave through the "tunnel" when he stopped, turned, and gave two more verbal orders on minor matters. With that, he departed from the Dalkon Shield case until the Eighth Circuit had ruled on the mandamus petition and he had ruled on the as yet unfiled recusal petition.

Unaware of the events that were at that moment transpiring back in Minneapolis, master Thompson was dutifully trying to ascertain the extent of his and Bartsh's task. In the morning, he was taken to a room at McGuire, Woods & Battle that was known as "the source file," where, he was told, most of the MDL documents had been placed. After lunch, he toured the A. H. Robins Company. As he would later explain it, "From our tour, it appeared that to comply with the discovery order, Robins must search approximately three-and-a-half file drawers and about eighteen boxes . . . in the legal department; about three file drawers (with, perhaps, only one file drawer's worth of documents relating to the Dalkon Shield) in the insurance department; and approximately four-and-a-half drawers, four boxes and a two-shelf bookshelf in the medical department."

However, as the master noted later, "Based on the large numbers of documents that eventually were labelled and searched at the Robins production site, [they] subsequently must have discovered substantial quantities of documents [elsewhere] that needed to be reviewed."

Thompson's tour that day led him to conclude that no one at Robins "had spent a great deal of time or effort" locating documents and cataloging them since learning several days earlier that it would be required of them. Faced with the enormity of the task, he returned home to Minneapolis that day to await further instructions.

On Monday, Jack Fribley telephoned Thompson from Richmond and told him that a system had now been worked out to effect the document search. After speaking with Magistrate McNulty, Thompson returned to Richmond that evening.

On Tuesday morning, he was joined by Roberta Walburn, one of Judge Lord's law clerks who had been temporarily assigned to Magistrate McNulty. She had been sent to Richmond by McNulty to assist Thompson. Once again, the Robins attorneys had an excuse for delay. They objected to anyone from Judge Lord's staff being involved at this stage. Later that day, McNulty ordered that Walburn be allowed to do the job he had sent her to do.

On Thursday, February 16, during a conference call with McNulty in the presence of Thompson and Walburn, Robins's attorneys made comments that to Thompson, at least, were "an attempt at intimidation." Ms. Walburn, for example, was warned against ever accepting a position with any law firm that had a lawsuit pending against Robins. If she did wind up at such a firm, Robins would take appropriate action (although what action it could take is unclear). To a lesser extent, Thompson recalls, that objection extended to him and Bartsh as well. The conference call also disclosed other problems the masters were facing, including repeated delays and arbitrary decisions on Robins's part regarding what should be produced.

That afternoon, McNulty reacted with an order of his own that rivaled Lord's in its description of Robins's tactics. "[A]n impenetrable wall has been erected around the A. H. Robins Company which demonstrates a collapse of voluntary unsupervised discovery procedures . . . ," the magistrate wrote. "[T]he focus of the decision-making on document production seems to lie in a single individual . . . who has not appeared before this court, [but who] is engaged in making unilateral decisions as to what is and is not proper before this court. . . .

"To this date, not a single document has been produced to the masters for examination. Instead, this court has been involved in a day-to-day and hour-by-hour process of definition, of redefinition, of defining and refining, further redefinition, and of discussion as to the propriety of production, the methods of production, the methods of examination, the persons who should be allowed to view, and many other technical hindrances. . . . This has exceeded the need for protection of rights and privileges, is obstructive and seemingly for the purpose of attempting to foreclose production or to delay it as long as possible. . . .

"As a consequence, the masters [and Ms. Walburn] have been directed to do more than masters are ordinarily requested to do and to supervise more closely than ordinarily required. The present situation warrants this supervision."

As McNulty was issuing his order, Slaughter filed the anticipated recusal motion with Lord, arguing that the judge should remove himself from the case because he had shown "an unprecedented degree of hostility" toward Robins and "has interjected himself into the proceedings not as an unbiased arbitrator, but as a partisan advocate." Among his proofs, Slaughter pointed out to Lord that he had forced the consolidation of twenty-one cases although the defense was ready for trial in only one case, and had granted two plaintiffs' motions for delays while acceding to only one such request on the part of the defense. (Slaughter neglected to also point out that the delay Lord granted Robins was for four weeks while the total time allowed in the two delays granted the plaintiffs was two and a half weeks and had been made necessary by Robins's own tactics of delay.)

At three that afternoon, the Eighth Circuit Court of Appeals heard Robins's appeal of Lord's discovery order. Slaughter argued that the order placed an "unreasonable burden" on Robins because of the enormity of the task. If the file drawers containing the requested documents were laid end to end, he told the three-judge court, they would stretch out more than a mile, a startling admission considering what it said about Robins's compliance with discovery orders in previous cases.

During the proceedings, members of the court urged both sides to remain in the room and try to settle the remaining cases still before Lord. The court was concerned over the fact that the empaneled jurors might read new accounts of the case or discuss it with others while waiting for the trial to begin. It urged that a mistrial be declared and a new jury empaneled when trial resumed. Six days later, Magistrate McNulty, following the Eighth Circuit Court of Appeal's urging, declared a mistrial.

By this time, Peter Thompson had returned to Minneapolis to take care of some unfinished business; Thomas Bartsh, meanwhile, had returned to Richmond late on the twenty-second to take over from Roberta Walburn the supervision of discovery.

The next day, February 23, the Eighth Circuit brushed aside Robins's arguments and gave the company fifteen days in which to comply. Lord wasted no time. Almost immediately upon hearing of the decision, he denied the motion to remove himself from the case. He then set March 26 as the new date for the trial. He also gave Robins ten days to catalog and turn over the documents so that he could rule on which to make available to the plaintiffs within the fifteen-day deadline set by the higher court. Finally, he set a ten-day deadline for the completion of all depositions.

Unbelievably, until this point not a single document had been turned over to the masters. The next morning, February 24, Lord was back in full command. He ordered everyone at Richmond to get cracking, or else. The documents began to trickle out.

Robins, however, was now up against it. Only one course remained: to settle the remaining cases before Lord's discovery process bore too much damaging fruit. Its attorneys were apparently ordered to settle the cases for as much money as necessary. In fact, the dollar amount of the settlement—a reported $4.6 million (the actual amount is sealed), more than the plaintiffs had sued for in the first place—proved to be the easy part. Mike Ciresi had completed those negotiations within hours of the Eighth Circuit's decision upholding Lord.

There were some problems, however. For one thing, two plaintiffs, Karen Gardiner and Deborah Michalik, after hearing impassioned pleas from Larson and Ciresi that there was more involved here than their injuries, that all Dalkon Shield victims needed their help, agreed to hold out for as long as possible in order to allow discovery to continue. "These women are owed a lot of credit for their courage," the attorneys agree. At any time before the settlement was finally signed, Robins could have withdrawn the money offer. One woman even kept the offer a secret from her husband because she feared he would pressure her into settling early.

Another problem was that Larson and Ciresi were playing hardball, demanding things that in the past Robins would never have agreed to in order to settle. Among these demands was the presence at the signing of the settlements of three top Robins executives (something Lord had suggested on February 24 when he first learned that there might be an impending settlement): E. Claiborne Robins, Jr., the company's president and chief executive officer; William A. Forrest, Jr., the vice-president and general counsel; and Carl D. Lunsford, Ph.D., the company's director of research and development. Their presence was required, Larson explained, because Robins had a history of not paying judgments by exhaustively appealing them, except in rare instances, and of not paying settlements, arguing that top management disagreed with those settlements. He did not want that to happen in these cases. He also wanted the Robins executives on record as having approved the settlements so that they could never again testify, as they had already done on other occasions (including during the consolidated proceedings) that they never had any real knowledge of what went on in Dalkon Shield litigation.

Another demand was that the two awards Larson's and Ciresi's firm had won for plaintiffs in the Strempke and Hahn cases would be paid as a part of the settlement of these cases (again because of Robins's history of not paying judgments, having paid only two until that point over the twelve-year history of Dalkon Shield litigation).

Larson and Ciresi also wanted to set up a system whereby the several hundred other Dalkon Shield plaintiffs in Minnesota, many of whom were clients of their firm, would be assured that discovery would continue after the consolidated cases were settled. As such, they wanted Robins to agree to have a nondestruct order entered by U.S. District Court judge Robert J. Renner, who was presiding over other Dalkon Shield suits, that would cover all documents ordered produced by Judge Lord.

The two attorneys also wanted guarantees that Robins would make no effort to have any of the remaining Dalkon Shield cases being handled by their firm transferred to other jurisdictions, as the Robins attorneys had attempted in the consolidated cases before Judge Lord.

It became a race for time under terrific pressure. The masters were down in Richmond, finally getting their hands on the documents Lord had ordered produced two weeks earlier. Robins had put an incredible money offer on the table that had been accepted but could still be withdrawn, which made for a great deal of tension. Soon, the pace became a frantic battle of wits and stamina, a test of endurance that Robins counted on winning merely because of the size of its litigation army.

"Some newspaper article after the settlement said we had worn down the Robins attorneys," Larson laughs. "Well, they had an army of attorneys, and here it was just Mike and me going at it, eighteen, twenty hours a day. We were the ones who were exhausted."

Over the February 25–26 weekend, a marathon round of talks were held at various sites, including the Robins, Zelle offices, at Faegre and Benson, and at the Oppenheimer firm. By Sunday night, with the talks then being held at the Faegre offices, Larson and Ciresi were close to reaching an agreement. They were too tired, however, to trust themselves to continue alone. They, therefore, called partner Larry Zelle to join them in an effort to make certain that they had not missed any Robins traps. The meeting that night lasted until 1:30 A.M. When Larson, Ciresi, and Zelle left for their respective homes, they believed that all of the major issues had been resolved. The settlement would be completed in the morning.

On Monday morning, the venue for the "final" talks was the Oppenheimer offices. Robins's out-of-state attorneys came in and put a check on the table for the agreed-on money settlement and said, in effect, "Take it or leave it; we're not going to agree to these collateral demands." Larson and Ciresi looked at each other in disbelief; all their hard work had just gone down the tubes. "You blew it," Larson told them and the meeting broke up. Ciresi went into another room and immediately made reservations to leave for Richmond that afternoon to continue the taking of the depositions. Larson, disheartened and exhausted, returned to his office to prepare for that day's meeting with Judge Lord.

The judge's pace through all this was no less exhausting. "It was obvious that Lord was putting in the same kind of hours we were—eighteen to twenty a day," Larson says. "He was always ready with his orders and they were always on point. He'd be spending his days and nights reading all of the deposition testimony, and the documents—and you knew he was because of what he would do and say—and he'd be taking phone calls from us on the continuing depositions to iron out problems, and getting reports from the masters and giving them instructions, he'd be holding hearings—he was in it as deep as anyone." On top of all that, Lord still had the rest of his case load to handle.

One of the reasons that the settlement negotiations had broken down was the method of continuing discovery. The Robins attorneys, for example, had agreed to preserve the discovered documents, but they refused to formalize that agreement with a nondestruct order, arguing that such an order would imply that Robins otherwise destroyed documents.

Also, Robins was willing to pay the *Strempke* and *Hahn* judgments, but only on condition that Larson and Ciresi would sit on their hands and not object when Robins moved to have those judgments set aside. This was a crucial point, however, for Larson and Ciresi and one they did not wish to abandon. The main reason Robins in the past had demurred in paying judgments, they reasoned, was that to do so could eventually lead to the approval of a collateral estoppel motion; a judge would point to the record of final judgments and say that, based on that record, Robins's negligence was now a proven fact. Therefore, even though it would pay the Strempke and Hahn judgments, it wanted no record of it.

Later on the twenty-seventh, as Ciresi flew to Richmond, Larson appeared in Judge Lord's chambers for the scheduled conference. He told Lord that the settlement negotiations had gone poorly and that, as a consequence, the plaintiffs wanted a formal hearing on a nondestruct order. The judge noted that he had prepared some remarks for the three Robins executives and had hoped to have had an opportunity to deliver them when the settlement was signed; now, apparently, he would not get that opportunity. Lord then ordered everyone into court for the nondestruct hearing.

As they were leaving Lord's chambers, Slaughter and other Robins attorneys approached Larson. "What do you think the judge will say to them?" Larson recalls being asked. "Will the judge sanction them? How harsh will [his] comments be? [He'll] tell them to recall the device. [He'll] give them a piece of his mind." Later, the Robins attorneys asked Lord similar questions in the hallway, as Slaughter himself recalled it.

Once in court, Larson formally requested the nondestruct order. Chuck Socha immediately objected. Lord asked the Robins attorney "what harm could come from a protective order that would require that no one destroy any documents or move them or shuffle them about."

"We have no objection, your honor, to the notion of not destroying documents," Socha said. "We do not destroy documents. We feel that entry of such an order . . . is an insult to the integrity of our lawyers, your honor."

"You may feel that way," Lord responded, "but I enter [non]destructive orders time after time ex parte, and it's no reflection on anybody."

"Well, your honor," Socha argued, "that does constitute a reflection, I believe, and I'm not—"

"I'll hear no argument on that," the judge cut in. "I've said that I do it ex parte and it reflects on no one."

Later on during the course of the hearing, judge and attorney clashed again when Socha would not give Lord a straight answer to a simple question. "Do you know where the documents are, for instance, the wicking file [referring to any documents ever in Robins's possession that referred to the wicking tendency of the Dalkon Shield's tailstring]?" Lord asked.

"Well, I don't believe there is any such thing as a wicking file, your honor," Socha parried.

"You take the generic name," Lord thrust back, "the tests and so forth we have referred to here as wicking files—do you know what that sort of generic description means?"

Socha had defended Robins many times and, each time, the central issue was whether the Dalkon Shield tailstring wicked bacteria into the uterus. Nevertheless, he answered Lord by saying, "Well, I don't know what you mean by it, your honor."

It was not the answer Lord was prepared to hear from Socha at this point. "Do you know what *you* have meant by it, as counsel [has] used that term?"

"Well . . . , I try to avoid using those terms, your honor. I think they are too vague to really give us a real grasp or a handle on what these documents refer to. And [there's] been a lot of confusion about that on the record."

"Has there?" Lord asked sarcastically.

"Yes sir."

"Who created the confusion?" Lord continued.

"Well, I think whoever it was that first coined the term 'wicking' and hung it onto documents."

Socha, of course, was keenly aware that the term "wicking" first appeared in an internal Robins memorandum dated June 29, 1970, and that it credited the term to the IUD's coinventor, Irwin Lerner. Lord was just as keenly aware of this. Frustrated and exhausted, he was understandably getting quite fed up with Socha's game-playing. "Where are the files that Mr. Robins [Sr.] directed be sent to him concerning wicking?" the judge demanded. "Do you know?"

"Well, I am not sure that Mr. Robins did that, your honor." Socha was not about to give in, no matter how angry Lord became.

"Will you answer my question?" the judge again demanded. "Let's assume he did it. Do you know where those files are?"

"Well, your honor, I—there is no way in the world that I can even respond to that—"

"Do you know?"

"I am telling you, your honor, I have no way to respond to that question."

". . . [D]o you know where those files are?"

"Well, your question, your honor, assumes there are in fact such files. . . . If I answer it, any way that I answer it I am conceding that . . . there are such files."

Lord's tone became more deliberate. "You disagree that there are such files?" he asked, deciding that it was time to do some setting up of his own.

"Yes sir, I certainly do."

"And you do that as an officer of this court with some knowledge of the subject matter?"

"Yes sir, your honor, I certainly do."

Lord was now determined to see how far Socha would go in his game. The judge, therefore, raised the stakes by baiting his purposely obvious trap for the Robins attorney. "That there are no files describing tests and things described in my first order, that they are non-existent, is that what you say *as an officer of the court?*"

"Oh, of course not, your honor," Socha said, stepping back a bit in order not to fall into Lord's trap. "But that is not what I understand you to be asking about. I understood you to be asking about something called 'wicking files,' and I don't think there are any such things."

"We will not use the term 'wicking files,' " Lord said finally.

"Okay," Socha quickly interjected, "then if you will reframe your question, I will do my best to answer it."

"I will not reframe my question." Lord now had his fill of Socha's tactics. "You answer it as it is written in the [February 8 discovery order calling for 'all documents containing opinions, reports of tests, examinations or studies concerning the safety or characteristics of the Dalkon Shield," i.e., its wicking tendency], or else cease talking. . . ."

"Your honor, what are we referring to now?" Socha inquired, ever so politely. He was clearly baiting the judge now.

"I am referring to something that will cause you to pin yourself down to what was written in the original order for production of documents that was issued a couple of weeks ago."

"I guess I don't understand what you are focusing on now, your honor."

"Then take your seat."

"Well, am I not to be permitted, your honor, to complete—"

"No."

"—making my record on the objections to the [nondestruct] order?"

"You should make objections based on something you know about," Lord snapped.

Subsequently, the judge issued his nondestruct order covering any and all documents referred to in his February 8 order.

Meanwhile, in Richmond, Bartsh and Thompson were pressing onward with their discovery task. Bartsh, for one, made an amazing find: of the 160,000-odd documents contained in the so-called source file room, approximately 100,000 of them had never been produced to the MDL. "The statements made by several of Robins's attorneys regarding the source file were . . . [thus] inaccurate . . . ," he has since stated. "There is no question that the production order required the production of thousands of documents which had not been previously produced."

Finally, early on February 28, Robins's attorneys decided it was safer to throw in the towel than to continue discovery under Judge Lord. They reached an agreement with Larson that, incredibly, allowed for almost every point requested by the plaintiffs' attorneys, including: a new nondestruct order to pick up after Lord's order terminated as of the moment of settlement; continuation at a later date of discovery (but without the use of court-appointed masters); the payment of the *Strempke* and *Hahn* judgments; and the attendance at the signing of the settlement of Robins, Jr., Forrest, and Lunsford. As part of the settlement, Larson insisted that Lord would have to approve portions of it and that the signing had to be done in open court. He says he had made it clear to the Robins attorneys that, if Lord "raised any problems at any time with the manner in which evidence or future court proceedings were being treated or affected by the agreement," the deal would be off. It was not made clear, however, whether Lord's approval was to be made in any official way.

For their part, Larson and Ciresi agreed not to oppose the effort to vacate the *Strempke* and *Hahn* judgments. (Those motions were nevertheless denied.) "It was a great deal, all things considered," Larson explained. "We even got agreement that Robins wouldn't move to transfer any of our out-of-state cases. It was time to settle. We needed about thirty days to rest before getting started on our other Dalkon Shield cases."

On February 28, the Robins attorneys appeared in St. Paul before Judge Renner, along with Larson, to enter the nondestruct order, which was nearly identical to the one Lord had issued the day before. Sitting beside Renner on the bench was Lord. Larson stated clearly for the record that "finalization of [the settlement agreement] requires the presence of [the three Robins officers] . . . in court before Judge Lord. The agreement will not be final until that occurs . . . and that is part of the settlement commitment that has been made by the defendant."

Larson then pointed out that the three Robins executives would be available as early as the next morning. Lord, therefore, scheduled the settlement agreement to be executed in his courtroom at 10 A.M. the next day, February 29. "I'll approve what you bring before me tomorrow," he added. No one objected.

The Robins attorneys, therefore, had agreed to put the settlement before Lord for his approval and they fully expected him to have a few words to say to Robins, Jr., Forrest, and Lunsford. They even had a pretty good idea of what those words would be. (When

Robins eventually filed its misconduct complaint against Judge Lord, Griffin Bell denied all of this, even though most of it was done on the record.)

What they did not know was the impact those words would have.

10

THE JUDGE HAS HIS SAY

For several days before the settlement was finalized, Judge Lord had considered his next move. These Dalkon Shield cases were the only ones in his jurisdiction on which he would be able to sit because of the conflict-of-interest situation created when Robins hired the Oppenheimer firm in which his son-in-law was employed. In other words, his time to gain justice for the victims of the Dalkon Shield was running out—and so were his options.

There was a great deal he had wanted to accomplish, Lord thought as he contemplated the inevitability of settlement over the February 25–26 weekend. He had wanted to influence the future course of events in some positive way. He had wanted, for example, to end the judicial logjam that the cases were creating nationwide. He had wanted to end Robins's intimidation via the "dirty questions" (as he had already done in the cases before him). He had wanted to convince the company to mount a nationwide effort to alert all women still using the Dalkon Shield of the possible dangers to them and to their unborn children, and to promote the removal of the device, preferably at Robins's expense. And he had wanted Robins to own up to what it had done, to accept responsibility for those actions and to rectify the situation as best as possible.

He knew, however, that there was very little he could do legally at this point. He had been outmaneuvered; Robins and its army of litigators had outlasted him, it was as simple as that. Something else was called for, something that might shock the A. H. Robins Company into positive action on behalf of the victims and potential victims of its IUD.

Perhaps, he thought, he could prepare a statement of some kind, one that would lay out all that he had learned over the course of his involvement in this litigation, that would appeal to a sense of decency that might yet reside in the A. H. Robins Company and its officers who would be present in his courtroom? The idea quickly appealed to him and the words and thoughts began forming in his mind. That weekend, he set about writing that statement. It was this to which Lord subsequently referred on February 27 when he heard that the settlement talks had broken down.

On the twenty-eighth, when Dale Larson announced that settlement had been reached pending Lord's approval of certain of its terms, another idea formed in the judge's mind as well. Perhaps he would give his approval by signing the settlement immediately under the words "So ordered." This could be tricky, and Lord knew it. To begin with, Larson's request apparently involved some form of review, but nothing formal. An out-of-court settlement is essentially a private contract; a judge's approval is unnecessary, although it is common practice in Minnesota to ask judges to formally dismiss settled cases. However, many more plaintiffs were waiting in the wings for their shot at justice and Larson wanted Lord to make certain that nothing in that agreement would impact negatively on those plaintiffs. Moreover, the settlement provided for certain mechanisms to be available to those future plaintiffs in pursuing their quest; putting the words "So ordered" on the settlement, therefore, would convert it into a decree, the violation of which would carry stiff contempt penalties.

Finally, Lord decided to play that one by ear. If, in fact, his understanding of Larson's intent was incorrect and his formal approval was required, he would sign it (provided he did, in fact, approve of it); however, if only his review and comments were required, he would decide what course to take as the hearing evolved.

Lord then set about the task of writing his "remarks." In doing so, he drew upon all of the deposition testimony he had read and that which he had supervised; the documents from the Robins files that had turned up during the multidistrict litigation proceedings;

and the testimony of experts in the five trials already decided in Minnesota.

There was, for example, the testimony that had been given during the Martha Hahn trial by Emanuel Friedman, M.D. His qualifications as an expert were (and are) beyond dispute: professorships at Columbia University, Chicago Medical School, and Harvard; prestigious positions at the Michael Reese Hospital in Chicago and Beth Israel Hospital in Boston; professional memberships and editorships at a variety of major obstetrics and gynecology journals; service on a number of U.S. Public Health Service and Food and Drug Administration panels, including the one which recommended that the Dalkon Shield not be allowed back on the market. (He had resigned from that committee when the FDA failed to heed its advice.)

"[D]irecting your attention to the Hugh Davis article [on which Robins based most of its claims] . . . , would that test be sufficient to form a basis, doctor, that the Dalkon Shield was safe?" Mike Ciresi asked Dr. Friedman during the Martha Hahn case.

"No. . . ."

"Would that test be sufficient to form a statement that the Dalkon Shield was trouble-free . . . , that the Dalkon Shield was dependable . . . , that the Dalkon Shield had a superior design . . . , that an individual who utilized the Dalkon Shield would have her fertility restored immediately upon removal . . . , that the Dalkon Shield would not produce any effect on the body, blood, or brain of an individual who utilized it?"

"No, sir."

"Was that study . . . conducted in accordance with [accepted] standards of testing . . . ? Is there anything in [Dr. Davis's article] that reflects that that study was conducted in accordance with those testing standards?"

"No, sir, none whatsoever. . . ."

Ciresi then launched into a question that, if the context were not so serious, might have qualified as an entry in the Guinness Book of World Records. Lasting about twenty minutes in length, it set out a series of "assumptions" Ciresi wanted Dr. Friedman to make. These "assumptions" were, in fact, part of the material that until that point in the trial had been placed into evidence, and parts of the testimony given at the trial either through "live" A. H. Robins witnesses or through videotaped depositions. Dr. Friedman was asked to "assume" these things because he had not been in court when they were introduced.

"Doctor," Ciresi asked finally, "based upon your training and experience, expertise, your consultation with drug companies, based upon the testimony I've asked you to assume . . . , do you have an opinion as to whether the Dalkon Shield was an unreasonably dangerous device when used for its intended purpose?"

"Yes, I have an opinion."

"What is that opinion?"

"It was. . . ."

"Do you have an opinion whether the Dalkon Shield was defective at all times during its marketing and use and in all of its models and designs?"

"I do have an opinion. . . . It was defective."

"And do you have an opinion as to whether the Dalkon Shield was adequately tested for safety prior to January 1st, 1971 . . . ?"

"It clearly was not."

"Do you have an opinion, doctor, as to whether the Dalkon Shield was ever safe . . . ?"

"It was never safe."

"And, doctor, do you have an opinion as to whether the Dalkon Shield was adequately tested for efficacy prior to January 1, 1971 . . . ?"

"It was never adequately tested for efficacy. . . ."

"And, doctor, do you have an opinion as to whether A. H. Robins . . . acted in disregard of the safety and welfare of women who used the Dalkon Shield by marketing this device."

"I have an opinion, yes."

"And what is that opinion . . . ?"

"They clearly did. . . . In regard to the safety and efficacy, [they] obviously were acting in disregard of such matters."

Of particular interest to Judge Lord, other than the depositions of Robins, Sr., and Robins, Jr., were the twenty-one volumes of deposition testimony of William A. Forrest, Jr., one of the three men whom the judge had suggested be in his court once a settlement was reached. In many instances, Forrest's testimony would try the faith of even the most believing of people.

The deposition was taken in Lord's courtroom, with Forrest sitting in the witness box and Mike Ciresi standing by a lectern about twelve feet to his right doing the questioning. Presiding was Magistrate McNulty, and a videotape crew recorded the proceedings.

"There was always something sad and melancholy about him," Ciresi's paralegal assistant, Ann Barcelow, says of Forrest. Especially on the first day, the Robins in-house attorney seemed ill at ease, often rocking back and forth in his chair, and snatching quick glances way over to his right beyond Ciresi to the defense counsel table, where Chuck Socha sat.

At one point during the first day of the deposition, February 10, 1984, Ciresi was questioning Forrest about a series of notes he had taken during the time the A. H. Robins Company was negotiating for purchase of the Dalkon Shield. "The next notes . . . show a date of June 5th, 1970, correct?"

"Yes," the dapper-looking Forrest agreed, arching his right eyebrow a bit as he looked down at a number of full-sized sheets of paper. The pages were joined together by a staple in the left corner and there was a black-bordered yellow exhibit label on the upper right-hand corner of the top sheet.

"And one of your notes is that [Dr. Hugh] Davis is not impartial, correct?" Ciresi asked, his hands now spread out to grip either side of the wide lectern.

"That is correct . . . ," Forrest said, looking alternately at the papers in his hand and at his questioner. "I took down that note to suggest that he had participated in the development of the product and I thought it was important that the product be checked out with other persons as a part of our acquisition process. . . . [Dr. Davis had an] interest in the Dalkon Corporation."

This was an important admission from the chief in-house attorney for Robins. To begin with, it was clear to Forrest that, because of Dr. Davis's financial interest in the Dalkon Shield, his data was suspect and "that the product [should] be checked out with other persons" before the company bought it. However, Robins never informed physicians of Dr. Davis's financial interest even while using his data to promote the Dalkon Shield, thus denying those physicians the knowledge that they, too, should check "with other persons." Also, the note showed that the A. H. Robins Company—and especially Forrest—knew of Dr. Davis's financial interest before they sent him to testify in Dalkon Shield litigation, testimony in which he denied under oath that he had any such financial interest.

During the long course of the Forrest deposition, the Robins vice-president and general counsel insisted that he would have advised the company to take responsible action if he knew the Dalkon Shield was dangerous, but that the number of cases he knew about was too small to make such a judgment. Ciresi tried a number of novel approaches to get Forrest to admit that even one case should have been sufficient. One such approach was of a highly personal nature.

"Mr. Forrest," Ciresi began this line of questioning, "I want you to assume that the [Dalkon Shield] tailstring was open-ended [and] multifilamented. I want you to assume that it had a wicking tendency. I want you to assume that it would wick . . . bacteria. I want you to assume that bacteria in the uterus can cause disease, meaning loss of reproductive organs or even death. Having all those assumptions in mind and assuming them to be true . . . , you would certainly expect [the medical department] to conduct the most basic wicking tests and that would be to wick water?"

Forrest's hands remained cupped on his lap. ". . . [I] think they would conduct or obtain information of any type relative to the characteristics of the product that would bear on its safety and effectiveness, yes, sir. . . ."

"And are you aware," Ciresi said the word slowly, for emphasis, "that the medical department never conducted a wicking test . . . ?"

"[T]hat's correct, sir," Forrest responded in his calm unemotional tone.

"You're not aware of such tests, are you?" the plaintiffs' attorney said, with perhaps just a trace of contempt in his voice.

"No, sir."

"Mr. Forrest," Ciresi began his next question, "I want you to assume you . . . were going to have an operation on your scrotum and you had a choice of sutures, one being a monofilament, solid on the interior, one being a multifilament [and] open-ended. And [the multifilament] suture was reported by your doctor to have a wicking tendency. And the manufacturer has stated that the sheath surrounding the filaments was meant to keep bacteria out but it can deteriorate in [place] and that the manufacturer knew that could happen, but . . . [not] how frequently it happened. And the doctor told you that if it could wick and if bacteria got in there and moved through, you might lose your reproductive organs. Now, do you believe that that . . . should be warned about . . . ?"

"Obviously, I am interested in . . . a suture which does not entail my getting a disease or getting injured by it, yes, sir. . . ."

"And you would want to know what the manufacturer knew with respect to the fact that that multifilament string might wick, might cause bacteria to get into your reproductive organs and may result in the loss of them. Is that a risk factor you would want to know about . . . ?"

"If it would cause disease, in fact cause disease, yes, sir."

"Yes," Ciresi smiled, "and it wouldn't make any difference to you if it caused disease in one man who lost his penis or a hundred, or a thousand, would it, sir?"

"In terms of one person, I'm not sure. I would be interested in it as an individual, yes, sir."

"Sure. I'm sure you would, sir," Ciresi said. Another smile crossed his face as he began asking his next question. "Now, directing your attention to the Dalkon Shield tailstring, do you think women would have wanted to know that the string was reported by its inventor to have a wicking tendency . . . , that the purpose of the sheath was to prevent the intrusion of bacteria into the interior of that string and . . . that it would wick body fluids, including bacteria . . . , that the sheath, nylon nature of it, would cause it to deteriorate in [place] over a period of time? Do you think women who had that device inserted in them would have wanted to know that risk factor regardless, sir, of whether it happened in one woman or happened in a thousand women?"

Unfortunately, the question was objected to and never got answered, but Ciresi had made his point.

On another occasion, Ciresi used the hypothetical example of an upturned carpet in the A. H. Robins Company headquarters. He asked Forrest what the attorney would do about it. Forrest said he would report it to maintenance. Would he tell maintenance to fix it? Ciresi asked a number of times and in a number of ways. No, Forrest would answer, "that's not my job." He might suggest that maintenance repair the carpet, but not fix it. What if one person was injured? Ciresi pressed onward. Forrest said he might go over the maintenance man's head to the maintenance engineer, but that was all. And if it still had not been fixed and a woman died, what then? He might go as high as E. Claiborne Robins, Jr., to point out the problem, Forrest said.

"Now," Ciresi asked at length, "what if [Robins, Jr.,] told you, '[I] checked on that and our department who has responsibility for that tells [me] that the carpet has been turned up there like that for four years. It has been literally thousands and tens of thousands of people who walked across. They think the woman that tripped and died, she was negligent, and they don't want to fix it, and [I] agree.' Now, what would you tell . . . Mr. Robins Jr. at that point?"

"I might tell [Mr. Robins, Jr.,] I think it's a mistake, that it should be fixed; but having done that, I think I have discharged my responsibility."

"You would tell [him] that that was a hazard, wouldn't you, sir?"

"I think, when I spoke to [him] about it, I would tell [him] it's a problem in my mind because I think someone might trip on it."

"And it wouldn't make any difference to you if only one woman tripped on that and died, correct?"

"I think it would be more impressive if a number of people had tripped in terms of the suggestion I made to management, yes, sir. . . ."

"The greater the number of people that go by it or walk over it, the greater the risk, correct?"

"I think that would be the case, yes."

"And you would also have in mind that some people might . . . even be blind who might be walking over that rug, correct?"

"That's a possibility, yes."

"And they might not even see that hazard, correct . . . ? And they need more protection than those who have eyes who can see, correct?"

"I think it's fair to say that a blind person generally needs more protection than a person that has eyes."

"And that is because the defect or the hazard is unknown to that blind person because he or she can't see it, right?"

"Yes, sir."

Having carried Forrest this far, Ciresi now sprang his trap. "Have you ever looked at a Dalkon Shield tailstring . . . ?"

"Yes, sir, I have looked at a tailstring."

"And, by looking at it, can you see that it is multifilamented, open-ended?"

"I don't know that a layman by looking at the string can tell that it's multifilamented or open-ended . . . ," Forrest grudgingly admitted. "[And] I don't know whether a doctor would be any better qualified than a lay person to tell."

At another point, Ciresi tried to elicit from Forrest what discussions were held by Robins before "Dear Doctor II" was sent out in September 1980, in which the company suggested that any patients then wearing the Dalkon Shield should be advised to have it removed because the device would have been in place at that time for no less than six years.

"Was there any suggestion during these conversations by anyone that reference should be made in the 'Dear Doctor' letter that the Dalkon Shield was associated with a higher incidence of pelvic inflammatory disease than other IUDs . . . ?" Ciresi asked, his right hand in his pocket and his left hand holding a pen and resting on the lectern.

"That assumes a premise with which I don't agree—that there was any indication or basis for concluding at that time"—Forrest put a greater emphasis on those last three words—"that there was any greater risk of PID in women wearing the Dalkon Shield than other IUDs, to the best of my knowledge."

Ciresi could not allow the implication made by Forrest's voice to pass. "At that time?"

"That's correct, sir," Forrest said matter-of-factly.

"Do you agree today that the Dalkon Shield is associated with a higher incidence of PID than other IUDs?"

"No, sir."

"So you don't even agree with that today, do you?" Ciresi asked, again that trace of contempt for the witness in his voice.

"That is correct, sir . . . ," Forrest responded. "I do not agree with it."

Perhaps the most incredible testimony Forrest gave during his exhaustive deposition, however, involved what Forrest may have told his wife about the Dalkon Shield. The line of questioning had grown out of Ciresi's frustration with the Robins general counsel's inability to admit that the problems he had learned about regarding the Dalkon Shield were serious enough to warn physicians and women about them. It would be inconceivable, Ciresi felt, that a man would not tell his wife how dangerous the device was even if he was helping to keep that information from other women. Ciresi had even hoped to get this across to the juries that eventually would watch the videotaped deposition. Forrest, however, would not cooperate with the plaintiffs' attorney's strategy.

"Mr. Forrest," Ciresi asked as the afternoon session of the first day of deposition testimony got under way, "it is my understanding that your wife wore the Dalkon Shield, correct?"

"She did, yes, sir . . . ," Forrest admitted.

"During what period of time did she wear it?" Ciresi's tone at this time was matter-of-fact to match Forrest's.

"She wore it for a period of time there, I don't recall the exact time, she wore it for a couple of years there; it was during the early '70s there, yes, sir." Throughout his answer, Forrest would pause as if to try and draw the information from some dusty file cabinet in his mind.

"During the early '70s?" Ciresi asked.

Again, Forrest's answer was given haltingly, as if trying to get the answer right. "During the period, I don't know, it was '71, '72, she had it inserted and wore it. Uh, I don't know when it was removed. It was removed sometime '75 or thereabouts. . . ."

Actually, as Forrest would testify much later, the Dalkon Shield was removed from Mrs. Forrest in July 1974, within two or three weeks of Robins's withdrawal of the device from the market at the behest of the FDA. Ciresi, however, was not aware of this at the time.

"Did you ever tell your wife that bacteria had been found within the interstices of the Dalkon Shield tailstring at any time before she had it removed?" Ciresi continued his questioning.

"I don't recall such a discussion"—a wisp of a smile appeared on Forrest's face—"because it wouldn't have been the nature of our relationship that I would have had that type of detailed discussion about the product. . . ."

When Ciresi had begun this line of questioning, he had expected yes answers; after all, that was the point he had been trying to make, that Forrest had told his wife what he would not tell other women. Nothing, however, that a Robins employee or officer could say surprised him anymore. Undaunted, he pressed onward.

"Did she have any problems with the Dalkon Shield, sir?" he asked in a follow-up question.

"Not that I know of, sir," came the response.

"You don't know of any infections or anything she had with the Dalkon Shield?" Ciresi asked.

"No," said Forrest. "I didn't inquire into—" The Robins attorney paused for a moment, then changed the nature of his answer. "Again," he explained, "this is a matter I thought between my wife and her gynecologist."

At one point, Ciresi asked Forrest whether his wife had another IUD inserted after the Dalkon Shield. She had not, he was told. This made Ciresi wonder why a woman who was still capable of having children would not have had another IUD inserted. True, the Forrests could have used another form of contraception, but something in the way the witness was answering these questions suggested another possibility. In what he admits was a long-shot question, he asked, "Did your wife ever have any operations to her reproductive organs after the use of the Dalkon Shield?"

"She eventually had a hysterectomy, yes," said Forrest. The long shot had paid off.

". . . And when did she have it . . . ?"

"I don't recall the year. . . ."

"At or near the time the Dalkon Shield was removed, sir?"

"Sometime afterward," Forrest stated.

"Shortly after?" Ciresi pursued the point.

"I don't recall. . . ."

"Did her doctor advise her that her hysterectomy was in any way related to the Dalkon Shield?" Ciresi asked.

"Not that I know of, sir," Forrest answered.

"Did you ever ask her that?" Ciresi went on.

". . . I don't recall. I may have asked her that. . . ."

"You just don't know one way or the other . . . ?"

"That's correct, sir. . . ."

"Was your wife ever diagnosed as having pelvic inflammatory disease?" Ciresi asked next.

"I don't know, Mr. Ciresi," Forrest responded.

"You don't know?" Ciresi asked incredulously.

"I do not know, sir," came Forrest's reply.

"You never asked that?"

"Again, I have suggested to you that"—again, a trace of a smile appeared in Forrest's face—"this is something that I preferred to leave between my wife and her gynecologist, and to my knowledge I don't recall any discussions. . . ."

"And are you telling the ladies and gentlemen of the jury, Mr. Forrest, that you and your wife have never had any discussion about whether or not the Dalkon Shield played any part in her hysterectomy?"

"I had no reason to believe that it did. . . ."

"Didn't she have the hysterectomy right at the time the Shield was removed?"

"I told you, I don't recall exactly when that occurred."

As it turned out, Mrs. Forrest's hysterectomy was performed in October 1974, just two months after the Dalkon Shield was removed. Ciresi would learn this much later in the deposition testimony.

On a subsequent day in the continuing deposition, Ciresi was asking Forrest a series of questions regarding the May 8, 1970, letter from the A. H. Robins Company to physicians that has come to be known as "Dear Doctor I." In that letter, Robins informed the physicians that problems had been reported to it about the Dalkon Shield and that, although it was standing by the product, women being fitted for it should be warned of the possibility that a therapeutic abortion might be necessary in the event of pregnancy. Ciresi had been trying to get Forrest to admit that the letter did not accurately represent what Robins then knew to be the true extent of the Dalkon Shield's problems. After several attempts, he decided to find out if Forrest had at least discussed "Dear Doctor I" and what had led to it with his wife.

"Around the time the 'Dear Doctor' letter was going to go out," he asked, "you had a discussion with your wife concerning the removal of [her] Dalkon Shield, did you not?" It was a reasonable assumption, rooted in humankind's natural concern for the health and safety of loved ones. Forrest's answer, however, was unnatural.

"I don't recall a discussion in that regard, no, sir," Forrest said with that same deadpan tone he had been using throughout.

"You mean," Ciresi said with more than a trace of disbelief in his voice, "after you met regarding the 'Dear Doctor' letter one, after that information had been brought to your attention by the medical department, you didn't have a conversation with your wife concerning the fact that she ought to go see her doctor relative to the removal of the device . . . ?"

"As I suggested to you," Forrest said, "I talk to my wife from time to time. I don't recall a specific discussion in which I said, 'You ought to go talk to your gynecologist to the end of having the Dalkon Shield removed, no, sir."

"Do you recall a general discussion concerning that subject matter, sir?" Ciresi followed up.

"The removal of the Dalkon Shield . . . ? No, sir. Again, this is something I left to my wife's gynecologist. . . ."

"Was she having problems of a gynecological nature at the time the Dalkon Shield was removed?" Ciresi pressed his line of questioning.

At this point, Chuck Socha, who was there representing Robins, objected. "I fail to see the relevance of this line of interrogation, this subject matter, which is highly personal to anything involved with this lawsuit," he told Magistrate McNulty.

"The entire lawsuit is entirely personal," McNulty responded calmly. "The objection is overruled."

"Yes," Forrest then said, "my wife had gynecological problems from time to time. . . . As I indicated, my wife was forty-one years of age at that time. She had had, I assume, some gynecological problems. I believe that was the case."

"Okay," said Ciresi, "at the time the Shield was removed, correct?" He was reaching, but it was worth a shot, he felt.

"Not necessarily at the time," Forrest responded coolly. "She may have had them before that time."

"I am not asking if she had it before," Ciresi countered. "I am saying at the time it was removed, she was having problems of a gynecological nature, correct?"

"I don't know this to be the case," Forrest responded.

"You just don't know one way or the other?"

"I don't know at that particular time that she had the Shield removed what, if any, gynecological problems she was having. . . ."

On the next day, Ciresi asked Forrest whether he had discussed his testimony with his wife over the last several days. He said he had. "Did you ask her whether she ever had any pelvic inflammatory disease?" Ciresi then asked.

"I didn't ask her that, no, sir," Forrest responded.

And then there was the testimony of Carl Lunsford, Ph.D. Dr. Lunsford, heavyset and double-chinned, with a receding hairline, had been deposed at the offices of Robins, Zelle, Larson & Kaplan under the supervision of another federal magistrate, Earl J. Cudd. Throughout the several days of testimony, he sat slightly slouched in his chair, hardly ever moving and with only one expression throughout: one that blended contempt for having been dragged into the proceedings with the painful look of a man who wished he were somewhere—anywhere—else.

His "hear no evil, read no evil, ask no evil, recall no evil" answers to Larson's questions were usually brief and to *his* point: namely that, as was the case with Robins, Sr., and Robins, Jr., he took no personal responsibility for anything relating to the Dalkon Shield because he only supervised the people responsible and had no direct involvement. In fact, Lunsford's answers often were so brief that getting information from him was like pulling teeth with rubber pliers.

"What's your profession?" Larson asked as the deposition got under way.

"I'm a chemist . . . ," Lunsford replied, his voice rising with the last syllable as if he had more to add, although he did not.

"Are you employed by the company that sold the Dalkon Shield?" Larson followed.

After a brief pause, Lunsford said, "Yes, I am employed by the A. H. Robins Company. . . ."

"What's your position?"

"My present position is director of research and development. . . ." Again, his voice rose slightly on the last syllable.

"Is the medical department of the A. H. Robins Company under your supervision and control, sir?"

"It is at the present time, yes," Lunsford answered.

"How long has it been under your supervision and control?"

"Since April of 1978. . . ."

"What amount of time did you spend concerning the Dalkon Shield during this year, 1984 [which is a month and a half old]?" Larson asked.

"Essentially none," came the reply.

"Have you talked to anybody in 1984 about the Dalkon Shield?" the attorney continued.

"I talked to [Robins attorney Frank] Tatum in preparation for this deposition. . . . I've talked to Dr. Robert Tankersely and Dr. Ed Martin [of the Robins research division]."

"Have you ever talked to E. C. Robins Jr. about it this year?"

"I have not."

"Do you report to him?"

"I do."

"He's your immediate supervisor, is that correct . . . ?"

"He is. . . ."

"Have you met with him in 1984?"

"I have met with him in 1984."

"Approximately how many times?"

"Oh, approximately four times."

"In his office?"

"Yes. . . ."

"Mr. Robins know you're here to give testimony?"

"He does."

"Did you tell him?"

"I did not tell him, no."

"Who told him?"

"I'm not sure who told him."

"How do you know that he knows?"

There was a long pause, lasting about eight seconds, before Lunsford replied. "I answered that question assuming that he is kept informed by the legal department of whoever is being deposed . . . ," he finally said.

"When did you talk to Dr. Tankersely this year about the Dalkon Shield . . . ?" Larson asked a few minutes later.

"Oh, approximately two weeks ago," was the reply.

"How long did that conversation last?" Larson inquired of the witness.

"Ten minutes, perhaps. . . ."

"Have you reviewed any documents before coming here to testify?" the plaintiff's attorney then wanted to know.

"Uhh, review? Yes."

"What have you reviewed?" Larson pursued the point.

"I don't recall, exactly. . . ."

"Did you ask anybody for any documents?"

"I did not."

"Did anybody give you documents?"

"Yes . . . , Mr. Tatum gave me some documents."

"What documents did you review?"

"I reviewed a previous deposition that I'd given."

"Anything else?"

"Yes, I reviewed a deposition given by Dr. [Fletcher B.] Owen. . . . ?

"Is Dr. Fletcher Owen in the medical department under your supervision and control?"

Lunsford nodded. "He's in the medical services department and heads that department."

"Is that department under your supervision and control?"

"It's under my supervision, yes, sir."

"Did you talk to Dr. Owen this year about the Dalkon Shield?"

"No, sir."

"Has he talked to you"—Larson emphasized the word "you"—"about the Dalkon Shield?"

"No, sir."

"He spends about seventy-five percent of his time on Dalkon Shield litigation, doesn't he, sir?"

"That is correct."

"And you haven't talked to him about the Dalkon Shield at all, correct?"

"Not the Shield, no, sir."

"Does he report directly to you?"

"He does. . . ."

At a subsequent session, Larson attempted to elicit from Lunsford the processes by which A. H. Robins drew up the "Dear Doctor II" letter. The board of directors' minutes obtained through Judge Lord's discovery had alluded to discussions of a possible recall of the Dalkon Shield. If this could be proven, it would further add to the case against Robins because, among other things, it would show that the company did take seriously the problems being caused by the device, something it denies up until this day. Once again, however, the witness was not being very informative.

"Did you keep notes of any of the meetings, Dr. Lunsford?" Larson asked at one point.

"I did not, no sir," Lunsford replied.

"Why not?" Larson inquired.

"It's not my habit to keep notes of meetings," the chemist explained.

"So you don't ordinarily keep notes of any meeting, is that right?"

"That's my ordinary, uh, practice, yes. . . ."

"Is it your testimony, Dr. Lunsford, that you never take notes concerning observations about the safety or efficacy of a device at meetings?"

"I believe I said that it's not my ordinary practice to take notes at meetings," Lunsford said after about seven seconds.

"But you do take notes about the safety and efficacy of devices or products, is that correct?"

"On occasion I might, yes, sir. . . ."

"Dr. Lunsford, did you keep any notes whatsoever about the safety or efficacy of the Dalkon Shield pertaining to any of the meetings you had [regarding 'Dear Doctor II'] . . . ?"

"No, sir."

Now it was Larson's turn to take a long pause. Somehow, he had to be able to get the witness to open up. "Who took notes of those meetings?" the attorney asked after about ten seconds.

"I don't recall anyone taking notes," said Lunsford.

"So you didn't see anybody with a piece of paper in front of him, and a pen, jotting anything down during any of those meetings, is that correct?"

". . . I don't recall anyone doing that."

"Did you receive any memoranda or correspondence concerning the subject of any of those meetings?" Larson tried again, using a different approach.

". . . I don't recall if I did," replied Lunsford.

"Did you generate any correspondence or memoranda concerning the subject matter of those meetings?"

"No, sir."

"So, as far as you know, all of these meetings took place and, uh, the 'Dear Doctor' issued without any memoranda, notes, or correspondence documenting either the facts, the background, or the history leading up to that letter, is that correct . . . ?"

"I don't recall any such documentation."

After another ten-second pause to rethink his approach, Larson tried again. "Do you have any policies or procedures," he asked, "within the . . . R&D department, as you call it, concerning the documentation of safety or efficacy information?"

"We don't have any specific policy, but if data is generated, either internally or externally, it is documented," Lunsford said after taking about ten seconds to frame his response.

"It is the R&D department's policy to document safety and efficacy information and opinions, is it not?" Larson thought he had Lunsford now.

"Sir, we don't have any specific policy, but if data is generated it would certainly be recorded and, therefore, documented."

"Well, if doctors within your medical department under your supervision and control come to the conclusion that there is a particular problem with respect to safety or efficacy, isn't it their custom and practice to document that information?" Larson tried yet again.

"That would ordinarily be the custom, yes."

"But you're not aware of any documentation within your department concerning any of these events or opinions exchanged leading up to the 'Dear Doctor' letter of 1980, is that correct?"

"I'm, uh, unaware of any documentation generated, yes, sir, in the medical department."

Such was the nature of the testimony by the people for whom Lord was preparing his remarks. It clearly helped him to define the approach he would take in that speech.

So did some of the other material Lord read. There was, for example, Ciresi's summation in the Martha Hahn case. Talking about "Dear Doctor I," Ciresi had told the jurors:

"They finally tell doctors about septic abortions, but they don't tell them about the other PID [problems], they don't tell them any of that, and they don't tell them to take them out of asymptomatic women because there's a time bomb ticking away within their uterine cavities." The ticking time bomb analogy was one that would appeal to Lord's sense of the dramatic, but he would want to make it uniquely his own, referring to the Dalkon Shield as "a deadly depth charge in their wombs, ready to explode at any time." He would use that in his speech, the judge decided.

As Dale Larson entered the courtroom on the morning of February 29, he had no idea what to expect. His instinct, however, told him it would be momentous. Sitting throughout the courtroom, various plaintiffs from the consolidated cases were waiting with great expectation for the events to follow. Some of them were looking at the officers of the company that had been responsible for their grief; others just seemed to look into themselves, as it were, still trying to understand what had happened to them and why; today, perhaps, they would get the answers to those questions.

"The opening scene—with all the officers and all their lawyers being there, there was a great deal of tension; you could cut the tension with a knife," Larson recalls. "Part of the tension was that we all wondered, I know I wondered, 'What the hell are these officers going to do, and what is Judge Lord going to do?' because he had told all of the lawyers about his desire to chat with these people."

As Larson proceeded to the plaintiff's counsel table at the front of the courtroom, he was approached by several of the Robins attorneys. "We had a bit of a colloquy—purely civil—about whether or not some of the other attorneys or I were going to subpoena these officers [now that they were in this jurisdiction and could be properly served]. I assured them that we were not, and that the assurances were good, but I also told them, 'You've got to assure me that no matter what happens here today, you're not going to bolt this courtroom.' And I was told, 'No, we're here for the finish.' "

Larson, admittedly exhausted by this point, was still not convinced that the settlement would be signed. That, however, was not the main reason for his wanting assurances that no one would leave the court until the session was over. "It wasn't so much that [the officers] were going to say no to the deal their lawyers had cut," he explains; "my concern was that either the officers or the lawyers for Robins would try to make it some kind of a platform for A. H. Robins by doing something like walking out of the courtroom, the negotiations were that tense. I wanted to be comfortable that I wasn't going to see any crazy antics from the defense."

The question of whether to sign the settlement was the first one

Judge Lord addressed as court convened. "[I]s there a place on that document for my signature?" he asked of Larson.

"There is not at this time, your honor," Larson said, still leaving the way open for just that.

"Is it anticipated that I will have to approve it?" Lord inquired further.

"It is not anticipated, your honor," Larson answered, adding, "but it is perfectly all right, if your honor would like to do so."

"Well, I'm not sure about that," Lord said, but he would consider it.

The judge then instructed that his clerks make copies of the settlement agreement and distribute it to all the other counsel in the consolidated cases, even though their particular cases had been settled previously. Because the dollar amount of the settlement was confidential, however, he warned members of the press seated in the courtroom that he would come down hard on anyone who posed as a consolidated plaintiff's counsel in order to get hold of a copy of the agreement.

The preliminaries out of the way, Lord got down to the signing by the Robins executives of the agreement itself. After that was done, he called on the signatories one by one.

"Now, Dr. Lunsford," the judge said, "have you reviewed this document?"

"Yes, sir," the Robins research and development chief said from his chair, with no trace of emotion.

"Do you know what is in it? You will please stand."

Lunsford rose. "Yes, sir."

"Do you know what the implications of it are?"

"I believe so, yes." Lunsford was clearly as uncomfortable now as he had been during his deposition.

"And you have signed this of your free will?"

"Yes."

"Very well, you may have your seat."

Judge Lord followed the same procedure with general counsel Forrest. Then he instructed E. Claiborne Robins, Jr., to stand.

"Have you read this document?" Lord asked the president and chief executive officer of the A. H. Robins Company.

"Yes, sir."

"Are you sure?" Lord's script had changed.

"Yes, sir."

"Is this the first document you have ever read in connection with the Dalkon Shield?" Lord asked.

"No, sir."

Larson smiled at an associate. He knew where the judge was headed. There were no smiles over at the defense table, however; they also knew what was coming.

"Someday maybe you'll tell how much you've read about it," Lord said grimly. "Did you sign this of your own free will?"

"Yes sir, I did," Robins answered, nodding his head.

After going through the same process with Alexander Slaughter, who had signed the agreement as counsel for Robins, the judge allowed himself a smile. "Well," he said, "we have it signed by the people who have no authority to revoke now, don't we . . . ? You see, one of the reasons I have asked for these people to come and to sign here, is because on another occasion in this same proceeding I dismissed some of the [out-of-town] lawyers and said 'now you proceed' to the Faegre and Benson lawyer [Jack Fribley] and they said, 'We have just taken his authority away from him to proceed.' So we don't want that to happen here."

Lord then made clear that he held Robins's local counsel at Faegre and Benson and the Oppenheimer firm in high regard. "Nothing I have said or will say should in any way reflect on those two local law firms," he said. "If there is anything that approaches censurable conduct, it has not happened in those law firms as far as I am able to determine."

The judge next began his review of the settlement itself. His major concern was its impact on other plaintiffs. He asked that the other plaintiffs' attorneys present read the settlement carefully and then report back to him later on in the hearing. He would decide then whether to take any formal action regarding the agreement.

Finally, Lord got to what, for him, was the high point of the proceeding. He handed his clerks two sets of documents. "The first set of documents . . . you can hand to counsel," as he spoke, the clerks were at the defense table, following the instructions he was giving as he gave them, "and you can hand it to Mr. Robins, and you can hand it to Mr. Forrest, and you can hand it to Dr. Lunsford, and"—now addressing the three Robins executives directly—"I am going to ask you to take time to read it and not leave this courtroom until you have read it. I may have a couple of questions about it.

"The particular document constitutes a speech that I made [on November 19, 1981,] to all the ministers in the state Council of Churches, where I talked about corporate sin and individual responsibility for the acts of a corporation. . . . And I'm going to ask you to stay here and read that. I may have a couple of questions about whether or not . . . you think anything in that speech . . . is anything that your company did."

Lord continued: "When you finish that, I have another document for you to read, a personal appeal to you about what you should do by way of a recall [of the Dalkon Shield]. I think it is a rather powerful document." Turning to E. Claiborne Robins, Jr., Lord added, a bit sarcastically, "And if your management style is such, Mr. Robins, that you could prevail upon your company to do what I have asked you to do in that document, I think your days on this earth and hereafter would be happier. . . ."

"I want you to read that document," Lord now addressed all three again. "I want you to read the next document. And if that doesn't change your ways, when you see what your lawyers have been doing in the name of Robins"—and again he turned to the young company president—"when you have the stamp of three generations on that company, you've got to have some personal feelings about what's going on, something besides the bottom line as your beacon and the low road as your route."

Lord then rose from his chair. "We'll recess now while you read the first document."

With that, he left the courtroom to return to chambers. There he received a telephone call from special masters Bartsh and Thompson in Richmond. They told him that they believed that at least 100,000 documents that should have been produced during the multidistrict litigation had not been produced.

While Lord was out of the courtroom, Robins, Forrest and Lunsford read through the Council of Churches speech. It was strong stuff, indeed.

"Having to sit in judgment of a fellow human being is not an easy thing to do," the Robins officers read Lord's words in that speech, "especially for someone who's very much aware of his own humanity. Nevertheless, it does provide considerable insight into the nature of persons and that condition we loosely refer to as sin.

"Now, what do I mean when I use the word 'sin' . . . Sin is the individual's transgression of the Law of God, the individual's moral failure, the individual's estrangement or alienation."

The judge then went on to explain that, just as God created the individual known as man, man created his own "individual," the corporation; unlike the Creator's individual, however, man's creation has no heart, soul, or conscience.

"This individual we've created is, in the eyes of the law, a person who has been, rightly or wrongly, afforded the rights and privileges and immunities that are accorded to natural-born people, those who *do* have a heart, soul and conscience," the Robins officers read on. "However, the corporate individual, unlike the person, does not have the legal or moral responsibilities imposed upon it.

"Many people denounce crime in the street, but few examine crime in the skyscraper. But just as the mugger in the street can cause problems as a member of our human family, so can the corporate individuals cause problems as they coexist with us, operating and exerting their influence on humanity. The mischief they can create is multiplied and magnified manyfold since the act of one is the act of many. . . ."

One paragraph in particular should have caused the Robins officers to sit up and take special notice, for it seemed to be both directed at them and a harbinger of things to come that morning:

"Unfortunately, with the corporations, we sometimes find people who are turning out foods or fibers or drugs and selling a product that is harmful and we can't find out exactly who's doing it. . . . If you go to the research department, you might find that somebody tested it on rats and wrote it up in a report. Where the report went, you'll never find out. Certainly, the people in the production department didn't know about it when they began the production. The sales department was never told. And it would be unthinkable to believe that one of the higher corporate officials got hold of information to the effect that what they are selling as a cure was actually poisoning people. The board of directors is the last to know."

As the Robins officers read on, they came across Lord's feelings regarding a concept known as the "cost-benefit analysis," an unfortunately common and socially acceptable computation in which the risk of harm a product may do is weighed against the benefit of that product to society in general and whether the cost of improving the product's safety is so high that fewer people will be able to benefit from it because of the higher expense. (By way of example, a major manufacturer some years ago was faced with the question of whether to correct a defect in the design of one of its products. It estimated that the cost to society accruing from the deaths and injuries that might be caused by that defect would total $49.5 million. The cost of making that product safer, a cost society must ultimately bear, came to $137 million. "Thus," the manufacturer asserted, "the cost is almost three times the benefits" and was thus not "cost-effective.")

"In the olden days—you know, golden olden days—if you killed somebody, if you produced something that would hurt somebody, you were stopped," Lord had said in his 1981 speech. "If you poisoned someone's cattle, you were stopped. If you burned all of the surface off someone's lands, you were stopped. Not today. Today, we have the cost-benefit analysis, where you weigh how much a human life is worth. Funny, I always thought life was a sacred and priceless thing. . . . When you put a price on the priceless, all is lost. . . .

"[W]e don't have much sense about how we do this cost-benefit analysis. There is no rhyme or reason to it. We sort of play Russian Roulette. . . . Even Hitler, when he was butchering people, articulated a reason for his madness. We don't even do that. We go along and make those sacrifices in easy stages. We poison them in the womb and in the milk of their mothers' breasts and the air that they breathe, the water that they drink, the food they eat. It is random selection imposed by the adults on the young and unborn generations. . . .

"THOU SHALL NOT STEAL applies to every corporate official who sells shoddy, dangerous or unusable merchandise in the name of profit. THOU SHALL NOT KILL applies to the corporation and agencies of those who are killing and maiming through industrial pollution. This is done by individuals, by corporate leaders who must some day appear in somebody's church. They should appear with the same attitude of contrition and humility which accompanies every other sin. They should ask to be forgiven and they should promise to mend their ways in the future.

"As to the rest of us who do our own kind of sin, the important thing is that it must be recognized as an individual sin. . . . [I]t is the individual who would destroy, pillage and ruin our earth and the people on it.

"It is up to you for, after all, when Cain asked God the question, we all had the answer: 'Yes, we *are* our brother's keeper.' "

As soon as Lord returned to the courtroom, he went about ascertaining whether everyone at the Robins table had read the speech. Satisfied that they had, the judge handed out to the three executives and their attorneys the second document. He prefaced doing so by saying that the words contained therein were based "upon my study and examining of thousands of documents, my reading of reports, cases, comments by other judges, [and] the briefs of other parties. . . ."

He then offered Robins, Forrest, and Lunsford an option: They could read it privately, or he could read it to them publicly. They chose a private reading. "It's fourteen pages double-spaced; it won't take long to read," Lord said.

As they read through the document the judge had prepared the preceding weekend, based on all that he had read regarding the case over the last several weeks, Lord urged them to take their time with it. "Please don't rush through that document," he pleaded. "It is a very important, profound document which I've been working on for weeks, and I hope it burns its mark into your souls."

As the executives continued their reading, Lord took up some of the questions other plaintiffs' attorneys had with the settlement agreement that had just been signed. He was concerned about a clause in the agreement that stipulated that "[t]he parties will not seek sanctions or attorney's fees for acts or omissions of parties or their counsel or their agents for conduct in any case."

The judge felt that "in any settlement, you ought to be kind of careful about that kind of language," he said. "If misconduct is committed by attorneys in court and if they are able to buy their way out of it when it is discovered—that's if"—he did not want any of the attorneys to think that he was pointing any finger at them, at least not in a way that would cause them to object—"then the court has no remedy for enforcing its edicts prospectively whatsoever or even retroactively."

As the discussion on this point continued, he noticed that the three Robins executives had completed their reading of his "document." The time had come to begin asking his questions of the men. His first question was directed at Dr. Lunsford.

"Just one question of you, Dr. Lunsford," Lord began. "Would you please stand up?" The Robins research chief rose obediently, but reluctantly. "Were you the man who in your deposition was surprised to hear that throughout the length and breadth of this country, when a woman claimed about having been hurt by the Dalkon Shield, that your lawyers examined into her sexual practices or sexual partners, even to interviewing wives of, husbands of the sexual partners? Did you express surprise at that?"

"Excuse me, your honor. I would object to this procedure and I would like to be heard." It was attorney Socha and Lord was in no mood to hear from him today. He still hadn't gotten over their exchange of two days before.

"You put it in writing and I will hear from you, sir," Lord said.

"I would like to be heard now, if the court pleases," Socha demanded.

The court, however, did not please. "You put it in writing," Lord ordered. "Marshal?" the judge called. The marshal moved a bit forward on his seat in the front row of the courtroom. "This man is going to sit down now. Have a seat, please." Socha got the message; he sat down.

"Your honor," Dr. Lunsford finally spoke up, "with all due respect, I have been advised by my counsel not to answer questions of this nature."

"Okay," Lord shot back, looking at the Robins attorneys, a copy of the settlement agreement now gripped firmly in both hands, "does he answer or doesn't he?"

Again, Socha rose to address Lord. "May the record reflect, your honor, that you are preparing to tear up the settlement if the witness," Socha caught himself, "if Dr. Lunsford does not—"

"Is that what the record reflects?" Lord asked, a bit playfully, it seemed; it was his turn for playing games and Socha clearly did not like that.

"Yes," the attorney said. "May it reflect that, your honor? I assume you have the settlement agreement in your hand and are preparing—" Socha did not finish the sentence with words. Instead, he used his hands to tear up an imaginary piece of paper.

"I don't intend to tear up anything," Lord retorted. "I'm just figuratively stating, 'Does he want this thing approved, or doesn't he?' "

"Well, your honor," Socha began, "it is not contemplated by us—"

Lord, however, no longer wanted to hear from Socha. "Have your seat, please," he instructed as Socha continued talking.

"—that it is necessary for you—"

"Go ahead, have your seat please."

Lord's voice was more threatening this time, but Socha plugged onward. "—to approve that, your honor."

"Shall I read the document?" the judge threatened.

"Well, if your honor please," Socha answered, "I object to the procedure. If you choose to overrule my objection and read the document, there is no way that I can do that. I would like to be heard on my objections to this procedure—"

Again, Lord demanded that Socha be seated. A moment later, he recessed the court to allow the other plaintiffs' attorneys to discuss the settlement agreement among themselves and to give himself some time to think. When court reconvened a short while later, Lord gave Socha the opportunity to state his objections.

"These individuals have come here at your request to finalize a settlement agreement," Robins's Denver attorney argued, "and that is the purpose of these proceedings. And it is my judgment that you have basically this morning made accusations against these men and their integrity."

"No accusations," Lord corrected. "I made some profound judgments." More important, no one other than the men and their attorneys knew what it was the judge had written to them, except from what they could glean from Socha's words.

"Well," the attorney continued, "however you characterize them, your honor, it is my judgment that, at this point, I respectfully submit that the court is exceeding . . . its jurisdiction; that these proceedings constitute an abuse of the court's discretion. And I respectfully request that you terminate these proceedings, your honor. . . . You decline to do that, your honor, then I suggest and respectfully request that we stay these proceedings while we seek relief at a higher level. And if you decline that motion, your honor, then I respectfully request that you abate these proceedings so that we could have a telephone conference with the Eighth Circuit [Court of Appeals]."

Lord remained calm throughout. When Socha had completed his laundry list of requests, the judge ordered his "document" to be filed with the clerk of the court. He then reached for his copy.

"I agreed that I would hand this document to [these three men] and I thought I could visit with them about it in a rather superficial way just to be sure they had read it," the judge began. "One of the reasons I wanted them to read it was so that they would never again testify in any court that they knew nothing about the dangers inherent in the Dalkon Shield. However, when you get a bifurcated presentation like this, it may lend itself to distortion—and I have seen plenty of that. So, as a consequence, I am going to read the whole speech, my appeal to these gentlemen."

Several plaintiffs' attorneys had been conferring quietly in the back of the courtroom. As they realized what Lord intended, they sat down to listen. The room was silent and attentive. A number of women who had been plaintiffs in the consolidated case moved forward in their seats as if to hear better. It was as if they knew their moment had come.

"It was incredible," Larson, who had been seated at the plaintiff's counsel table and had not been involved in the conversations, recalls the scene. "First of all, he had given that speech to them to read in the courtroom—but he didn't give it to us. So we didn't know precisely what it was all about, and we wondered about it. Then he made his comments that this was something he didn't necessarily want to put on the record right now but he wanted them to read, and then he tried to talk to them. So, you know, I had no idea of what they'd read or, indeed, what his questions were going to be. But they quickly took again that very 'the hell with you, judge' sort of an attitude, which is waving a red flag in front of any federal judge. They could have handled that situation totally differently and the speech would never have been read, I'm sure.

"The judge's frustration was evident; this is not the way he wanted those proceedings to be going. It was also very clear that, whatever this was, he had given it great thought. There was a pausing in his voice and he just sort of sat there mute for a while, and then he turned to the clerk and said, 'Please file the speech,' and he said, 'I'm going to read this to you,' which was by itself a tremendous dramatic entry into this."

"Mr. Robins, Mr. Forrest and Dr. Lunsford," Lord began in a moderate, even tone, "after months of reflection, study and cogitation—and no small amount of prayer—I have concluded it perfectly appropriate to make to you this statement, which will constitute my plea to you to seek new horizons in corporate consciousness and a new sense of personal responsibility for the activities of those who work under you in the name of the A. H. Robins Company.

"It is not enough to say, 'I did not know,' 'It was not me,' 'Look elsewhere,' " Lord said, alluding both to his own experience and the experience of Judge Theis, who had overseen Dalkon Shield discovery for nine years.

"Time and time again," Lord continued, "each of you have used this kind of argument in refusing to acknowledge your responsibility and pretending to the world that the chief officers and directors of your gigantic, multinational corporation have no responsibility for the company's acts and omissions.

"In a speech I made several years ago—the document which I have just asked you to read," Lord extemporized, "I suggested to hundreds of ministers of the Gospel, who constitute the Minnesota Council of Churches, that the accumulation of corporate wrongs is in my mind a manifestation of individual sin.

"You, Mr. Robins, Jr., have been heard to boast many times that the growth and prosperity of this company is a direct result of its having been in the Robins family for three generations. The stamp of the family is upon it. The corporation is built in the image of the Robins mentality.

"You, Dr. Lunsford, as director of the company's most sensitive and important subdivision, the medical division [the research and development department has responsibility over the A. H. Robins Company's medical personnel], have violated every ethical precept to which every [medical] doctor under your supervision must pledge as he gives the Oath of Hippocrates and assumes the mantle of one who would help and cure and nurture unto the physical needs of the populace.

"You, Mr. Forrest, are a lawyer who, upon finding his client in trouble, should counsel and guide him along a course which will comport with the legal and moral and ethical principles which must bind us all. You have not brought honor to your profession, Mr. Forrest.

"Gentlemen, the result of these activities and attitudes on your part have been catastrophic. Today, as you sit here, attempting once more to extricate yourselves from the legal consequences of your acts, none of you have faced up to the fact that more than nine thousand women have made claims that they gave up a part of their womanhood so that your company might prosper. It is alleged that others gave their lives so you might prosper. And there stand behind them legions more who have been injured but who have not sought relief in the courts of this land."

As Lord spoke, Larson turned back to look at the courtroom behind him. "There were a bunch of plaintiffs," he recalls. "They were crying; the emotions were high. There were tears in their eyes. You could hear their sobbing throughout the courtroom."

"I dread to think what would have been the consequences if your victims had been men rather than women," Lord continued, "women who seem through some strange quirk of our society's mores to be expected to suffer pain, suffering and humiliation. If one poor young man were by some act of his, without authority or consent, to inflict such damage upon one woman, he would be jailed for a good portion [of] the rest of his life. And yet your company, without warning to women, invaded their bodies by the millions and caused them injuries by the thousands.

"And when the time came for these women to make their claims against your company, you attacked their characters. You inquired into their sexual practices and into the identity of their sex partners. You exposed these women, and ruined families and reputations and careers, in order to intimidate those who would raise their voices against you. You introduced issues that had no relationship whatsoever to the fact that you planted in the bodies of these women instruments of death, mutilation, and of disease."

Lord paused for a moment and looked at the three men. "I wish to make it absolutely clear that I am specifically directing and limiting my remarks to that which I have learned and observed in these consolidated cases," the judge said. "If an incident arises involving another product made by A. H. Robins Company, an independent judgment would have to be made as to the conduct of your company concerning that product. Likewise, a product made by any other company must, of course, be adjudged upon the individual facts of that case."

Judge Lord then returned to reading his text. "Gentlemen," the judge continued, "you state that your company has suffered enough, that the infliction of further punishment in a form of punitive damages will cause harm to your ongoing business, will punish innocent shareholders and, conceivably, depress your profits to the point where you would not survive as a competitor in this industry.

"Well, when the poor and downtrodden in this country commit crimes, they too plead that these are crimes of survival and that they should be excused for illegal acts which helped them escape desperate economic straits. On a few occasions when these excuses are made and a contrite and remorseful defendant promises to mend his ways, courts will give heed to such a plea. But no court would heed this plea when the individual denies the wrongful nature of his deed and gives no indication that he will mend his ways. Your company in the face of overwhelming evidence, denies its guilt and continues its monstrous mischief."

At the defense table, the three Robins executives sat stony-faced and motionless. Their attorneys, too, put on airs of cold detachment. Over on the plaintiffs' side, Dale Larson smiled sadly. He had expected little else from Robins's officers, but seeing them sit there with such apparent unemotional detachment nevertheless disturbed him.

"I watched them all the way," he says. "From about the first few lines that the judge spoke, it was evident what he was going to say, and—given my belief that these people have been lying about their involvement all the way along and that nothing was going to get to them other than in a monetary sense; they would never have to deal with it—I just turned my attention and watched them through the whole thing. And I saw nothing. It was remarkable, I thought; at least somebody ought to wince, they should have some reaction."

"Mr. Forrest," Lord read on, "you have told me that you are working with members of the Congress of the United States to ask them to find a way of forgiving you for punitive damages which might otherwise be imposed." The judge was referring to efforts on Capitol Hill that Robins supported that would relieve manufacturers from having to pay for knowingly producing products that can cause harm to people. "Yet the profits of your company continue to mount. Your last financial report boasts of new records for sales and earnings with a profit of more than fifty-eight million [dollars] in 1983. And all the while, insofar as this court is able to determine, you three men and your company still engage in the same course of wrongdoing on which you originally commenced.

"Until such time as your company indicates that it is willing to cease and desist this deception and seek out and advise [Dalkon Shield] victims, your remonstrances to Congress and to the courts of this country are indeed hollow and cynical. The company has not suffered, nor have you men personally. You are collectively being enriched by millions of dollars each year. There is as yet no evidence that your company has suffered any penalty whatsoever from these litigations.

"In fact, the evidence is to the contrary. The case law indicates that the purpose of punitive damages is to make an award which will punish a defendant for his wrongdoing. Punishment traditionally involves the principles of revenge, rehabilitation and deterrence. There is no evidence I have been able to find, in my review of these cases, to indicate that any one of these factors has been accomplished."

Again, Judge Lord looked up from his prepared text to the defense table. "Mr. Robins, Mr. Forrest, Dr. Lunsford, you have not been rehabilitated by the punitive damage awards that have been made so far. In fact, I don't think one of them has ever been paid yet, up until this settlement." The judge then returned to his speech.

"Under your direction, your company has in fact continued to allow women, tens of thousands of them, to wear a device—a deadly depth charge in their wombs, ready to explode at any time. Your attorney, Mr. Alexander Slaughter, denies that tens of thousands of these devices are still in the bodies of women. But I submit to you that Mr. Slaughter has no more basis, for his denial, than the plaintiffs for stating it as truth—because we simply do not know how many women are still wearing these devices; and your company, run by three men, is not willing to find out.

"The only conceivable reasons you have not recalled this product are that it would hurt your balance sheet and alert women who already have been harmed that you may be liable for their injuries. As I said before, and out of context," the judge ad-libbed slightly from his text, "you have taken the bottom line as your guiding beacon and the low road as your route. This is corporate irresponsibility at its meanest. Rehabilitation involves an admission of guilt, a certain contrition, an acknowledgement of wrongdoing and a resolution to take a new course toward a better life. I find none of this in the instance of you and your corporation.

"Confession is good for the soul, gentlemen. Face up to your misdeeds. Acknowledge the personal responsibility that you have for the activities of those who work under you. Rectify this evil situation. Warn the potential future victims and recompense those who already have been harmed.

"Mr. Robins, Mr. Forrest, Dr. Lunsford, I see little in the history of this case that would deter others from partaking of like acts.

"The policy of delay and obfuscation practiced by your lawyers in courts throughout this country has made it possible for your insurance company and you, the Aetna Casualty and Assurance Company and the A. H. Robins Corporation, to delay the payment of these claims for such a long period that the interest you earn in the interim covers the costs of these cases.

"What other corporate officials anywhere could possibly learn a lesson from this? The only lesson could be that it pays to delay compensating victims, and to intimidate, harass and shame your victims, the injured parties.

"Mr. Forrest, Mr. Robins and Dr. Lunsford, you gentlemen have consistently denied any knowledge of the deeds of the company you control." Lord looked up from his speech. "You, Mr. Robins Jr., I read your deposition. Many times you state that your management style was such as to delegate work and responsibility to other employees in matters involving the most important aspects of this nation's health. Judge Frank Theis, who presided over the discovery of these cases during the multi-district litigation proceedings, noted this phenomena in a recent opinion he wrote. I quote:

" 'The project manager for Dalkon Shield explains that a particular question should have gone to the medical department, the medical department representative explains that the question was really the bailiwick of the quality control department, and the quality control department representative explains that the project manager was the one with the authority to make a decision on that question.'

"'Under these circumstances,' Judge Theis noted, 'it is not at all unusual for the hard questions in Dalkon Shield cases to be unanswerable by anyone from Robins.'"

Lord then began addressing the specific reasons for his anger: the obvious attempt by Robins and its counsel to prevent the full story of the Dalkon Shield from ever being aired in public.

"Your company," Lord declared, "seeks and has sought to segment and fragment the litigation of these cases nationwide. The courts of this country are now burdened with more than 3,000 Dalkon Shield cases. The sheer number of claims and the dilatory tactics used by your company's attorneys clog court calendars and consume vast amounts of judicial and jury time.

"Your company settles those cases in which it finds itself in an uncomfortable position, a handy device for avoiding any proceeding which would give continuity or cohesiveness to this nationwide problem. The decision as to which cases to try rests almost solely at the whim and discretion of the A. H. Robins Company. In order that no plaintiff or group of plaintiffs might assert a sustained assault upon your system [of] evasion and avoidance, you have time after time demanded that able lawyers who have knowledge of the facts must, as a price of settling their cases, agree to never again take a Dalkon Shield case nor to help any less experienced lawyers with their cases against your company.

"Minnesota lawyers have filed cases in this jurisdiction for women from throughout the United States. The cases of these women have waited on the calendar of this court for as many as three years. Until such time as this settlement came about, the evidence that the women were to present was simply their own testimony and/or that of their doctor, usually taken by deposition, and then the generic evidence concerning the company's actions—which is as easy to produce in Minnesota as anywhere else. Yet your company's attorneys were persisting in asking that these cases be transferred to other jurisdictions and to other judges unfamiliar with the cases, there to wait at the bottom of the calendar for additional months and years before they could have their day in court.

"Another of your callous legal tactics is to force women of little means to withstand the onslaught of your well-financed, nationwide team of attorneys, and to default if they cannot keep up with the pace. Your target, your worst tactics were reserved for the meek and the poor.

"Now, again I point out that Faegre and Benson and the [other] local law firms do not come under any of the strictures of that which I have said. As far as I have been able to know and has been reported to me, they have acted honorably with the evidence that was available to them.

"Despite your company's protestations, it is evident that these thousands of cases cannot be viewed in isolation, one at a time and that is one of the main reasons why I feel free to make this statement here today. If every judge is terminated as soon as he catches on to what's going on, if you settle the case and flee the jurisdiction, that leaves no one to follow up to make any cohesiveness to this.

"The multi-district litigation panel of the federal district court found these cases to have sufficient similarity on issues of law and fact to warrant their reference to a single judge [Judge Theis] who, for varying periods of time, conducted discovery depositions and proceedings designed to devise an efficient method of handling these cases. Yet I find, as I previously indicated, from the report of the masters as late as this morning, that the multi-district litigation unit was only given about a third of the documents, and the most relevant documents are in the hands of the lawyers for the defendant.

"So that is twelve years of delay.

"In each of the thousands of cases, the focal point of the inquiry is the same, the conduct of your company through its acts and omissions. Indeed, when I speak here of when judge[s], [of] judges being spun off from time to time, Judge Gerald Heaney of the Court of Appeals—I believe he said it—of the Eighth Circuit, recently urged judges in Minnesota to work together to devise a coordinated system for dealing with all of their Dalkon Shield cases.

"These litigations must be viewed as a whole." Once again, Lord looked up from his text and extemporized:

"If a judge were to wait until all the cases were over before he spoke out on the evils he sees inherent in the system and in the trial tactics, then no one would ever speak out. There is a time when measures must be taken, when steps must be taken to see that fair play and ethical standards apply to the disposition of all the cases that are come to the future, regardless of what might have happened in the past."

Lord then returned to his prepared speech:

"These litigations must be viewed as a whole. Were these women to be gathered together with their injuries in one location, this matter would be denominated a disaster of the highest magnitude. The mere fact that these women are separated by geography blurs the total picture. Here we have thousands of victims, present and potential, whose injuries arise from the same series of operative facts. You three gentlemen have made no effort whatsoever to locate them and bring them together to seek a common solution to their plight.

"If this were a case in equity I would order that your company make an effort to locate each and every woman who still wears this device, and to recall your product."

Lord put down his speech and paused a moment. Looking straight at the three men who represented the upper levels of management of the A. H. Robins Company, he now added something that he had not even hinted at in the text he had supplied them.

"I would order you now," Lord said solemnly, "to take to the Food and Drug Administration a correct and proper report on what's happened with these devices. If I did that, they would order you to recall. So, while the governmental agencies are set up to protect the public, there is evidence here that you didn't tell the truth to the governmental agencies. I believe that evidence. I've made it—I've made a judgment on it. These matters of which I speak are not matters about which I speculate. They are matters contained in the evidence that has gone before me in the briefs of counsel, in the admissions and in the documents—some of which I have seen and no [plaintiff's] lawyer has seen, but I haven't disclosed anything about them except my conclusion about the matters about which I hear spoke.

"I do not have the power to order you to do this. I must therefore resort to moral persuasion and a personal appeal to each of you.

"Would you believe it, gentlemen, I am not angry with you; I don't dislike you personally? I am not happy with some of the things you have done. I would really like to try to talk you into doing this. It's just awful, and you can't get hung up in that corporate thing; you can't worry about whether or not the stocks are going to drop.

"You've got lives out there; people, women, wives, moms—and some who will never be moms. Can't you move in on this thing now?"

Judge Lord picked up the speech one last time, found his place and continued reading. "You are the people with the power to recall. You are the corporate conscience. Please, in the name of humanity, lift your eyes above the bottom line. You, the men in charge, must surely—"

The judge by now was filled with emotion. He put the speech down and again spoke from somewhere deep within himself, "I know you have hearts and souls and consciences—and I am not a great 'Bible pounder,' but this almost takes you into a biblical reference, you can only explain it in that way. If the thought of facing up to your transgressions is so unbearable to you—and I think it will be difficult for you—you might do as [former Robins attorney] Roger Tuttle did and confess to your Maker and beg forgiveness and mend your ways.

"The options are few. Either you go along stonewalling it, like you are going, or you face up to what you have done, and then you have to start thinking about how you might make amends for that.

"Please, gentlemen, give consideration to tracing down the victims and sparing them the agony that will surely be theirs.

"And I just want to say I love you; I am not mad at you."

As Lord finished, an indignant Chuck Socha jumped to his feet. "Your honor, on behalf of my client, I object to the court's remarks."

11

THE JUDGE ON TRIAL

"It is apparent to me, your honor, with all due respect, that you have become an advocate for the plaintiffs' position," Chuck Socha said, continuing on with his objection. Socha's face bore a look of disgust, Larson recalls, but he believes it was more likely a lawyer's posturing than real emotion.

There were few in the courtroom that Leap Day who would have disagreed with that statement, including Miles Lord himself. "I certainly have [become an advocate for the plaintiffs]," Lord declared from the bench, emotion still welling up inside him. "Let me, let me interrupt you. At the end of this case, after reviewing thousands of documents, looking at the briefs, reading the depositions and studying the depositions, I have concluded that the plaintiffs are right and that the things I say are based—they are my judgment based on the record. . . . You don't have to argue that I am prejudiced at this point. I am."

"And, your honor," Socha picked up his objection, "I would then respectfully submit and, on behalf of my client, we disagree vehemently with the allegations and assertions you have made. And I reiterate and reincorporate all my objections to these proceedings. I again move to terminate them. I make the other motions I previously made. I ask for return of the settlement agreement. It is not contemplated by us that you approve it—you may, if you wish—but we have a settlement; we have signed stipulations. And upon those bases, and those other bases I have just articulated, I move to terminate these proceedings."

"As far as these Robins people are concerned, they just don't give a damn," Dale Larson thought as he watched Socha's performance; "it's the same old Robins deal. It's typical." It angered Larson that no one at the defense table seemed to care. "I remember feeling so strongly, that I had the inclination that it would be nice to just stand up, turn around and personally introduce these men to each of those plaintiffs back there who were in tears," he said later. "That was depressing, in a sense, that here the judge had done this [very moving thing] and that for these folks it was part of the game."

Lord, for his part, clearly was no longer interested in any Robins game. He ignored the objection and moved on to discuss the settlement with the other plaintiffs' attorneys who had not had a hand in preparing it. After a few more minutes of discussion, the judge said:

"[A]s of now, having bared my heart and begged people to try and get this thing on the road and do right by the women that are not yet represented and have no concept of how their trust has been betrayed, that about winds me up. I am going to sign the order and approve the settlement. . . ."

He then wrote "So ordered" on the agreement and signed his name below that. Turning to Robins, Forrest, and Lunsford, a spent Miles Lord added, "I want to thank you for attending. I hope our visit might bear some fruit. Maybe you shouldn't listen too close to lawyers and insurance companies. I don't know what you [can] do; you're in a tough spot, all of you, but I hope you work it out.

"Thank you, folks. We'll stand in recess." With that, Judge Lord rose and walked through the little corridor to his chambers.

As Lord stood up, so did Dale Larson. He felt he had to say something—"It was probably the most dramatic judicial event that I'd ever be likely to see in a courtroom"—but all the exhausted and now emotion-filled attorney could get out was a simple "Thank you, your honor."

"It was monumentally historic that a judge would tell parties and lawyers what he thought, what he had seen, what he'd been shown, laid it out in no uncertain terms, clearly with no individual animosity, and literally pleading with them to stop doing this," Larson explains. "I remember being so moved emotionally by it, I went back [to my office] and I tried to call Manny Friedman, the Harvard physician who had been going through a lot of hell over the years knowing he was right, and I couldn't get through reading it to him, so I got [my secretary] to read it and then I took the phone back and Manny was so emotional that he couldn't say anything—and Manny is a pretty hard-nosed physician."

Robins and Forrest, on the other hand, appeared to have taken this emotional day in court in stride. Not so Carl Lunsford; he did show some concern: for his image. He had looked around the room and had noted how many press representatives there were, and even noticed that a court artist was present. It bothered him greatly. That concern apparently began to show in the company plane on the ride back to Richmond. At one point, young Robins turned to him and said, "You look like you feel pretty bad. I didn't think that was so bad." Robins's public comments had been more cautious, however. "It's something I'm going to think about," he said when asked whether the speech had changed his thinking in any way. "I'm going to read it again."

(Robins subsequently adopted the company line, telling A. H. Robins's stockholders that Lord "wasn't prepared to be impartial, as befits a judge. Instead, he was prepared to destroy, to tear down and to demean.")

Later that day, Roscoe E. Puckett, Jr., Robins's manager of public information, expressed the company's disappointment "that [Judge Lord] abandoned [his] role as an impartial arbiter of the proceedings and, acknowledging [his] prejudice against the company, became an advocate for one side."

That Lunsford, at least, had not been sufficiently moved to act by what Lord had said is evident from deposition testimony he gave over the course of the next few months. On April 23, 1984, for example, Larson questioned Lunsford on whether he had "discussed with any corporate employee or officer since hearing that opinion or advice to you, the subject of recalling the device from women users?"

"I have not, no sir," came Lunsford's reply.

Q. Have you discussed with anyone, or raised the questions as to whether or not the company should seek to compensate women who have been injured by [the Dalkon Shield]?

A. I have not, no sir.

Q. Have you made any inquiry to obtain any more knowledge yourself about the safety or lack of safety in the Dalkon Shield?

A. I have not, no sir.

Q. Have you asked any company employee or representative, since [leaving Judge Lord's courtroom on February 29], as to whether or not the device is unsafe and hazardous to women users?

A. I have not, no sir.

Q. Have you made any effort to find out whether or not the company knew the device was unsafe or potentially hazardous to women dating all the way back to 1970?

A. I have not made any such effort, no sir.

Q. So you haven't tried to gain or learn any more information about the device than what you knew the last time you were testifying [which was prior to February 29], is that correct?

A. That's correct.

Q. If I were to go through Judge Lord's speech—comments, whatever you wish to refer to them as—line by line, would it be accurate to say, Dr. Lunsford, that you have made no effort whatsoever to find out whether or not the statements made are true or accurate?

A. That would be accurate, yes sir. . . .

Q. Have you ever had any curiosity as to why your company has been found guilty of such conduct . . . ?

A. Not to the point that I've asked questions, no sir.

The Lunsford deposition was continued in mid-June. In the interim, two events of some importance had taken place. The first was a letter sent to Lunsford by Charles M. March, M.D., associate professor and chief of the gynecology section at the Los Angeles County–University of Southern California Medical Center, dated May 1, 1984. "On Sunday, March 18, 1984, Mrs. Christa Berlin, age 41 . . . , was admitted . . . because of lower abdominal pain and fever. A diagnosis of pelvic abscess was made and antibiotic therapy was initiated. She had had a Dalkon Shield in place for approximately eight years. Because her condition deteriorated despite high-dose parenteral antibiotic therapy, a total abdominal hysterectomy [removal of the uterus] and bilateral salpingo-oophorectomy [excision of a uterine tube and an ovary] was performed. Postoperatively she improved initially and then her condition deteriorated. Despite intensive care and cardiorespiratory support she expired on the 18th postoperative day."

The second event was a decision by the Colorado Supreme Court, in the case of *Carie M. Palmer* v. *A. H. Robins Company, Inc.*, upholding a $6.2 million punitive damage award against Robins. In a very lengthy majority decision, in which it reviewed in exhaustive detail the evidence presented at the original trial in 1980, the state's high court declared on June 4, 1984, "We see no reason to review the verdict as other than the conscientious decision of a jury to punish a wrongdoer [the A. H. Robins Company] with a penalty commensurate with the seriousness of [its] misconduct . . . and, concomitantly, to deter Robins and others from similar acts of misconduct in the future."

A little over a week after that decision was handed down and a month after Lunsford had learned of the death of Christa Berlin, Larson again sought to determine whether Robins's research chief had done anything regarding the Dalkon Shield.

Q. Right up to today, irrespective of the Colorado Supreme Court decision, or Judge Lord's plea, or any verdict, or the reports of the death of a woman, you haven't asked anybody to review any evidence concerning the safety of the device, right . . . ?

A. I have not made that request, no.

Q. And you have no intention of doing so, right?

A. At this point in time, that's correct.

Larson next asked Lunsford what he thought of Lord's speech, considering that he had done nothing to determine whether the judge had accurately portrayed him and the A. H. Robins Company.

"First of all, Mr. Larson," Lunsford said, in a departure from his otherwise brief answers, "I objected to being lectured to on matters that I felt that I had no personal responsibility for and lectured in a manner that I did not think was appropriate for a court. . . . I objected to the adverse publicity that I received personally as a result of that. I heard from friends and relatives around the country that commented on this, at least three or four different instances. There were subsequent publications that were based on the judge's remarks that I felt were unfair to my own reputation. In all those published reports, I was referred to as the chief medical officer of the A. H. Robins Company; I deny that being true. . . . [I am] head of the research and development division. In that position, the medical department reports to me. They, in turn, are personally responsible for the medical monitoring of the Dalkon Shield cases in litigation."

Larson then asked Lunsford whether he was "the highest officer in the company with specific responsibility for the safety of the Dalkon Shield."

"In that those individuals who are monitoring the Dalkon Shield problems, the litigation and the medical problems that are reported to us, those medical individuals report to me," Lunsford said after some verbal fencing and objections by counsel. "In that regard, I have responsibility."

"Do you accept any personal responsibility at all for the safety of the Dalkon Shield?" Larson demanded, again to a chorus of objections.

"[A]s far as a personal decision," Lunsford declared, "I do not accept any responsibility."

Perhaps, it was this kind of attitude or the fear that Lord would involve himself again in the case to protect the integrity of his nondestruct order that, in April, caused Griffin Bell to file the misconduct charges against Judge Lord on behalf of both the company and the three executives personally.

"By exceeding his authority in compelling complainants' presence on February 29 and then subjecting them to public scorn and ridicule in this manner," Bell's complaint read, "Judge Lord grossly abused his office, thus bringing the courts into disrepute and prejudicing the administration of justice."

Lord, according to the complaint, had deliberately set out to "humiliate and castigate" the Robins executives after concluding, without benefit of proper judicial proceedings, that the plaintiffs were right.

Along with the complaint, Robins appealed the judge's involvement in the settlement itself to the Eighth Circuit Court of Appeals. Thus it was that at 9:30 A.M., on Monday, July 9, 1984, Chief Judge Donald Lay opened the first-ever public hearing under the controversial Judicial Discipline and Conduct Act enacted by Congress four years earlier.

"Pursuant to that act, the chief judge of the circuit is required to appoint a committee composed of an equal number of district and circuit judges to serve with the chief judge to conduct an expeditious investigation and report to the Judicial Council of the circuit . . . ," Lay told the overpacked courtroom. "As chief judge, I've appointed Circuit Judges Myron H. Bright and Richard S. Arnold to serve on the investigative committee along with Judge Albert G. Schatz of the District of Nebraska and Judge Howard F. Sachs of the Western District of Missouri."

Lay took several minutes to explain for the record the rules and procedures to be followed during the course of the extraordinary two-day hearing. Today's session, he explained, would be given over to the actual case against the judge in question, Miles W. Lord, chief judge of the U.S. District Court in Minnesota, who had been charged with "gross abuse of judicial discretion and power." Each side would have two and a half hours to present testimony and evidence, Lay explained. Tomorrow would be set aside for final arguments, with each side having one hour. Objections should be kept to a minimum, Lay advised. The rules of evidence would be followed, but as informally as possible. Speed was the order of the day. The attorneys on both sides should assist the committee in moving the proceedings along as quickly and as expeditiously as possible, "[b]ecause of the time restraints involved." No recording equipment (other than the committee's own) or cameras would be allowed.

Ramsey Clark still found it difficult to believe that this was really happening. "At the behest of a very powerful corporation, the judge was now the defendant," he explained to us recently. "This corporation—a corporation that had spent millions upon millions of dollars defending itself against such charges [as Judge Lord had made in his February 29 speech], this corporation that first brutalized women physically and then brutalized them out of their rights, now attacked the judge in order to divert attention away from what it did, in order to tell courts all over the country, 'you fool around with us and we'll jerk you before a disciplinary committee, so just take it easy.' "

There was something of a circus atmosphere to the proceedings;

Lord lent to that atmosphere that morning by being as casual and friendly as possible before the start of the session. He would enter the courtroom and make his way down the aisle to the front row as if he were a candidate for public office, or a conquering hero, joking with people and shaking hands with anyone and everyone who offered one to him—which many, journalists included, did. His mood, however, would change dramatically as the day wore on. He would become somber and reflective—and somewhat disbelieving.

Extra folding chairs had been added to the federal courtroom in St. Paul to accommodate the standing-room-only crowd; forty seats were designated for the media, including local newspapers, radio and television, two commercial networks, out-of-town press, and even national news magazines. All forty seats were filled.

Despite this circuslike atmosphere, however, no one in the courtroom that day took lightly what was to happen there; for, behind the specific issue of this hearing, Lord's February 29 speech, there was an even greater question that had to be answered, many felt: whether powerful U.S. corporations such as the A. H. Robins Company, by virtue of unlimited funds and equally unlimited influence, could harass and intimidate the judicial system into doing its bidding, and justice be damned.

"If [my] judgment on this is going to be reviewed and second-guessed, with the possibility that I may be personally subjected to serious sanctions," Lord had told the five-judge committee in a written statement, "this will undoubtedly have a chilling effect upon my exercise of judicial authority in the future. It will, I believe, also adversely affect the willingness of other federal court judges to properly exercise their authority to control and supervise litigation. . . ."

Lord was not alone in expressing such feelings. "I would respectfully suggest that anything less than a full and unambiguous vindication of Judge Lord would be not only an injustice to Judge Lord," Professor Monroe H. Freedman would testify later that morning to the investigative committee, "but a serious impairment of the independence of the federal judiciary."

Freedman, a law professor and expert on judicial and legal ethics, has oftentimes testified on matters of judicial conduct, including at hearings held by committees in both houses of Congress. He called Lord's speech, which his counsel had now characterized as a reprimand, "the most appropriate means . . . of speaking on behalf of society in disapproval of . . . seriously antisocial behavior on the part of" A. H. Robins.

That Ramsey Clark was Lord's defense counsel and Griffin Bell his prosecutor lent a sense of irony to the proceedings because both men were Democrats and unabashedly so, as was Lord himself.

There was irony, too, in Bell's role against Lord and that of Bell's associate at the counsel table, Charles Kirbo. One would have expected such men from an administration that had set the preservation of human rights as its cornerstone to side with Miles Lord in this matter and even to sympathize with him, not to prosecute him.

There was irony also in the way the media perceived the case because of opposing counsel. "In a way, it became something of a distraction," Clark said of the media's focusing on the Battle of the Attorneys General. "I thought the case was extremely important on several levels—the health of women, the responsibility of corporations, the role of the judiciary in the administration of justice, the power of economic concentration in our society. To me, if the press had to play up the notion of two attorneys general doing battle, the real story might have been why a former attorney general represents interests like this [Robins] and what he's paid for it."

Ironic, too, was the fact that, for doing what had to be done and saying what had to be said, Lord's fate would soon be in the hands of five colleagues; and if Lord lost, justice would lose. Indeed, some said that on the day Miles Lord lost, on that day justice would die in America.

"Pursuant to the statute, any judicial officer against whom a complaint has been filed has a right to a hearing," Lay continued his recitation. "Under the statute, the judicial officer may request a public hearing, and, if the chief judge of the circuit consents, the hearing is then opened to the public. In this case, Chief Judge Miles W. Lord has requested a public hearing, and I have acquiesced in that request."

Lord smiled contentedly to himself. All previous hearings under Section 372 had been closed, but "Judge Lord felt very strongly that a secret proceeding would be very harmful to the judiciary," Clark explained. An open hearing thus had been his first "victory" in the case.

Lay then outlined what testimony and submissions the committee would allow. Finally, the procedural matters were out of the way. "We are now ready to proceed with this hearing," Lay said. "I have appointed Judge Howard F. Sachs of the Western District of Missouri to serve as chairman of this investigatory committee and to preside at this hearing and make whatever rulings are necessary. Now I turn this hearing over to Judge Sachs."

Judge Sachs, too, had "housekeeping" matters to present. The statute, he explained, allowed the judge in question to cross-examine witnesses; the complainants, however, had no similar right conferred on them. Nevertheless, Sachs said, both sides would have the right to cross-examine. However, "Because of the limited time, we do suggest that cross-examination be brief."

Judge Sachs then formally introduced counsel for both sides and the proceeding finally got down to the business at hand.

Throughout all this, Ramsey Clark had been absentmindedly engaged in playing with his ball-point pen, sliding it through the fingers first of his left hand, then of his right, returning it to the breast pocket of his shirt, then retrieving it and beginning again. All the while, his mind was half on what was being said and half on the charges Bell had filed against Judge Lord that brought them together. Now he rose to address the panel.

"Mr. Chairman," Clark began, "may it please the committee, we will present the oral statements of several witnesses, some additional documentary evidence, and other factual matters . . . [in order to show] that Judge Miles Lord's [conduct] throughout the relevant period was . . . in the highest tradition of an independent judiciary and that none of his acts were in any way improper by judicial or other standards."

Clark, with the committee's permission and Bell's acquiescence, then began reading into the record Judge Lord's written statement.

"My primary purpose . . . ," Clark quoted Lord, "was to rebuke and sanction [the Robins executives] for what the Court otherwise felt would be an affront to its authority and dignity, and a frustration of its efforts to provide for the proper administration of justice. . . . [T]he Court had come to discover compelling evidence of serious discovery abuses which had taken place before the federal courts. . . . In attempting to correct that through ordering additional discovery . . . , the Court found that its authority was still being frustrated when it became evident that A. H. Robins was feverishly settling the cases before the Court so as to be able to get out from underneath further discovery and effectively flee from the jurisdiction of the Court."

As Clark read on, Lord played the words over in his mind, recalling some of the tactics of abuse to which he and the victims of the Dalkon Shield who were before him seeking justice had been subjected.

Sitting on a bench some rows behind Lord, Mike Ciresi laughed silently and knowingly as these words evoked the memories of all that had gone by: the prodding and baiting of Judge Lord by Socha, Slaughter, and the other Robins attorneys; the tactics of delay and obfuscation; the sideshow quality of the depositions taken in Richmond; the seemingly endless stream of Robins attorneys in and out of the drama; his own hurried attempt to complete the Lord-ordered round of depositions before the settlement was finalized; the hectic pace of the two special masters supervising the gathering of evidence from the files of Robins and its attorneys before they were ordered to stop. Ciresi understood only too well what Lord was talking about in his statement to the panel.

"If the Court, at that time, had allowed this to go on, without even adverse comment, it would have made a mockery of the Court's responsibility to protect the integrity of the judicial process and maintain the public's esteem and confidence in the court system . . . ," Lord's statement continued. "[T]he Court took the actions which it did based upon a good faith belief that they were within the Court's authority and that they would properly serve the ends of justice and promote the expeditious administration of the business of the courts."

Griffin Bell sat silently throughout Clark's reading of Lord's statement. No sooner had the sixty-sixth attorney general of the United States finished, however, than the seventy-second attorney general rose to comment. "Your honor," Bell said, "I don't wish to object to the reading of the statement, or the statement [itself], provided it's understood that we can rebut some of the findings of fact recited in the statement."

"Fine," Judge Sachs responded and he signaled for Joe Walters to get on with the case. Walters rose and presented Judge Lord's first witness, Ernest Friesen, dean of the California Western School of Law in San Diego, California, a former assistant attorney general, a founding dean of the National Judicial College, onetime director of the Administrative Office of the United States Courts and a founding director of the Institute for Court Management, among other credits; in other words, a man expert in the proper role of judges in the pursuit of justice.

Dean Friesen's direct testimony was given in the form of a statement. He began by reciting the judicial history of the 1980 act under which Lord had been charged. The bottom line of that act, he stated, was the "effective administration of justice" and it is in that context that Judge Lord's actions must be viewed.

"[W]hat are the purposes of the courts . . . ?" Friesen asked rhetorically. "I suggest to you that the five basic purposes in civil courts are [as] follows: to do individual justice in individual cases; to appear to do individual justice in individual cases; to provide a forum for ending a dispute through governmental sanctions; to protect individuals against the arbitrary use of government power; and to provide a formal record of legal status.

"It seems to me that in several of these respects Judge Lord's comments might be interpreted to make the justice system more effective. . . . It is certainly . . . a proper view that Judge Lord's admonitions and concern in this case . . . indicate that he has undertaken to avoid the abuses of discovery and to control discovery and to push the matter towards a timely, informed, call it prepared settlement.

"I, for the last five years, have been a member of the American Bar Association Action Committee on the control of court costs and delay. We're just finishing our report. . . . We discovered, of course, that the basic abuses of discovery are in large, complex cases—products liability [such as the Dalkon Shield case], large medical malpractice, multiple defendants cases, places where the complexity is significant. . . . [The ABA committee] will report that the solution to the problem is [activist judges] . . . taking early judicial control by the court, maintaining consistent judicial control, heading off the kinds of problems you get when people try to avoid discovery by getting the parties . . . to agree without motions to enforce and motions to resist, and to get that whole process going.

"Seems to me that Judge Lord's behavior, as it's described in the papers here, supports the idea that he was becoming and was an activist judge in this process. . . .

"Each judge is accountable for the effective administration of the business of the courts. And the behavior that we are considering today may well be in the highest respect providing accountability to the public for suggesting that the processes needed to be dealt with quite differently."

As Dean Friesen completed his statement, Bell rose to cross-examine the witness. "Mr. Friesen," Bell began, avoiding adding more weight to the witness's testimony by calling him "Dean" (although Bell encourages people to call him "Judge Bell," a memorial of his long gone days on the Georgia bench), "you spoke of the duty of the court and the activist judge. And you've taught a court management [course], judicial administration, over the years, is that right?"

A. That's correct.

Q. Have you taught due process?

A. Yes, I taught civil procedure for twenty-eight years.

Q. Now, when you speak of the activist judge, do you mean that the rules of due process can be suspended; you mean that to be activist within the context of due process?

A. . . . [O]nly within the context of due process . . . ; we do not give up any due process in being activists. As a matter of fact, by being activists, you enhance the due process of law because you get rid of the witnesses lost and the memories lost, and all of the things that happen when people drag out litigation over long periods of time.

Q. Now, in due process of law, would you say that one is entitled to notice?

A. Absolutely.

Q. Before being charged?

A. Before being charged.

Q. Before losing a right?

A. Before losing a right. . . .

Q. Would you think that you are entitled to an opportunity to confront witnesses?

A. In due process, you certainly are.

Q. Opportunity to a hearing?

A. Yes.
Q. Opportunity to cross-examine?
A. Correct, and have the right to compulsory witnesses.
Q. Opportunity to counsel?
A. Opportunity to have counsel.
Q. And would you be entitled to a neutral judge?
A. Yes, [an] objective judge.

"Thank you," Bell said as he began to return to his seat. He had managed to turn Lord's first witness against him, or so he thought. Dean Friesen, however, had been keenly aware of what Bell was doing, and he wasn't quite finished with his lecture. "There's a difference between being objective and being ignorant. They're not the same. You don't have to be ignorant to be objective," Friesen said as Bell walked away.

Bell, however, was not interested in pursuing Friesen's point. "I'm not asking anything about ignorance," he said, "but I thank you very much." With that, he sat down. Almost simultaneously, Joe Walters was on his feet.

"[H]ave you had an opportunity to review . . . the transcript [of the] February 29th, 1984, hearing before Judge Lord?" he asked on redirect.

"I read the transcript and the settlement agreement," Friesen responded.

"Okay," Walters continued, "in your opinion, you believe there was a violation of due process?"

"No, I do not," Dean Friesen said pointedly. "I've nothing further," said Walters with a smile.

Bell, his carefully made point now a shambles, quickly tried to gain back some of his lost ground. "Did you, in view of that last answer, did you see anything in the record about notice to the individuals or to the company that they were going to be reprimanded?" he asked.

"No, not that they were going to be reprimanded," Friesen answered.

"You don't think that was necessary?" Bell challenged the witness. "You just got through testifying that you thought a person was entitled to notice, did you not?"

"Well," Friesen explained, "I think that you and I are probably looking at the [February 29] proceeding differently. You're assuming that it had something"—the dean groped for the right words—"that it was a trial of an issue of fact and that the issues of fact were what were before the hearing. . . ." Clearly, the February 29th hearing was not a trial of an issue of fact, Friesen said.

Q. Did you see in the February 29 proceedings, which you say you read, did you see any findings of fact . . . in that transcript?
A. I would not have described it as findings of fact in the civil procedure sense, no.
Q. Did you see any conclusion of the facts?
A. Not in the civil procedure sense. . . .

By this point, Bell was becoming frustrated with Friesen's cautious responses. "What about not in civil procedure sense but just walking-around sense?" he asked with a twinge of Southern sarcasm.

"I believe that Judge Lord drew some conclusions," Friesen said, and Bell tried to press the point home.

Q. So you did see some conclusions?
A. Yes, sir.
Q. But you didn't see any findings . . . ?
A. No. I'm saying he drew some conclusions about matters of fact. . . .

At that point, Bell gave up and allowed Dean Friesen to be excused. Judge Sachs then recessed the hearing for ten minutes. When the committee reconvened, Clark introduced Monroe Freedman. As with Dean Friesen, there was to be no direct examination of the witness, he explained; Professor Freedman would give his testimony by way of a statement to the committee.

Freedman wasted no time in letting everyone know, Bell and Kirbo included, that he had done his homework thoroughly before reaching his conclusions.

"Mr. Chairman and members of the committee," he began, "in preparation for this testimony I have read [Judge Lord's] order of February 9, 1984, with regard to discovery . . . , the complaint of judicial misconduct [filed by Robins] . . . , the five affidavits in support of that [complaint], the brief of the complainants, the [February 29 transcript] . . . , the statement of Chief Judge Lord which was submitted to this committee . . . , the brief of respondents and several other documents which I skip-read. . . . I've also reviewed the Code of Judicial Conduct and the reporter's notes to the code and some other research sources."

Freedman then proceeded to make his case for Judge Lord. "[W]ith respect to the so-called reprimand, or admonition of the Judge," Freedman testified, "I think it's important to note the context in which the Judge made a determination, first [of] callous disregard of the health and lives of the women involved [on the part of the A. H. Robins Company], and second of what he viewed to be, and not unreasonably in my view, a massive obstruction of justice with regard to discovery."

Mindful of Bell's questioning of Friesen, Freedman chose his words with great care. "Now, [irrespective of] whether Judge Lord was right or wrong as a matter of fact in that conclusion, it was beyond any reasonable question, in my view, well within his judicial discretion to make those judgments on the record . . . ," Freedman stated. Then he began to pick apart Bell's arguments one after another:

"When I was asked whether I might be able to testify in this case as an expert witness, one of the first questions that I raised . . . was my concern with due process of law. . . . [I]t appears to me clear, on my reading of the documents that I referred to, that the parties who were subject to the judge's admonition were aware *in advance* that something like that was going to happen, although they did not receive *formal* notice; that they were indeed *on notice;* that they *were* represented by counsel; that the judge offered them *an invitation to respond;* that counsel spoke on their behalf and *did not* request a hearing; that counsel *did not* request an opportunity for rebuttal. . . . And I am satisfied on my reading of the record that there was *no* due process violation." (Emphases ours.)

"Professor," Bell began his cross-examination as soon as Freedman had concluded his statement, "you say you read the transcript of the February 29 hearing. And you based your testimony that there was no denial of due process based on your reading of that transcript?"

"Yes, sir."

"Did you find anything in there about any notice that these plaintiffs were going to be reprimanded . . . ?"

"Mr. Bell, it is my reading that the respondents and their lawyers were on notice that the judge might have partially critical things to say about the behavior of the company and the conduct of the litigation."

Once again, Bell was thwarted. Try as he did, he could not get Professor Freedman to agree that the Robins executives were denied due process. He finally gave up the effort and sat down. Joe Walters then introduced Lord's final witness, Robert J. Sheran, former chief justice of the Minnesota Supreme Court. Sheran got right to the point of his testimony:

"[T]he purpose of this proceeding is not to ascertain whether the statements made by Judge Lord . . . were or were not supported by the record, but whether Judge Lord should be disciplined, and I'm assuming that discipline would include, under the statute, censor and reprimand for having made those statements. And it is my judgment that the administration of justice is not furthered if judges generally and trial judges in particular are disciplined, censored, reprimanded for statements made in the course of litigation and in good faith. . . . I feel that the experience that I had as eight years of Chief Justice of Minnesota, my contact [as chairman for five years of the State and Federal Relationship Committee of the Conference of Chief Justices] with all of the chief justices in the country, and my concern for judicial administration combine to lead me to express this opinion, for what it may be worth, that the Congress couldn't have intended this statute to encompass a situation of this kind. . . ."

In other words, Sheran said, the committee had no legal jurisdiction in the matter.

Bell decided to impeach Sheran's testimony by showing that it was based, not on the information in this case, but on the judge's prejudice against the act under which the matter was brought in the first place.

"Judge Sheran," Bell said, "I'm struck by your testimony. You [are] just opposed to this kind of a procedure, as I understand it? You oppose this federal statute? You think it's an ill-advised tactic?"

"I don't recall having said anything that would suggest that," Sheran countered.

"I mean that's my impression of that," Bell parried.

"Let me correct that impression, then . . . ," Sheran thrust back. "I think the statute performs a useful function interpreted in such a way so as not to intrude upon the independence of the judge who sat in good faith."

Again, Bell decided to not make matters worse by pursuing cross-examination. He allowed Sheran to be dismissed.

At this point, Walters read into the record a statement signed by two of Lord's colleagues on the U.S. District Court in Minnesota, Robert J. Renner and Paul A. Magnuson. Once again, the theme was judicial independence.

"Frequently," the statement said, "federal court litigation is complex, difficult . . . and acrimonius. Accordingly, it is often our duty to take . . . controversial action. However, we can perform the duties of this office effectively only if we may act without fear of retaliation directed at us by litigants or others who are dissatisfied with our actions. . . .

"If we are to be true to our oaths, and to be allowed to devote our thoughts and talents and convictions to the proper resolution of the business brought before us, then we must be free to act without fear of personal reprisal. We must be free to act untrammeled by fear, answerable only to the Constitution and to our consciences."

Walters then presented the bulk of Lord's case, by methodically reviewing the history of Lord's involvement with the Dalkon Shield litigation, and then describing all of the various documents and exhibits that had been submitted on Judge Lord's behalf.

There was, for example, the affidavit from U.S. district judge Frank Theis, the one other U.S. district judge who was in the best possible position to know the frustrations faced by Miles Lord when Robins and its battery of attorneys appeared before him with anything but candor. In his affidavit on his colleague's behalf, Judge Theis noted that Lord's handling of the cases before him had called into serious question all that Theis had been told over the years by Robins's officials and counsel.

"The object and purpose of these multidistrict proceedings was to coordinate nationwide discovery on the generic aspects of product liability of Robins and to avoid duplication, and disparate requests and responses," Theis's affidavit read. "It was my intention to effectively complete all document discovery and depositions so that a trial package could be available [to other courts] containing all relevant and admissible evidence."

In the course of the last eight and a half years, Theis noted, "thousands of documents had been produced and I was satisfied that appropriate discovery had been made . . . , that all available relevant evidence in the possession of A. H. Robins and its attorneys had been made available to the plaintiffs."

Lord, however, uncovered many thousands of documents that were not supposed to have existed. This, Theis declared, appeared to run "contrary to the representations made to me by counsel for A. H. Robins. . . . It would appear to me that [these representations] are open to serious question. . . .

"I do not believe a judge should be hobbled or censored for good faith remarks he makes with full knowledge of facts and circumstances which appear to him to inhibit the processes of justice and the inherent right of free speech of a judge to prevent possible fraud upon the court. . . . Judge Lord's remonstrance to the responsible company officials," Theis wrote in his affidavit, "was mild punishment indeed considering the strong possibility that such apparent misrepresentations and trial tactics [to which Lord reacted in his speech] seem to permeate the proceedings [in my court] and elsewhere."

"I read about [the disciplinary proceeding] against Judge Lord and I thought I should do something to help him if I could," Judge Theis explained to us afterward; the affidavit would in January 1985 lead to a recusal petition filed by Bell, asking Judge Theis to remove himself from any further involvement in the multidistrict litigation because of his "obvious" prejudice against Robins. "I really objected to the star-chamber approach of disciplining Judge Lord," Judge Theis explained. "If the Robins folks did not like what he said, they had a means of redress through the Court of Appeals. They did not have to resort to a complaint of that type.

"I have long admired his courage. I have always admired the way Miles took on the big interests in the past, be it mining or drug companies. . . . I might not—in fact, I probably would not—have done it the same way. If what Judge Lord says is right, and I can't prejudge whether it was or wasn't, I would have probably cited them for contempt."

Lord's counsel also introduced a memorandum filed by Robins in a recent South Carolina case—a memorandum that showed clearly that Robins intended to use the proceedings against Lord to intimidate other courts, as Clark put it to us, to "just take it easy" where the company was concerned. The memorandum referred to Judge Lord's massive discovery order:

"This order was entered in a proceeding which was irregular in the extreme," the Robins attorneys told the South Carolina court. "Because Judge Lord's order is irrelevant, it is unnecessary here for Robins to detail Judge Lord's unorthodox and objectionable conduct. It is enough to say that Judge Lord took no evidence and had no proper basis for any statement relied upon by plaintiff but instead acted as an admitted partisan for plaintiffs."

It was a typical Robins fudging of the facts. Nowhere, for example, did it say that Lord's discovery order was upheld by the Eighth Circuit Court of Appeals. Not only did that court find Lord's order relevant, but it found that Lord "did not abuse [his] discretion in entering the discovery orders. . . ." By claiming that the judge "took no evidence," it ignored the fact that the judge actually supervised the taking of several depositions and read all of the depositions he had not been present to hear live. As for Lord acting "as an admitted partisan for plaintiffs," the only time he even came close to saying something like that had been on February 29—twenty-one days *after* he issued the discovery order.

It was in a pointed footnote, however, that the Robins attorneys added their veiled warning: "The proceedings before Judge Lord are now the subject of judicial investigation by the Eighth Circuit Court of Appeals. This is the first time in the Eighth Circuit that a complaint of judicial misconduct has been certified for investigation by the Chief Judge."

The implication was that the *discovery* proceedings were under investigation. Again, this was a deliberate misstatement. Discovery was not the issue at hand; Lord's reprimand of the Robins executives was the only matter before the investigative committee. The Robins attorneys, however, were less interested in presenting the facts than they were in issuing their warning.

On July 11, 1984, the Special Investigative Committee of the Eighth Circuit U.S. Court of Appeals Judicial Council listened to the final arguments by Griffin Bell and Ramsey Clark.

"When Judge Lord made [his] speech to the Minnesota Council

of Ministers [sic] in 1981 about the evil of the American corporation . . . he put himself on a cloud," Bell argued. "And there's no lawyer that could ever appear in his court on a product liability, bad product liability case of some sort, pollution case [such as Reserve Mining], that wouldn't think about moving to disqualify him on the basis of that speech. So when you go into his court, you go in under the law of the United States, all the decisions of the courts, but you also go in on his personal philosophy that the American corporation is evil. . . . In that instance, I don't think we had a fair judge, and that is one of the things that you are entitled to as part of due process."

It was, of course, a gross mischaracterization of Lord's Council of Churches speech in which he had been talking about very real abuses committed in the name of profit, abuses that put cars with exploding gas tanks on our roads, deadly asbestos fibers in our homes, and Dalkon Shields in our bodies.

As one of his proofs of Lord's biased stance, Bell pointed to the February 8 discovery order. "Whose . . . discovery order, are we talking about?" he asked. "Did a lawyer ask for it? I can't find any reference of a lawyer asking for it. . . . Judge Lord made up this discovery order, and we've sent two masters to Richmond, appointed two masters, one wasn't enough. He then sent his law clerk over to Richmond to help out. He then, himself, went twice to take a deposition. All this having to do with discovery in a situation where there'd been hundreds of cases, all sorts of discovery, two multi-district hearings together had gone on for eight and a half years."

In making his arguments, Judge Bell often misspoke himself; whether by design or out of ignorance we cannot tell because he has refused to discuss it with us. Although Judge Lord did initiate discovery, for example, the record does show that he had been requested to do so on a number of occasions by plaintiffs' lead counsel, Larson and Ciresi. It was obvious to all concerned that one master would not do because even Robins's attorneys talked about the massive effort discovery would entail. Lord's law clerk, Roberta Walburn, was sent to Richmond by Magistrate McNulty after the judge had temporarily withdrawn from the consolidated cases pending the Eighth Circuit's ruling on Robins's mandamus petition. And Lord made only one trip to Richmond to oversee the deposition-taking—and he only made that trip after both sides agreed that his presence might help speed the process along.

Bell even tried to show that Lord's remarks on February 29 could not have been based on in-depth knowledge of the cases before him. As proof, he cited the instance during the taking of E. Claiborne Robins, Sr.'s, deposition, in which Lord asked the chairman of the A. H. Robins Company why no recall had been issued. Amid objections and discussions between attorneys, Robins had told Lord that his company had sent out a letter to doctors in 1980. Robins was not referring to a recall but to "Dear Doctor II." To that, Lord said, "Well, see, I wasn't even aware of that, that's how new I am to this case." Bell argued that this proved Lord's ignorance of the issues.

However, aside from the fact that this occurred in January and that Judge Lord had a whole month to learn everything he needed to know about the Dalkon Shield, the record clearly shows that Lord knew all about "Dear Doctor II" before Robins brought it up. In fact, it was Lord, on the record at the previous deposition session, who suggested that the elder Robins be given a copy of that very letter to refresh his memory. It was clear, as Ramsey Clark would argue, that the way Robins had phrased his response to Lord's question about a recall (and given the chaotic conditions at the deposition site), that the judge thought that Robins had issued a recall.

"[T]o have uncaring judges would be a tragedy of enormous proportion . . . ," Clark argued on behalf of Lord. "I think . . . that he was terribly and tragically right and not to have said [what he did], how can we live with ourselves when we see this . . . ? [F]or a judge to feel no obligation to comment on that, I think would be a terribly disabling thing. . . . This is the heart of all that he had seen and all that was before him. . . . I think that he had a judicial responsibility in the best sense and the finest tradition of the judiciary to comment on this. . . .

"The people need fearless, courageous, independent judges.

"This judge acted with passionate discipline. When you think of the things that he could have done under the procedures available to him, he took the course that he believed was best calculated to help the problem—to help the problem of congestion in the courts;

to move the cases; to help the problems of the women in the streets with the Dalkon Shield who didn't know they were in danger.

"He tried to help. . . . [A]nd I urge you . . . to make announcements that could help restore this invaluable, precious quality in the American vision of individual freedom: the independent and fearless judiciary."

It was during the second day of hearings that the subject of Robins's appeal was brought to the attention of the committee. Clark argued that the appeal was the proper course for redress and that, having been taken, there was no further need for any action against Lord. Bell found it difficult to argue the point. The investigative committee apparently agreed. Later that day, it put off any decision on the misconduct charges until Robins's appeal was decided by the Eighth Circuit U.S. Court of Appeals. Because the appeal only covered Lord's formal involvement in the settlement by affixing the words "So ordered" above his name, the committee also urged Chief Judge Lay to widen its scope to cover the question of whether Lord's speech should be stricken from the record. That same day, Lay issued an order widening the appeal and set August 27 as the hearing date.

On November 2, 1984, the Eighth Circuit agreed to expunge Lord's speech from the record and to remove his name and the words "So ordered" from the settlement agreement, saying that he had "crossed the line separating permissible judicial comments from impermissible public accusations" by delivering the blistering attack. It took no action, however, against the judge personally.

Despite the harsh wording of the opinion, Lord saw it as a vindication. "I am, of course, greatly pleased that the A. H. Robins Company has failed in its attempt to personally punish me as a federal judge for reprimanding the company for its misdeeds," he said at the time. "A. H. Robins never seriously contested the truth of my remarks, nor did the Court of Appeals question the accuracy of my statement. Jurors in Minnesota and across the nation have found this corporation to have acted with willful indifference to the rights and safety of women."

On the day after Christmas 1984, on the advice of its investigative committee, the Judicial Council of the Eighth Circuit, made up of five U.S. district judges and nine U.S. appeals court judges, dismissed the disciplinary proceedings against Lord, on the grounds that "[a]ll relief deemed appropriate has been granted." In other words, while Judge Lord had technically overstepped his authority, he did not deserve to be punished for it.

That message, however, was not the "full and unambiguous vindication of Judge Lord" that Professor Monroe Freedman had told the investigative committee was necessary to maintain "the independence of the federal judiciary." In fact, the message was misinterpreted by many, including the A. H. Robins Company. New complaints were quickly filed against Lord, apparently by ordinary citizens, again seeking some form of punishment for the judge. It did not take long for Judge Lay and his colleagues on the Judicial Council to realize that they could not get away with saying nothing. The issue had to be met squarely and firmly. On Thursday, January 24, 1985, therefore, the council issued a ruling fully exonerating Lord.

"A trial judge should not fear that because of comments he or she makes from the bench, which in good faith the judge feels are related to the proceeding before the court, he or she ultimately may be subject to a disciplinary sanction by the Judicial Council," the Judicial Council stated. "Disenchanted litigants or other citizens should not be able to attempt to influence a federal judge about a judicial decision through the threat of disciplinary sanction."

Lord called the ruling an "emancipation proclamation" for all judges, adding, however, that "[i]t will neither increase nor decrease my voluble nature. I'll just say what I have to say."

Referring to the Eighth Circuit Court of Appeals' ruling that ordered his February 29 speech struck from the record, Lord said that the Judicial Council's ruling was doubly appreciated by him. "They found me not to have done anything improper because the comments were made in the midst of a judicial proceeding," he said. "It gives me great comfort."

Said Clark afterward, "[I]n terms of both truth and justice, Miles W. Lord has prevailed."

12

AFTERMATH

However correct or incorrect Miles Lord was that Leap Day 1984, it is important to look beyond what has been said about his actions to what has happened as a result of them. It was Lord's goal to influence the future course of the Dalkon Shield story in a positive way. And, indeed, he did just that.

He had sought, for example, to lighten the burdensome load of Dalkon Shield cases weighing down the nation's courts and to bring to the victims of that device some measure of justice. As an attorney for Robins told Mike Ciresi, Lord's actions had "ground into dust all of the defenses that we had painstakingly built up." Judges now sitting on similar cases began moving in much the same way he did, especially as regards continuing discovery. As a result, Robins has been settling cases almost with abandon, thus helping to break the judicial logjam:

· In Minnesota, Ciresi and Dale Larson were vigorously pursuing discovery on the 198 cases remaining in their firm. Among the cases were two involving deaths of children, eleven involving the health of children born to women who had used the device, and one involving a mentally retarded child with cerebral palsy. On November 14, 1984, all of these cases were settled for $38 million. This worked out to an average settlement of $192,000 per claim; until that time, settlements had averaged only $39,000 per claim.

According to Robins spokesman Roscoe Puckett, Jr., the unusually high settlement was "directly attributable" to "Judge Miles Lord's public attacks and utterances over the past several months." Ciresi agreed, but from a more positive perspective. Lord's involvement, he said, had been "monumental and pivotal."

· In Florida, plaintiffs' attorneys sought to obtain eight "secret" Dalkon Shield studies that had been commissioned by Robins attorneys on which the company until now had successfully claimed privilege. Using a novel argument first put forth by Ciresi and Larson, the attorneys argued that the studies were a part of a drug company's legal obligation to continually monitor its products and thus were not privileged no matter who commissioned them. In Gainesville, Florida, Judge Maurice Paul bought the argument and ordered Robins to produce the studies under threat of sanctions no later than October 5, 1984. On October 4, Robins settled. In Fort Lauderdale, attorney Sid Matthew also won the right to see the documents; Robins settled his case on the courthouse steps.

· In South Carolina, Judge C. Weston Houck gave Robins fifteen days to produce the studies. Robins settled on day fourteen. "From zero to settlement in a week," said plaintiff's attorney David Norton of Charleston, South Carolina, adding: "I've got a feeling there are some things in those papers Robins doesn't want anyone to see."

Another calendar-clearing event would be the granting of collateral estoppel on the issue of liability; in effect, a decision by a judge that liability has now been proven and no longer needs to be tried. In Colorado, Lord's actions have contributed to an almost certain granting of collateral estoppel the next time a Dalkon Shield case comes up for trial in that district. If that occurs, it will undoubtedly have carry-over effects in other districts as well.

Following Lord's lead, U.S. district judge Richard Matsch in Denver consolidated eight Dalkon Shield cases for trial. Following that trial, he made a wide-ranging ruling which declared that the issue of liability had now been proven; thus, all that is now required for collateral estoppel is a formal motion in the next case. Robins, in an effort to stave off such a motion, has since offered to concede liability on the issues of negligence and strict liability in the district —in itself an extraordinary action—in exchange for the plaintiffs' agreeing to drop their punitive damage claims. Most of the attorneys, however, consider the offer worthless. Says Denver attorney Norman Kripke, "Liability is no longer an issue here. I pitched their letter."

Judge Lord also had wanted to put an end to the vile "dirty questions." After February 29, more and more judges began refusing to allow those questions to be asked. "This court considers these questions to be beyond the reach of normal discovery and cannot be asked," is how Minnesota's Judge Jonathan Lebedoff bluntly worded his order.

In one thing, Judge Lord failed. He had wanted Robins to own up to what it had done to women and to accept responsibility for it. Instead, almost from the moment Lord had finished his remarks, A. H. Robins and its attorneys made it clear that it was business as usual.

As part of the February 29 settlement, Robins had agreed that the discovery begun under Judge Lord would continue under U.S. district judge Robert Renner. It also agreed to the issuance of a nondestruct order by Judge Renner that would continue Lord's order. Renner's order said in part:

"No party or their attorneys shall damage, mutilate, or destroy any document having potential relevance to [the Dalkon Shield proceedings]. . . . A document is deemed to be of potential relevance . . . for the purpose of this order if it in any way relates to the documents encompassed by Judge Lord's [discovery] order of February 8, 1984. . . . Each party shall upon receipt of this order promptly make reasonable efforts to notify all its attorneys . . . employees, agents, experts, and *other persons who now have access to any of the aforedescribed documents.*" (Emphasis ours.)

Robins's attorneys, anxious for a settlement so that they could escape Lord's court, had no problem with Renner's order when they agreed to it. Less than a month later, however, they moved to have the order either vacated or stayed pending an appeal. Suddenly, a key provision of the settlement agreement meant nothing (which is precisely why both Judge Lord and Dale Larson had wanted Robins, Forrest, and Lunsford to sign the agreement personally). Suddenly, Robins's attorneys argued that they did not understand the language of the order.

Coincidentally, on the day the motion to vacate was filed, March

22, 1984, or on March 23, the nondestruct order was violated when twenty boxes of documents in the basement of a former Robins outside counsel were thrown away. Robins said that it was an accident.

Harris Wagenseil, a former Rhodes scholar and Harvard Law School graduate, had represented Robins while practicing law in San Francisco. In June 1983, Wagenseil left private practice and in August moved to Columbus, Indiana, to assume a corporate position. All of the files from his years of private practice went with him and were stored in the basement of his new home, along with "a lot of furniture and toys and all kinds of that stuff."

In November, Wagenseil and his wife decided to buy a new and larger home. The following February, they put the old house up for sale. The real estate agent suggested that cleaning out the basement would improve the chances for a sale. At the time, Wagenseil was spending his weekends in Philadelphia, where he was working on an M.B.A. degree at the Wharton School of the University of Pennsylvania. Despite the fact that the couple was now living in a larger home (and thus had more room in which to store the "furniture and toys and all kinds of that stuff" and which in fact was moved there), Mrs. Wagenseil, on either March 22 or 23, telephoned her husband in Philadelphia and said, "I'm throwing out that stuff in the basement. Do you have any problem with that?" His reply was, "No, go ahead."

Wagenseil testified that he would not have allowed his wife to throw out the twenty cartons of Dalkon Shield documents if he had known about the nondestruct order. However, he did not learn about the order until a month after the documents were destroyed.

Why? As Griffin Bell would argue at a hearing in August 1984—a hearing called to determine whether sanctions should be imposed on Robins—the company did not notify Wagenseil of the order that specified "other persons who now have access to any of the aforedescribed documents" because it was too vague; "ambiguous in the extreme," is how Bell put it. He pointed out that Judge Lord "had gone to the trouble to add former employees," but that Renner on reissuing the order had dropped the phrase.

The Wagenseils were not alone. It was later revealed that five outside experts hired by Robins had also destroyed documents that fell within the scope of the order. These documents included research notes, computer printouts of preliminary data analysis, and laboratory notes. Here, too, none of the experts were notified of the nondestruct order. Although there would seem to be nothing vague about the word "experts" in that order, Griffin Bell insisted that these five were not "experts" as Robins read the order, but "former experts," and thus were not thought to be covered.

Then there was the question of what happened to a set of handwritten notes pertaining to a critically important and heretofore undisclosed February 17, 1975, all-day Dalkon Shield meeting attended by William Zimmer III, Robins's then president, and other top officials. They had all brought their notes and papers with them to refresh their memories. The meeting is considered critical by plaintiff's attorneys because it could show who-knew-what-when among Robins's top officials.

Taking stenographic notes of the meeting was Patricia Lashley, a Robins paralegal whom E. Claiborne Robins, Jr., has called "one of the two most instrumental [individuals] in the Dalkon Shield situation in our company." It was during deposition testimony that Ms. Lashley gave on February 28, 1984, that the 1975 meeting was first mentioned. Ms. Lashley then revealed that she had taken stenographic notes of the meeting, but that no formal report of the proceedings was ever prepared. As the meeting broke up, she added, several of the officials left their notes in her care. She put all those notes into a file for safekeeping.

"And where are those notes today?" Mike Ciresi asked.

"In that file," responded Ms. Lashley.

Ciresi, arguing that the notes clearly were covered by Judge Lord's discovery order, then asked that Ms. Lashley bring them with her at the next deposition session.

On April 19, the Lashley deposition was resumed. Immediately, Ciresi asked for the notes. Ms. Lashley explained that she went to the file and found that the file folder was empty. Somehow, the notes had disappeared. She also said that the only people besides herself with access to that file were her boss, William Forrest, outside counsel Clifford Perrin and William Kogar, and a "Mr. Norrell."

Jon Mueller, a young associate in the McGuire, Woods & Battle law firm (Ciresi calls him a "poor kid" who was "hung out to dry" by Robins), would later testify at the August sanctions hearing that he had seen the file more than a year before Lord's nondestruct order was issued, but that all it contained at that time was a misfiled letter from a local defense counsel and a page from a 1970 calendar. Thus, if the notes were ever in the file, they had disappeared long before the nondestruct order was issued.

The folder itself was then presented and, indeed, it did contain the letter and the calendar page. This, of course, conflicted with Ms. Lashley's sworn testimony that the folder was empty when she looked at it after February 28, as Ciresi pointed out to Magistrate McNulty, before whom the sanctions hearing was held.

Mueller also testified that he had kept a log of the files he had reviewed that day, adding that the log substantiated his testimony. This led to yet another case of Robins playing loose with the facts. Ciresi demanded that the log be introduced into evidence. Robins objected on grounds of privilege. To resolve the question, McNulty asked if the log was available to the masters, who were back at work in Richmond. Jack Fribley stated that master Thomas Bartsh had seen the document in February and had "deemed [it] 'not responsive' to Judge Lord's document production request."

McNulty, however, knew better. "Mr. Bartsh called me a few minutes ago on another matter," the magistrate told Fribley. "I interrogated him regarding this document, describing to him its length, its contents and so forth. He denies ever seeing it."

The biggest post-Lord bombshell, however, came from Roger Tuttle, the born-again Christian law professor at Oral Roberts who once was in charge of Dalkon Shield litigation at Robins. Ciresi had long been curious about the apparent change of attitude on Tuttle's part, as evidenced by his 1983 *Oklahoma Bar Journal* article cited at length in Chapter 5. Tuttle had been deposed as part of the MDL in 1977, but it was a deposition filled with evasions and objections. Ciresi wanted a shot at the "reformed" Tuttle. Robins vigorously opposed the request, even to the point of obtaining an injunction against it in Oklahoma, but in the end Ciresi won the right to redepose the attorney.

That deposition may well become one of the most significant events in the history of the Dalkon Shield litigation. It began shortly before 10 A.M. on July 30, 1984, in the same federal courtroom in St. Paul where twenty-three days earlier Judge Lord had been forced to stand in the dock. Overseeing the deposition was Magistrate Earl Cudd.

During the afternoon session on the first day, Ciresi asked Tuttle a series of questions about Patricia Lashley's missing stenographic notes. A moment later, for no reason other than because Ciresi believed that Lashley's notes had been deliberately destroyed, he asked Tuttle a question for which he expected a resounding no: "Have there ever been any documents destroyed by the Robins Company concerning the Dalkon Shield?"

"Yes, sir." Tuttle's reply was immediate and direct.

Ciresi was momentarily stunned. "You're *aware* of documents that have been destroyed by the Robins Company . . . ?" (Emphasis ours.)

"Yes, sir . . . ," Tuttle reiterated.

Ciresi had trouble believing what he had just heard. Over the twelve-year history of Dalkon Shield litigation, many people had suspected that documents had been destroyed, but no one had ever hoped to prove it. There was thus no way to counter arguments such as those of Chuck Socha, who, in objecting to Judge Lord's February 27 nondestruct order, declared, "We do not destroy documents." Now, under oath, Roger Tuttle had said, "Yes, sir." Recovering himself, Ciresi turned to his paralegal, Ann Barcelow, and quietly said, "Here we go." He then began to question Tuttle again.

"Do you have personal knowledge that records were destroyed, sir?" he asked Tuttle.

"As to being physically present, no, but I have every reason to believe that the people who reported back to me that it had been done did it," Tuttle replied.

"Did you give instructions to physically destroy documents?"

"Pursuant to orders, I did."

"Who gave you the orders to have documents destroyed?"

"Mr. Forrest. . . ."

Forrest, Tuttle testified, had ordered him in February 1975 to gather up all "legally damning" documents from the files of E. Claiborne Robins, Sr., and several other company executives and to make certain they "would no longer be in existence." (Forrest, under oath, has denied the charge.) The order came after a memorandum damaging to Robins had surfaced in a case then pending in

Wichita. Tuttle claimed to have asked Forrest about the legality of such an act, but was told not to worry about it.

Several days later, under Tuttle's instruction (he did not want to participate, he said), what was assumed to be the entire lot of "damning" documents was destroyed by people Tuttle assigned to the task. Unknown to anyone, he claimed, he kept about forty "of the most sensitive" documents.

As proof, Tuttle then presented a number of those documents to the court. Some were "old hat" by now, with one major exception: "For the first time," says Ciresi, "we were looking at the originals. You have to understand that, for years, we've seen these things, but Tuttle had the originals." That in itself tended to support his story. Some of the documents were new, including further evidence that A. H. Robins had misled the FDA about the effect of copper in the Dalkon Shield.

The business-as-usual attitude of Robins also extended to the MDL proceedings in Wichita. Until Lord, those proceedings had been used to foreclose new discovery. Now, because of Judge Lord, MDL lead counsel Bradley Post in January 1985 asked Judge Theis to reopen the MDL discovery and to allow a new round of depositions of all major Robins figures. He also wanted to introduce into the MDL record the Tuttle deposition.

Robins thereupon attacked the Tuttle deposition as an outright lie that should be ignored. As for the rest of Post's requests, Griffin Bell filed a motion in mid-January 1985 saying that Judge Theis was no longer fit to sit in judgment of such matters because he had come to Judge Lord's defense and had thus shown his prejudice against the company. As a consequence, Robins asked Theis to remove himself from the case. He also asked that the MDL itself be shut down as no longer necessary. On February 1, 1985, Judge Theis refused the Robins request. He would stay on the case. Robins immediately appealed to the Tenth Circuit U.S. Court of Appeals in Denver.

In February 1985, Tuttle's testimony received an indirect boost from Peter Thompson and Thomas Bartsh, the two special masters appointed by Judge Lord a little over a year earlier who had continued their work for Judge Renner. In a report filed with the U.S. District Court in St. Paul, Thompson and Bartsh charged that Robins, "with the knowledge and participation of in-house counsel, engaged in an ongoing fraud" that, among other things, "involved the destruction or withholding of relevant evidence."

In April, the Tenth Circuit U.S. Court of Appeals dismissed the Robins appeal seeking to have Theis removed from the MDL. The company wasted no time in asking the U.S. Supreme Court to review the case. The nation's highest court had not responded to that request as of early June, when this book went to press.

Theis also wasted no time. Not bothering to wait for the Supreme Court, he plunged right back into the Dalkon Shield case. On May 2, he issued a "short order" admitting the Tuttle deposition into the MDL and ruled it admissible by plaintiffs in all Dalkon Shield cases nationally.

Almost immediately, Theis's decision began to hurt Robins. Within a few days of Tuttle's deposition being admitted to the MDL, it was presented to a Kansas jury which was then nearing the end of a Dalkon Shield case. Within another few days, that jury handed down a $9.2 million verdict against Robins. Of that $9.2 million, $7.5 million was for punitive damages, making it the largest such award ever in a Dalkon Shield case to date. All parties to that suit admit that the Tuttle deposition played a crucial role in that decision.

Robins, therefore, decided to step up its attacks on Tuttle's allegations. Robins attorney James Crockett, Jr., told reporters at a May 23 press conference in Richmond that the memo Tuttle insists outlined the records destruction was indeed written by Tuttle—but it was written at least a year after he had left the company.

Crockett insisted that company records proved that Tuttle at the time was in El Paso, Texas, representing Robins in a court case unrelated to the Dalkon Shield litigation. As proof, Crockett presented those records: the expense account of another Robins employee who supposedly had accompanied Tuttle to El Paso. What Crockett did not produce, however, were Tuttle's expense accounts for that trip.

Crockett also presented the memorandum that Tuttle claimed he had written to himself at the time of the alleged records destruction. The paper was clearly the kind used by the A. H. Robins Company, but the company name had been cut off. Crockett also presented other memoranda written by Tuttle while at Robins and after he left the company. The same paper was used for all those memoranda, but only those written once Tuttle left the company had the Robins name removed. This, said Crockett, proved that Tuttle had not written the memorandum until much later than he had testified.

Tuttle insists that he often removed the company name from its memorandum paper when he wrote personal notes—and the destruction memorandum was a personal note. "I'm bound to believe that the ultimate judge of whether or not I have been impeached on the veracity of my testimony is the juries in the cases," Tuttle said.

Theis may have delivered an even greater blow to Robins on May 29. On that day, he issued what is known as a "crime or fraud exception" order that effectively wipes out any Robins claim of privilege for its documents.

In simple terms, a crime or fraud exception means that the attorney-client and attorney work product privileges do not apply when the attorney's services are engaged to perpetrate a future crime or fraud.

The privilege claim has been the biggest barrier to plaintiffs' cases in the twelve-year history of Dalkon Shield litigation because Robins has used it to keep many potentially vital documents from the women suing the company. MDL lead plaintiff's attorney Brad Post had argued that from the time the Dalkon Shield was withdrawn from the market in 1974 Robins's attorneys handled all matters relating to it and helped to orchestrate a cover-up. Therefore, any communications between the attorneys and Robins and any work product connected with the Dalkon Shield should be subject to discovery.

In a landmark thirty-page opinion issued May 29, Judge Theis basically agreed with Post. Theis did not rule on the substantive question of whether Robins and its counsel did in fact perpetrate a crime or fraud. However, he did rule that there was sufficient evidence suggesting that they had. As such, Theis declared that documents and work product relating to (a) the withdrawal of the Dalkon Shield from the marketplace, (b) the issuing of the two Dear Doctor letters, (c) the existence of a design flaw or product defect in the Dalkon Shield, (d) counsel's involvement, if any, in the wording and issuing of various communications relating to the Dalkon Shield, and (e) the company's alleged failure to warn of a defect in the product are now subject to discovery.

In his opinion, Theis wrote: "Plaintiffs have established a prima facie case for the purpose of a crime or fraud exception to the attorney-client privilege and the work product doctrine that Robins failed to adequately test the Dalkon Shield before marketing it; attempted to develop hard evidence which misrepresented the nature, quality, safety and efficacy of the Dalkon Shield; ignored the mounting evidence against the Dalkon Shield with knowledge of the potential harm caused by the product; relied upon invalid studies in an effort to refute or ignore the dangers potentially caused by the Dalkon Shield; and attempted with the assistance of counsel to devise strategies to cover up Robins's responsibility and lessen its liability with respect to the Dalkon Shield."

"This does not mean that Judge Theis has found that Robins actually committed a crime or fraud," Brad Post explained. "It simply means that we have made the necessary showing in order for documents which otherwise would be protected to be released."

In an obvious effort to get out from under Theis and the MDL, Robins engaged in a major effort in U.S. district court in Richmond to have the 4,500-plus Dalkon Shield cases still pending consolidated into a single class action suit on the issue of punitive damages. Obviously, if Judge Theis had removed himself, Robins's motion for a class action in friendly, hometown Richmond would have been helped along a great deal. As this book went to press, however, the class action suit had not yet been decided.

It was also business as usual as far as Robins's defense of the Dalkon Shield as safe was concerned. Herein, however, lies Judge Lord's greatest success, one which he said made it "well worth the anxiety, discomfort or inconvenience" that the misconduct complaint "caused me or my family":

The A. H. Robins Company recalled the Dalkon Shield.

Naturally enough, Robins did not use the word "recall." Practically, however, that is what Robins did on October 29, 1984, when it announced a multimillion-dollar national media campaign to get women still wearing the devices to have them removed at company expense.

The campaign was carefully worded to avoid admitting liability. The "Important Message," as the advertisements were called, was addressed to "IUD Users," not "Dalkon Shield Users," thus reinforcing the argument that the Dalkon Shield was no worse than any other IUD. According to the text of the advertisement, "It is important that each Dalkon Shield be removed, since there is substantial medical opinion that its continued use may pose a serious personal hazard." The message did not say that the company agreed with that opinion, however. In fact, in announcing the removal campaign, E. Claiborne Robins, Jr., made it clear that the company did not agree, reiterating yet again the Robins position that the Dalkon Shield is safe when used properly.

The company president also alluded to Judge Lord's part in the decision to mount the "removal" campaign. "Our effort," he said, "grows out of our concern for the health of these women and, quite frankly, our concern about the adverse publicity our company and the Dalkon Shield have received in recent months, which we firmly believe is unwarranted."

Curiously, while Robins refuses to this day to characterize the program as a "recall," its own attorney, Griffin Bell, has been making it clear that a recall is just what Robins had done. Bell told the Richmond *Times Dispatch* that he had urged Robins's board to undertake the campaign as a dramatic way of improving the company's chances in the thousands of lawsuits still ahead.

"I wanted the recall campaign, what they [at Robins] say is the 'removal' campaign," the former attorney-general said. "I recommended that to the board, because the Dear Doctor letter in 1980 apparently hadn't impressed judges or juries. We needed this as an act of good faith to warn people about continued wearing of the Dalkon Shield."

Whether it was a "recall" or a "removal," the fact remains that the campaign itself would seem to support Judge Lord's claim that "tens of thousands" of women were still wearing the Dalkon Shield in 1984. According to Robins's own figures, as of March 31, 1985 (the end of the campaign's twenty-second week), 4,437 women had had their Dalkon Shields removed at a cost to Robins of $1.1 million, and the company was then processing an additional four hundred and fifty claims. More to the point, the company informed the FDA on April 3, 1985, "Robins continues to receive more than one hundred new claims each week." At that rate, the company will have received an additional three thousand claims by the time the removal campaign is one year old. Considering that only a fraction of people ever respond to advertising campaigns of any kind, it would be safe to assume that the number of women who have responded thus far represent only a fraction of all those to whom the campaign was directed, thus clearly vindicating Lord.

E. Claiborne Robins, Jr., called the campaign "unprecedented in American medical history." Judge Lord's comment, however, was more to the point:

"Fourteen years too late is better than never."

POSTSCRIPT: In 1984, the Association of Trial Lawyers of America, which had honored Judge Lord as the nation's outstanding federal trial judge in 1981, gave him its Presidential Award of Merit "in recognition of his judicial independence, courage and integrity of purpose."

It was the kind of honor that Lord would have loved to have used for his long-threatened exit from the public stage. The investigation of his behavior in the Dalkon Shield case, however, hung over him at the time, and he was determined not to go out under that particular cloud.

On May 19, 1985, that cloud no longer existed. Miles W. Lord, having been finally vindicated by his peers and, more importantly, by events, announced his retirement as chief judge of the U.S. District Court for the District of Minnesota, effective immediately, and as an active judge, effective July 1, 1985.

"It has indeed been satisfying and rewarding to work with so many wonderful people in helping shape the direction in which our beloved state and nation has traveled and in making government more responsive to the needs of people," Lord said in his announcement.

Hubert Humphrey had said that Miles Lord would be "people's judge." And so he was.